contents

wdp World Destinations Publishing

Publishers:
James Buchanan, William Colegrave

Editor:
Vicki Ingle

Editor, Wedding Features:
Carole Hamilton

Art Director:
Horacio Monteverde

Design Assistants:
Kicca Tommasi, Biljana Lipic

Advertising Editor:
Tracey D'Afters

Advertising Administrator:
Rebecca Kendall

Picture Editor: **Joseph Fullman**

Contributors: **Philippe Barbour,
Liz Booth, Brenda Birmingham,
Rodney Bolt, Dana & Michael Facaros,
Joseph Fullman, Marc Harris, Vanessa
Letts, Antony Mason, Matthew Tanner,
Tim Ware, Ian Wisniewski, Stewart Wild**

Production Managers:
Andrew Wilson, Rupert Wheeler

Sales Executives: **Kate Collins,
Linda Johnston, Lucie Winter**

Reproduction:
The Setting Studio, Newcastle

Printed and Bound by:
Hunters Armely Ltd, Leeds

A catalogue record for this book is
available from the British Library

ISBN   1-86011-004-5

Published by:
World Destinations Publishing Ltd
Silver House
31–35 Beak Street
London W1R 3LD

Distributed in North America by:
The Globe Pequot Press
6 Business Park Road
PO Box 833
Old Saybrook
Connecticut 06475-0833

Copyright: © 1998
World Destinations Publishing Ltd

The publishers are especially grateful to
Marc Harris of Africa Archipelago for his
expert contirbution to the Africa section
of this guide.

Dear Honeymooner

Welcome to the first edition of Special Honeymoon Hotels.

As you are no doubt beginning to appreciate, choosing where to spend your honeymoon can be a daunting decision, involving a large part of your wedding budget, but there are no comprehensive sources to guide you. We set out to make your decision as easy as possible with this definitive guide to honeymoon destinations around the world.

In this association between the experienced editors, authors and researchers from Britain's foremost wedding and honeymoon magazine You & Your Wedding, and leading travel publishers Cadogan Guides, we bring you a rollcall of the finest — the most stylish, romantic and exciting destinations around the world. All 115 luxury hotels, resorts, cruise lines and safaris have been selected by our panel of travel experts, including Brian McArthur, Travel Editor of The Times in London.

Our combined knowledge, together with the trust and understanding You & Your Wedding magazine shares with its readers, will make the new Special Honeymoon Hotels indispensable to couples looking for the ideal place to get married, hold a wedding reception or go on honeymoon.

Take time to enjoy the many wonderful places featured in the book, we hope you will find it inspirational when choosing the perfect destination for your dream holiday. Wherever you go, we wish you a truly memorable honeymoon.

Best wishes

Carole Hamilton
Editor-in-Chief, You & Your Wedding

Vicki Ingle
Editorial Director, Cadogan Guides

detailed contents

you & your
wedding

We have over 12 years experience in recommending perfect honeymoon hotels for our readers. We visit the countries, stay in the hotels and sample the service. Then we recommend. We are unrivalled in the quality and depth of our honeymoon coverage, helping you, the bride-to-be, to choose from a brilliant selection of wonderful honeymoon destinations.

We apply the same research and understanding of your needs to the rest of the magazine. Our aim is to provide you with inspiration and advice, including fashion and flowers, gift lists, planning and shoppers' guides and much more. If you haven't bought You & Your Wedding yet, treat yourself. You deserve it.

Britain's Biggest

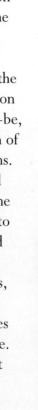

you & your wedding

Banish Wedding Day Nerves

Big Day Beauty Tips

Ceremonies With a Difference

50 pages of Inspirational Fashion

FREE Wedding Planner INSIDE

The Sexiest Bridal Lingerie

How to Give a Great Speech

and Best Bridal Magazine

planning your dream honeymoon

It sounds simple. Go to the travel agents, flick through glossy brochures, pick out somewhere that looks like paradise and hand over your money. Honeymoons have a lot to live up to, and are viewed by most love-struck couples as the trip of a lifetime with long, lazy days filled with champagne and romance.

In order for the dream to live up to the reality, it is important that you approach this very special holiday with your eyes wide open and your feet firmly on the ground. Great honeymoons do not just happen. They take careful planning and a true understanding of each other's likes, dislikes and dreams.

First, decide where you want to go. Choose a destination that neither of you has visited before. Do not even consider going somewhere you have stayed with a previous spouse or lover. Your married life should have a fresh place to start.

Work out how much time you can both afford to take off work or spend away from home. Do not use up all your annual leave with pre-wedding plans, and remember that if you are going to a long-haul destination you will lose two days of holiday travelling.

For the female half of this partnership, a word of advice. If your husband-to-be is a traditional kind of chap who wants to keep the destination a surprise, try dropping a few hints. A surprise honeymoon is certainly romantic, but it can make packing your suitcase a nightmare. If he is determined to keep it a complete surprise, see if you can find a friend or family member to do your packing.

A time to indulge all your fantasies and dreams...

think ahead

Think carefully about what you both want. After the stresses of arranging a wedding, the chances are that relaxing is going to be top priority. But what is your idea of relaxation? That isolated island in the brochure may look like paradise, but will there be enough to do?

A good compromise is to book a two-centre honeymoon. Unwind first at a beach resort and then visit a city for some sightseeing, or incorporate activities such as a few days on a boat or under canvas close to nature.

Get your friends to recommend destinations they have first-hand experience of, and use your travel agent. Ask the staff lots of questions. Many agents have dedicated wedding co-ordinators who will have plenty of holiday ideas and will be able to tell you the best time of year to visit certain places.

If you prefer a more high-tech approach, the Internet is a growing information source. After a few hours surfing the net, you should have plenty of ideas for your hideaway heaven.

There are plenty of possibilities for sporty honeymooners, too. Many resorts provide all the usual watersports at no extra charge, and some include scuba diving. Diving holidays often combine exotic locations with stunning sport; the Red Sea, the Cayman Islands, the Seychelles and the Philippines are all hot spots for divers and honeymooners alike.

When you are agreed, book as soon as possible so that hotels can reserve the honeymoon suite for you.

And remember that it is a good idea not to travel too far on your wedding day. Rather, you should spend a night or two at a local hotel, and arrive at your destination refreshed.

Long, lazy days filled with champagne and romance...

your dream honeymoon

costs

Set your honeymoon budget early, along with the rest of the wedding budget. Money considerations may not be very romantic, but you do not want to start married life completely broke.

Pay attention to what is included in any package price. If only breakfast is mentioned this may be why the hotel sounds like such a bargain. Additional meals at luxury hotels can be extremely expensive. Drinks, tips, service charges and airport tax all need to be thought of, too. An all-inclusive resort or hotel may seem expensive at first glance, but the price you pay includes all food, drinks and most activities, and the system frees you from constant worrying about how much everything costs.

Finally, put aside some money for emergencies and impulse spending. This is a holiday that could easily cost more than planned.

health matters

Talk to your doctor well in advance about health requirements and injections.

Some vaccinations need to be given at least a month before you travel, and you may need to start a course of anti-malarial tablets before you leave.

beds and basics

Make sure everyone involved in your holiday arrangements knows you are on honeymoon. You will be amazed how many gifts and special offers suddenly come your way. Many hotels will provide a free bottle of champagne on arrival. Most will give upgrades if a better room is available, especially in the low season, and offer such perks as a romantic candle-lit dinner for two served on your balcony or breakfast in bed. Your travel agent will be able to check exactly what is on offer, what is free and what is not. Take along your marriage certificate as proof of your new status.

It may sound obvious, but check that your hotel room has a double bed. In Europe, in particular, many establishments have twin-bedded rooms only – not the most romantic arrangement to start married life! And to save yourself embarrassment, check with your travel agent whether the hotel restaurant has a dress code.

time out

Many newlywed couples feel that they have to spend every waking hour together 'being romantic'. It is worth remembering that there is nothing wrong with pursuing individual interests; most couples come together afterwards feeling fulfilled, and romantic.

It may sound obvious, but check your hotel room has a double bed...

forms and formalities

You will save yourselves time, money and possibly heartache by researching and completing all necessary documentation well in advance.

Do take out comprehensive travel insurance. Keep your passports in your hand luggage along with tickets, hotel confirmations and your marriage certificate.

Think ahead if you are changing your name and want to travel under your new name. Make sure the registrar or minister has signed the relevant form to apply for a new passport in advance. Inform the airline so that the name on your ticket matches the name on your passport.

Fewer and fewer countries now require British passport-holders to have a visa, but your travel agent will be able to advise you. Do not leave it too late. The last thing you want to do before your wedding is spend two days queuing at an embassy – once to submit the application and a second time to collect the visa. There are companies that will take care of such formalities for a small fee.

travel checklist

don't leave home without...

Paperwork
Passports
Airline tickets
Car documents if driving
Hotel booking confirmations
Tour/drive confirmations
Travel insurance
Foreign currency
Traveller's cheques
Credit cards
Vaccination certificates
Marriage certificate

Health and Beauty
Vaccinations
Malaria tablets
Mosquito night-burning oil
Insect repellent
Sting cream
Headache tablets
Sun cream
After-sun lotion
Lip protection
Beauty/skincare products
Haircare products
Make-up
Hairdryer with adaptor

Clothing (hot)
Swimsuit
Shorts
Tops
Sundresses
Sun hat
Evening wear – casual
Evening wear – smart
Beach shoes
Sports gear

Clothing (cold)
Woolly jumpers
Hats
Gloves
Warm boots
Coats
Sports gear
Evening wear – casual
Evening wear – smart

General (hot)
Sunglasses
Mosquito net
Luggage labels
Books
Guide books

Added extras
Romantic music
Candles
Bath oil
Sexy lingerie
Perfume/after shave

getting married abroad

The thought of a wedding without arguments over the guest list, the seating plan and even the colour of the mothers' hats is more than enough to justify escaping to an exotic clime. Add the spice of a tropical wedding, exchanging vows on a deserted sandy beach with palm trees rustling in the breeze, and the idea becomes totally tantalising.

Wherever you get married, the more effort you put in at an early stage, the happier and more relaxed you will be on the day itself. Some tour operators have a wedding department and a dedicated brochure, with staff to guide you to the right destination and give plenty of practical advice. They like at least four months' notice to deal with all the formalities, and to ensure the right hotel is available on the right date.

Many hotels in the Caribbean now limit the number of weddings held each day, so each couple feels truly special. Most of the time this is no problem, but if you are determined to get married on a specific date then booking ahead should ensure your wishes are granted.

Countries that are already popular honeymoon destinations have realised that they can take advantage of the growing trend to marry overseas and are changing their local regulations. Trinidad and Tobago was one of the last Caribbean countries to relax previously stringent residency requirements. Even the Far East, where one might have thought strong local culture may have made overseas marriages difficult, has become a relatively easy option. St Lucia remains the top destination for weddings, but is facing some tough competition from Mauritius, the Seychelles, Sri Lanka and near neighbour Barbados.

Bali, Thailand and Australia are becoming increasingly popular, along with Kenya and a whole host of Caribbean islands such as Tobago, Grenada and St Kitts and Nevis. In most places, arrangements can be tailored to your wishes.

The easiest way to arrange your wedding is to buy a package through a tour operator. Typical deals include the services of a minister, the necessary paperwork, a cake, flowers, accommodation and possibly some photographs. Some hotels offer a free wedding package if you stay two weeks or longer, while others will waive the cost of the wedding if you travel with a sufficiently large party of friends and family. Check the small print carefully for any extras you may be charged for.

If the two of you want to travel on your own, most hotels will arrange witnesses for you; some groups of hotels will offer accommodation and the honeymoon at another resort. Young Island Hotel in the Grenadines, for example, will sail you away on its private yacht for your wedding night.

Most ministers are non-denominational and weddings overseas are usually feasible for those with strict religious beliefs. Catholics may face particular difficulties in marrying overseas, and the authorities in some countries such as Bali require that both bride and groom are of the same religion.

The only other major hurdle that couples will face is their age. Certain destinations will not marry couples under a particular age. For example, the groom must be

Remember

- Pack all the originals of your required documents, otherwise you cannot get married.

- Brides, buy a simple dress in a cool natural fabric like chiffon or georgette. Ask the airline whether you can carry your dress as hand luggage.

- Hang your dress in a steamy bathroom the minute you arrive to minimise creases.

- Grooms, wear a light coloured suit in cotton or linen.

- Make friends with the hotel's wedding co-ordinator — you are much more likely to have any unusual demands met.

- Go easy on the sunbathing to avoid looking like a lobster in your wedding pictures.

- Arrange to video the ceremony, to appease unhappy friends and relations who have been left behind.

- Do not expect too much from the ceremony. It will be quick and informal, although most registrars are happy to include a reading or two that means something to you.

23 in Bali, while in Sri Lanka both parties must be over 21. Most places, however, set the limit at 18.

Most hotels have an on-site wedding co-ordinator who will make sure the day runs perfectly. She is a friend and mother rolled into one, quelling last-minute nerves and smiling happily as the vows are made. She will run over all the details of the day itself, arrange equipment if you want to play a CD or tape, and will organise a rehearsal and tour the property with you if there is a choice of locations.

The co-ordinator will usually travel with you if you need to visit the local authorities and will arrange the wedding breakfast with the hotel. If you want separate rooms on the night before your wedding, book in advance – it can usually be arranged, but might incur a single-supplement charge.

Brides should think carefully about what style of dress they want to wear. A huge billowing silk dress may not be practical in the heat of the tropics while high heels could prove a nightmare on a sandy beach. The best advice is to stay with natural fibres and avoid skin-tight dresses.

Having settled on the destination, the hotel and the dress, it is time to start thinking about your packing. Many airlines suggest the dress is boxed separately and is then placed carefully in the hold; others will allow you to bring it in a suit carrier as hand luggage. As soon as you arrive, hang the dress up to allow any folds to fall out – the natural humidity of tropical heat will help.

original weddings

More couples are searching for ever more unusual ways to say 'I do...'

The days of formal wedding services held exclusively in church are over. Couples have an increasingly wide choice of the weird and the wacky.

In the United Kingdom, though, couples do have to marry in a place which does not undermine the sanctity of marriage. This rules out skydiving as you say your vows — but does not stop the vicar from joining you mid-air for a blessing after the formalities.

If you are determined on a wedding with a difference, the place to head to is America. Countless tongue-in-cheek documentaries have ridiculed Las Vegas for its weird and wonderful moments but the city reigns supreme in its desire to make people's dreams come true.

For those who do not want any fuss at all, there are drive-through kiosks where you can be married in seconds. Wedding chapels line the main roads; you simply cruise along and find a style you fancy. For those wanting a little more to mark the occasion, there are wedding chapels galore. You choose your theme and find people to oblige — from an Elvis Presley lookalike to serenade you and then drive you around town in his pink Cadillac, to those who will marry your pets at the same time. You can become almost anyone your imagination allows — from a medieval bride to a cowboy — or take to the skies in a hot air balloon, sky-diving or wing-walking.

Leaving Las Vegas behind you, in Florida the minister joins you underwater in scuba gear. On dry land, hundreds of couples choose to spend their big day with Mickey Mouse and his friends at Disney World, for a fairytale wedding at Cinderella's Castle, a drive through the park in the glass wedding coach, or to hover above the park exchanging vows in a helicopter.

For something more exotic, some wed in the Far East. But be aware that local regulations may force you to spend some time in your chosen destination, and create some complicated paperwork.

Tour operator Kuoni, which specialises in traditional weddings, is able to help organise local costumes for bride and groom, and even fortune-tellers; in Sri Lanka the casting of seven beetle leaves will ensure happiness, joy and health for the next seven generations.

unusual honeymoons

Having married in an unorthodox fashion, you are likely to want your honeymoon to be equally unusual. Try riding an elephant through the African grasslands of Botswana, heli-skiing in Australia and New Zealand, or white-water rafting or skiing in America; spend two weeks on a ranch out west, go pony trekking in Kashmir or mountain climbing in Nepal.

The less energetically inclined can try cruising in the Dominican Republic, looking for whales or swimming with dolphins in the Bahamas. Cycling through the Pyreenees can be arranged at a leisurely pace, or you might prefer simply to find a romantic folly or ancient castle in which to hide away.

While some feel honeymoons are best spent in glorious isolation, others are happier joining a tour; one couple recently booked a six-month trip travelling through Africa in an old army bus, sharing sleeping space with 20 others. On the wildlife trail, you might search for manatees in South America or travel with scientists into the Amazon jungle seeking out new and exotic species.

Or you could chose to stay at a religious retreat, where the peace and quiet provides a soothing balm to the frenzy of wedding celebrations.

cruising

Cruise Companies

BA Holidays Cruise & Stay
+44 1293 723260

Carnival Cruises
+44 171 729 1929

Celebrity Cruises
tel +44 171 355 0606

Clipper
+44 171 436 2931

Costa Cruises
+44 171 323 3333

Cunard
+44 1703 634 166

Kuoni Cruise & Stay
+44 171 374 6601

P&O
+44 171 800 2222/1280

Princess Cruises

+44 171 800 2468

Royal Caribbean International
(0500) 212213

Seawind Cruise Lines

+44 181 385 9000

Star Clipper Cruises
+44 1473 292229

Sailing an ocean liner has always been one of the most romantic ways to travel, and a truly great way to spend your honeymoon.

Imagine sitting in the Jacuzzi, sharing a bottle of champagne and watching the sun set on another glorious day as you sail away from the sandy shores of a paradise island. Dream of slipping into formal evening wear and strolling down to a sumptuous candlelit dinner before heading to the casino, the evening show or simply a walk on deck under moonlit skies.

Ships cater to a wide variety of different destinations, styles and budgets. If you want to explore tiny islands is the South Pacific or cruise the Caribbean, there are ships to do it. Just remember that, as a general rule, the smaller the ship the higher the bill — and, probably, the more personal the service and the more adventurous the itinerary. Before booking, it is wise to decide whether you will find time to explore every port of call or whether you want a few days at sea to really enjoy the ship and its facilities.

The Caribbean remains the favourite destination for cruisers, particularly in the balmy winter months. In summer, some head north to explore scenically stunning Alaska, an area where ship numbers are limited in a bid to preserve the environment. Others voyage way south to the southern tip of Southern America and explore the Galapagos islands, a haven for wildlife. Equally popular is the exotic Far East with its bustling harbours and excellent shops, fascinating culture and, again, stunning scenery.

To the south, Australia and the Pacific Islands are areas once inaccessible to the British traveller but now opening up to increasing numbers of ships. Mauritius and the Seychelles are top of the list for many honeymooners, so why not take a cruise and visit more of the Indian Ocean islands — weird and wonderful Madagascar, and the spice island of Zanzibar. By contrast, the Norwegian fjords provide one of the most dramatic backdrops to any cruise, while the Mediterranean offers a wonderful mix of pretty islands, exotic tastes and balmy days.

Having more or less decided on your destination, the major decision is, which ship?

Deciding on a budget will help narrow the process. At the top end of the market are some wonderfully luxurious cruise lines. Silversea Cruises prides itself on its six-star service; staff almost outnumber passengers and everything is included, even champagne. Every cabin is a suite and the onboard theatre, shops and spa rival some of its larger competitors. In the same category, passengers on the Sea Goddess say that even a bath in champagne would prove no problem for her wonderful crew.

Both the above companies operate relatively small ships. By contrast, Star Clipper Cruises vessels are four-masted sailing boats with the back-up of 20th-century technology. The atmosphere is casual but upmarket and there are special offers for honeymooning couples. Clipper can take you to the inland waterways of the Amazon and the Orinoco to the hidden islands of Alaska from Santa Fe to the Grand Canyon or even golf cruising along Florida's Gold Coast. Smaller still is the Schooner Mondriaan. This yacht and others like it can be booked solely for two, for cruises through the Caribbean islands from its base in St Vincent and the Grenadines.

On a much larger scale, you still find luxury combined with endless entertainment and exotic locations. Costa Cruises was originally an Italian company, and still has that European flair combining style and good service. Royal Caribbean International not only has some of the largest ships afloat, but also some of the best in their class. Celebrity Cruises, Seawind and Carnival are all popular names in the Caribbean, while Princess Cruises is famed for its Alaskan itneraries. Star Cruises is the company of choice as you head to the Far East. For Africa and the Indian Ocean, the African Safari Club offers a traditional style ship with an intimate and friendly atmosphere.

Celebrity Cruises

Worldwide

Contact:
17 Old Park Lane
London
W1Y 3LG
England

tel +44 171 355 0606
fax +44 171 412 0908

Contact:
UK Reservations:
tel 0500 332 232

What could be more romantic than getting married or honeymooning on a five-star cruise ship as it glides effortlessly through the high seas? Travelling to some of the world's most exotic and fascinating destinations from tranquil Bermuda to the sun-splashed Caribbean, through the mighty Panama Canal or the awe-inspiring glaciers of Alaska, Celebrity Cruises offer diverse and original excursions in every port of call. Marriages can be arranged either on board in port or ashore in venues such as New York, Key West in Florida, Barbados, Grand Cayman, Cozumel in Mexico or Juneau in Alaska.

On board any one of the five state of the art liners, luxury and elegance are premium.

 UK£1,199 (823) 9 nights

 UK£2,675 (52) 9 nights

 included

 Included

Honeymoon specials

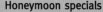

Breakfast in bed including champagne, boxed set of engraved glasses, floral arrangement, single rose on pillow, *Celebrity* bathrobes, personalised certificate, costs UK£80. Cabin upgrade available (restrictions apply). Weddings are arranged through Weddings Abroad, International House, 154 Ashley Road, Hale, Cheshire, WA15 9SA. tel +44 171 941 1122.

The state rooms and suites are modern and spacious with warm wood-finish furniture, artworks on the walls and soft, atmospheric lighting. Some come with verandahs while others enjoy a full butler service.

The tables in the expansive dining rooms are set with fine linen, sparkling crystal and polished silverware and graced with fresh flowers. A new menu is on offer every evening. Appetizers such as North Atlantic Shrimp might be followed by a chilled Gin and Tomato Consomme, a Roquefort salad, Yakutat Bay Halibut steak and Pear Flan Soufflé to finish. After dinner there are convivial piano bars, intimate night clubs, casinos and pulsating discos to enjoy.

During the day, the trips ashore are equally varied. Whether it be renting a moped to visit picturesque Bermudian villages, visiting the Alaska Chilkat to see one of the largest colonies of bald eagles in the world, tasting the frenetic excitement of the Big Apple or just soaking up the sun on a Caribbean beach, Celebrity Cruises provide some of the best the world can offer.

Local attractions

Depending on the cruise: Panning for gold or whale watching in Alaska, train rides through the Rocky Mountains, travelling the length of the Panama Canal, sightseeing in Niagara Falls, visiting the Elmorro Fortress in San Juan, shopping for souvenirs in Nassau's straw market or sampling Grand Cayman's famous rum cake.

Leisure facilities

On board: numerous bars and lounges, health clubs, aqua spas (including massage, fitness programs, aromatherapy, etc), shops, pools, wine tasting, auctions, cookery classes, West End-style shows and productions, casino,
On shore: golf, tennis, watersports, fishing, diving, sailing, canoeing, walking, hiking.

Royal Caribbean International

Worldwide

Contact:

Royal Caribbean House
Addlestone Rd
Weybridge, Surrey
KT15 2UE

tel +44 1932 820 230

fax +44 1932 820 286

londonoffice@miamail01.rccl.com

Member of:
Passenger Shipping Association

Tour operator:
Royal Caribbean International

Inspired by a bygone age when travel was a romantic adventure rather than a means to an end, a Royal Caribbean International cruise removes the problem of picking just one honeymoon destination. The warm sandy beaches and gentle trade winds of the Caribbean, the bright coral reefs of the Bahamas, the bustling seaports and quaint villages of Bermuda, the ice-blue glaciers and pristine wilderness of Alaska, and the ancient medieval cities of Europe – all can be visited by passengers on a majestic cruise ship, sailing sedately through the world's great oceans and seas.

Most of the luxury cabins offer magnificent ocean views, some have private balconies and sitting areas. All are bright, well proportioned and decorated to a high standard, with discreet lighting, pretty fabrics and solid, well-built furniture.

 from UK£999*

 from UK£2,505*

 included**

 included**

Honeymoon specials
Complimentary bottle of Moët et Chandon.

*based on Majesty Of The Seas, sailing 28.11.98

**beverages are not included

Guests wake every day to a new culinary adventure: pastries on deck at sunrise, pancakes and maple syrup in the lavish dining room, afternoon tea by the pool, a barbecue on a private island, or a romantic dinner for two served in the luxurious privacy of the cabin.

Royal Caribbean International also offer a special Royal Romance wedding package on selected cruises. From as little as US$600, couples can be married on board and expect VIP priority check-in, onboard co-ordination, a wedding cake for two, flowers, a marriage certificate, photographs and, of course, the ceremony. Should couples really want to splash out, US$1,200 will buy numerous extras including a chauffeured limousine. A whole host of extras are available such as island weddings, receptions, live music, video packages, ice sculptures, and pampering appointments with beauticians and stylists.

Local attractions

Depending on the cruise, the many shore excursions on offer include guided tours through the Canadian Rockies, shopping in New York, whale-watching in Alaska, visits to the volcanoes of Honolulu, the Bridge of Sighs in Venice, or the Peter and Paul Cathedral in St Petersburg. These cost extra.

Leisure facilities

On board: beauty salon, boutiques, casino, indoor/outdoor pools*, library, miniature 18-hole golf course*, fitness centre and spa, solarium*, video games room, nightclub. On shore: depending on the cruise, guests might go snorkelling in the Caribbean, paddle-boating in Haiti, gambling in Monaco, horseriding in Mexico, salmon fishing in Alaska, mountain biking in Curaçao, sailing in Marseille or submarining in Aruba.

*on selected ships

CADOGAN

inspiration and practical advice

Cadogan Guides is one of the world's
leading guides series. Based in London,
we have writers and researchers throughout
the world. Our 80 titles cover all seven
inhabited continents, inlcuding Antartica.
Our authors take you right to the heart of
each destination with a blend of good writing,
entertaining anecdotes and personal advice.
They reveal hidden treasures, as well as sights you know
you want to see, and give the full low-down on places to
eat, drink and stay for all budgets; as well as shopping,
festivals, entertainment and nightlife.
When you choose your honeymoon destination
make sure you take a Cadogan Guide,
and let us help you have a wonderful,
truly memorable honeymoon.

North America

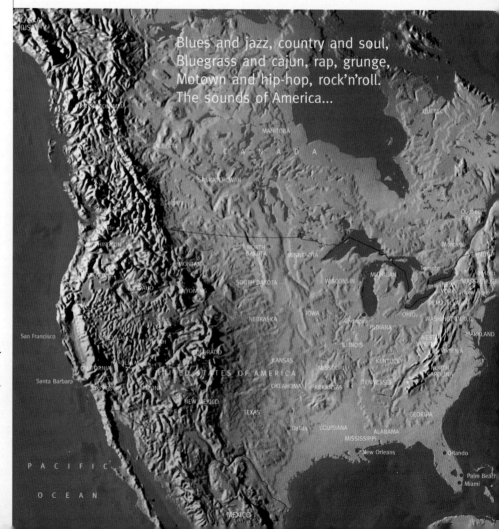

Blues and jazz, country and soul,
Bluegrass and cajun, rap, grunge,
Motown and hip-hop, rock'n'roll.
The sounds of America...

flying times
From London expect to spend between 7 hrs (NY) and 18 hrs (Hawaii) in the air. In North America, flight times are long (NY–Hawaii 12 hrs).

climate
Varies enormously according to location. Most areas have distinct hot and cold seasons, but southern states enjoy mild, sunny winters.

when to go
There is glorious autumn foliage; skiing in the highest resorts into summer. High season in northern US beach resorts is May–Oct; in the south resorts open all year.

currency
The US dollar.

language
English, and French in Canada.

health
Medical expenses can be high. Take proof of insurance.

getting around
Flying is the most practical way to combine destinations. Long-distance bus or train journeys can be adventures in themselves. Fly-drive is the ideal way to tour.

The United States & Canada

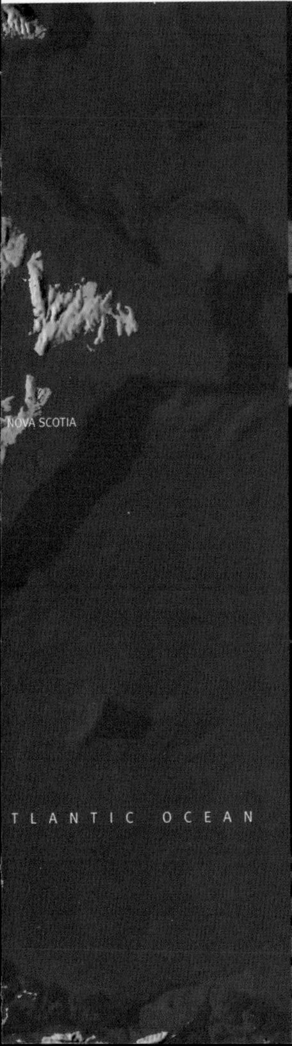

The American terrain is incredibly diverse, encompassing the icy wastes of Alaska and the soaring peaks of the Colorado Rockies, the tropical warmth of Florida's Gulf Coast and the blistering heat of the Mojave Desert.

An American journey embraces not only dramatic and varied scenery but a melting pot of cultures, contributed to by generations of immigrants, and absorbed into the American way of life — not least into the American kitchen with its Italian pizzas, German hot dogs, Chinese noodles, spicy French Creole gumbo....

With some of most spectacular scenery in the world, including the awesome Grand Canyon, Niagara Falls and the vast expanses of the Great Parks and Lakes, there is no better place to take up the challenge of nature. Activities such as white-water rafting, hiking, riding with cowboys on a working ranch are all readily available. In locations such as California, Colorado, Canada, New Mexico and New England you can you can combine skiing, snowboarding and snowmobiling with sightseeing.

More leisurely options include a hot-air balloon rides over spectacular scenery, and a cruise on a Mississippi paddle steamer. Add lazy days on the beach, a hectic city break, a gourmet wine-tasting tour — America has it all.

NOVA SCOTIA

ATLANTIC OCEAN

California

Perhaps the most interesting and varied of all the American states, with snow-capped mountains, incredible forests of giant redwood trees, national parks, sun-burned deserts, Pacific beaches, theme parks and all-action cities, California is also the most perfect touring destination.

Start off in San Francisco — so picturesque and impossibly hilly that, even if it does not steal your heart, it will take your breath away. Let a clanging cable car carry you up to lofty heights for splendid views over San Francisco Bay, then hold on tight as it

Grandiose, pink-painted mansions hiding behind tall gates, swimming pools glinting in the intense, sunny spotlight that bathes Beverly Hills...

flying time
To: LA/San Francisco
London: 11 hrs
Miami: 4–5 hrs
NY: 5–6 hrs

climate
California weather varies
from year-round hot
desert to distinct seasons
in the cooler north.

when to go
Theme parks and beauty
spots like Yosemite
National Park get crowded
in the summer holidays.
You can catch the
San Francisco 49ers in
football action Aug–Dec.

getting around
Consider flying into one
Californian city and out of
another, driving the
distance between.

hurtles downhill towards the seafood restaurants of Fisherman's Wharf.

Drive north and soon you are in the Napa Valley, touring the vineyards, and tasting vintages from California's leading winemakers. Head inland and you come to the blue waters of Lake Tahoe, surrounded by pine forests, mountains and ski resorts with snow from December right through until May.

One of America's most scenic drives follows Highway 1 south of San Francisco, passing seals playing on the wave-lashed grey rocks. It twists around the craggy Pacific coast between Monterey (where you should be sure to see the vast aquarium), and pretty Carmel, with its quaint shopping streets and old Spanish mission. Indeed, the further south you go in California, the stronger the Hispanic connection. Hacienda-style buildings, mission churches and place names are all Spanish legacies; and from San Diego you can take a trolley bus to the Mexican border and walk into Tijuana.

Los Angeles rewards those who brave its smog and sprawl and make time to get to know it. For LA is not only Hollywood, but also the wacky seaside strips of Venice Beach and Santa Monica; the shopping street of the stars, Rodeo Drive; the hip restaurants serving up imaginative Californian cuisine; and the wealth of theatres, galleries, museums, and venues for music and dance. ●

San Ysidro Ranch

900 San Ysidro Lane
Santa Barbara
CA 93108
USA

 Santa Barbara 20km

tel +1 805 969 5046
fax +1 805 565 1995
yanisyr@west.net

Open all year

Member of:
Relais et Châteaux

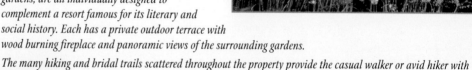

Idyllically nestled amid the rugged, natural beauty of the Santa Ynez Mountains in Santa Barbara and adjacent to the blue Pacific, San Ysidro Ranch has been welcoming guests since 1893. Once a magnet for movie stars and later frequented by politicians, including the Kennedys who honeymooned there in 1953, it remains a haven of tranquillity for those seeking serenity and seclusion.

The 21 guest cottages, approached by cobbled pathways meandering through jasmine-scented gardens, are all individually designed to complement a resort famous for its literary and social history. Each has a private outdoor terrace with wood burning fireplace and panoramic views of the surrounding gardens.

The many hiking and bridal trails scattered throughout the property provide the casual walker or avid hiker with splendid scenic vistas. Tennis, swimming and a complete spa programme are also available.

The world-acclaimed Stonehouse Restaurant features hearty American and regional cuisine. For more informal dining the Plow & Angel Pub, built in 1893 as an original wine cellar, offers cocktails and a casual dinner menu. After dinner, guests can enjoy the sounds of live jazz or dance the night away to a classic 1952 Wurlitzer jukebox.

This is an idyllic spot for those contemplating a wedding ceremony abroad. The beautiful terraced wedding garden has, in the past, served as the site where Lawrence Olivier and Vivien Leigh exchanged their vows.

 US$325–3,000 (37)

 US$325–3,000 (20)

 US$50

US$13

Honeymoon specials
The wedding couple have the luxury of booking the entire ranch for their wedding party. Flowers and champagne in the room on arrival.

Sightseeing and leisure
The Mission, Santa Barbara Aquarium. Pacific Ocean and beaches are a short distance from the ranch. Wineries of Santa Ynez valley and scenic walks in the mountains. Spa facility on site with complete health, fitness and beauty treatments available. Tennis, hiking and swimming.

Shutters On The Beach

One Pico Boulevard
Santa Monica
California 90405
USA

✈ Los Angeles Int. 16km

tel +1 310 458 0030
fax +1 310 458 4589

Toll Free:
US/Canada: 800 223 6800
UK & Northern Ireland: 0800 181 123

Open all year

Member of:
The Leading Hotels of the World

Shutters On The Beach is the only luxury hotel nestled right on the warm California sands of Santa Monica Bay in Los Angeles. Recalling the architecture of historic Southern Californian beach resorts of the early 1900s, the hotel has the look and feel of a sumptuous ocean-front home. The structure comprises three separate buildings, visually linked by elaborate slate-grey shingled siding, flower-covered trellises, balconies and striped awnings.

Each of the rooms and suites has warm walnut desks, round-backed lounge chairs and sliding shuttered doors opening onto the balmy ocean breeze and panoramic coastal views. All rooms have large marble bathrooms and whirlpool bathtubs with glass windows providing spectacular views. The suites feature wooden parquet flooring and fireplaces adorned with hand-made tiles.

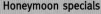

One Pico, the hotel's more formal restaurant, offers a front row seat to the Pacific Ocean and the stirring sunsets. With the emphasis on local and regionally-grown produce, celebrated chef Desi Szonntagh creates entrées with a discreet and unobtrusive quality, such as Roast Chilean Seabass with Black Bean Sauce and Applewood Smoked Salmon. Pedals, a casual restaurant at the edge of the beach promenade, recreates the atmosphere of a warm café with an Italian trattoria feel.

The hotel is situated near the historic pier in this Southern Californian seaside resort and is within minutes of many fashionable shopping districts, fine restaurants and art galleries.

📖 from US$315 (186)
US$750–2,000 (12)
US$40
US$14

Honeymoon specials
Two or four night packages include champagne and chocolates, dinner for two, daily breakfast, mountain bike hire, his and her massages and facials, limousine to and from the new Getty Centre and keepsake.

Sightseeing and leisure
Museums (including the new world class Getty Centre), art galleries, outdoor Rodeo Drive boutiques and speciality bookshops are just minutes away. Pool, jacuzzi, spa, health club, aromatherapy, massage, reflexology are available at the hotel

Florida

They call it the Sunshine State, but it could just as easily be known as the Sunshine State. Florida is a fun place.

Every evening is party time in old Key West, as street entertainers and visitors from all over the world gather to celebrate the glorious sunset. Then it is time for some bar-hopping along Duval Street, catching a snatch of music from a sixties band here, a jazz band there, maybe ending up in Ernest Hemingway's old haunt, Sloppy Joe's, for a drink and a dance.

Two hundred miles away at Miami's South Beach, the stylish set preen and pose outside the pastel lemon and lilac Art Deco façades, deciding which restaurant to grace that night. Meanwhile, in the world's theme park capital, Orlando, just as many adults as kids get delightedly dizzy on Disney World's Tower of Terror and the Test Track high-speed car ride. The theme park rides stay open until late, and when

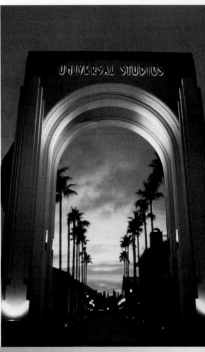

Skimming from island to island on the Florida Keys, driving far out across the ocean on a ribbon of bridges, enveloped in the hypnotic, wrap-round blue of sea and sky...

flying time

To: Fort Lauderdale,
Miami, Orlando.
London: 9–10 hrs
LA: 4–5 hrs
NY: 3 hrs

climate

Winters are mild, at
15–20°C with mainly
sunny days. Summer is
hot and humid,
especially in central
Florida, and you will
be thankful for an
air-conditioned car.

when to go

Avoid the busy US
public and school
holidays when visiting
the theme parks. May,
June and November are
generally good months
to visit.

getting around

Driving is by far the
best way to explore as
road and rail services
are limited. If your
budget allows, hire a
convertible and feel the
wind in your hair.

they close there is a good time to be had at Rosie O'Grady's saloon or the bars and clubs of Pleasure Island — where they celebrate New Year's Eve every night of the year with fireworks and a street party.

If sports are your idea of fun, Florida is your dream destination. It has more than a thousand golf courses, and excellent tennis centres where you can get tuition from leading professionals. All sorts of watersports are on offer, with scuba diving off the Keys and exciting deep-sea fishing trips from Miami and Fort Lauderdale. Around the state's 1,800 miles of coastline are beaches to suit everyone, from the pristine white strands of the Panhandle area up in the north west corner to the broad, hard-packed sands at Daytona, where Malcolm Campbell once drove at 276mph. Nowadays the motor racing is in the Daytona International Speedway, but you can

still drive on the beach, if you stick to the normal speed limit of 10mph.

From all-action Orlando, it is only an hour or two's drive west to the quiet Gulf Coast beaches of Sanibel and Captiva, or east to the Space Coast beaches and Cape Canaveral, where you can tour the rocket launch pads, and maybe see a shuttle blast-off.

The highways get you around quickly, and in a two- or three-week trip you can sample not just theme parks and beaches but also splendid art collections like the Ringling Museum at Sarasota, historic plantation mansion houses and, of course, Florida's natural wonders. These include lakelands and state parks to explore, where you can meet pelicans and dolphins. Or you can view riverbank wildlife from a canoe, and sweep across the Everglades in an air-boat under an alligator's watchful eye.

The Breakers

1 South County Rd
Palm Beach
Florida 33480
USA

 Palm Beach 7km

tel +1 561 655 6611
fax +1 561 659 8403

Open all year

Member of:
The Leading Hotels of the World

Tour operators:
UK: British Airways Holidays
US: GOGO Worldwide Vacations

Set amid lush landscaped gardens, The Breakers is the only oceanfront resort located in the heart of Palm Beach and surrounded by an active and lively community atmosphere.

Elegantly appointed rooms feature modern amenities and services that blend past tradition with contemporary luxury.

There are a variety of recreational activities on offer including golf at two championship courses, tennis, snorkelling and diving. The hotel is happy to arrange bicycle excursions for those who want to discover the charm of the island. After an exhausting day spent shopping in the many boutiques, guests can relax by the resort's two oceanfront swimming pools, sunbathe on pristine beaches or enjoy an invigorating masssage in the spa.

There are seven restaurants to choose from encompassing a wide range of international dishes featuring the freshest seafood, prime grade steaks and the chef's daily specialities.

After dinner, guests can enjoy a drink in the Italian-style piazza before taking a romantic stroll into Palm Beach where a myriad of entertainment possibilities await.

There are two Mediterranean-style courtyards available for wedding receptions of up to 800 guests.

US$145–600 (572)
US$345–1,650 (54)
US$65
US$20

Honeymoon specials
Champagne and strawberries in room on arrival, souvenir gift, breakfast in room, gourmet dinner, round of golf or a day's tennis, private beach cabana for one day, choice of a massage or facial. The package costs from US$864 for 2 people staying 2 nights and includes room tax and service charges.

Sightseeing and leisure
Trips to Flagler and Norton museums, Worth Avenue, Coral Sky Amphitheatre. Access to Palm Beach polo club, horse and greyhound tracks. Shopping trips bicycle hire, garden, historical and kitchen tours can be arranged. Two 18-hole golf courses. Tennis, swimming, scuba diving, snorkelling, deep-sea fishing.

Sonesta Beach Resort
Key Biscayne

350 Ocean Drive
Key Biscayne
Florida 33149
USA

✈ Fort Lauderdale Int. 45km
   Miami Int. 18km

tel +1 305 361 2021
fax +1 305 361 3096
seidelberg@sonesta.com

Contact:
Toll Free Reservations:
US: 1 800 SONESTA
UK: 0800 898 410

Open all year

Tour operators/booking:
UK/US: Utell International

The tropical island of Key Biscayne sits off the coast of Florida in the Atlantic Ocean. Home to two historic national parks, the island hosts the Lipton International Tennis Tournament and the Royal Caribbean Golf Classic. Overlooking a private beach on the shores of the Atlantic, the Sonesta Beach Resort is surrounded by beautifully lanscaped parkland and coconut groves.

The comfortable rooms, furnished with crisp modern elegance, lead out onto private balconies with sweeping ocean and island views.

An award-winning combination of cuisine, combining flavours from Florida and the Caribbean, is served in the refined surroundings of the Purple Dolphin restaurant. Other dining options include the exotic Asian dishes of Two Dragons, and the casual American favourites prepared by the Jasmine Cafe.

Guests can explore the island's parks on bicycles or mopeds, visit the oldest light house in the south eastern states, or shop in the bustling streets of nearby Miami. Watersports abound and the adventurous may try parasailing or wave runners. All the facilities needed for keeping in shape are on hand with fully-equipped fitness and beauty centres.

The attentive staff are happy to assist with all wedding arrangements, and recommend a themed outdoor area on the beach for an unforgettable private ceremony.

 US$160–395
 US$575–1650
US$60–120
US$12–25

 VISA

Honeymoon specials
Romantic rendezvous package costs US$1,104–1,664 for two people for four nights, and includes a welcome cocktail, champagne and strawberries on arrival, breakfast, private dinner on the beach, one hour catamaran cruise, beach cabinette daily, unlimited tennis, admission to fitness centre and bicycles for two for one day to explore the island.

Sightseeing and leisure
A full array of watersports, Olympic size swimming pool, jacuzzi, tennis, fitness centre, hair salon and beauty centre are available at the hotel.
Championship golf nearby. Bicycles and mopeds for rent to explore the island. Shuttle to nearby attractions and shopping.

Hawaii

flying time

To: Honolulu, Oahu Island
London: 18 hrs
LA: 6 hrs
NY: 12 hrs

climate

Sunshine and mild
temperatures all year.
Aug and Sept are humid
and hottest (25–30°C).
Winter (Oct–Apr) is cooler
and wetter, rain being
most likely Feb–Mar.

when to go

If possible, avoid Christmas
and New Year, and school
summer holidays, when
rates are high and hotels,
golf courses and beaches
busy. Try to catch the
islanders celebrating
during the Aloha Festival
(mid Sept–Oct).

getting around

Internal flights link the six
main islands; island-
hopping to two or three is
recommended. Helicopter
sightseeing trips show off
the dramatic scenery. Car
hire is popular but driving
can be hair-raising on roads
with steep, hairpin-bends.

Hawaii is an excellent choice for a honeymoon destination, a place where American efficiency overlays romantic South Seas traditions. You will be guaranteed a warm welcome — greeted with a garland of flowers, invited to dance the *hula* and to taste the Polynesian barbecue known as a *luau*. Try to visit at least two of the islands during your stay. Of the six main islands — Oahu, Hawaii, Maui, Kauai, Molokai and Lanai, many people vote Kauai the most beautiful. Nicknamed the Garden Isle because of its lush, colourful scenery, it has featured in movies including 'South Pacific' and 'Jurassic Park'.

Be sure to surf the swells — body-surfing on a board is is the easy option; and make the most of a rare opportunity to go whale-watching. And, should one of the islands' volcanoes decide to perform while you are there, prepare yourself for a spectacle more thrilling than anything America's theme parks can offer. ●

Balmy heat and exotic floral scents hanging heavy in deep, green-carpeted valleys...

The Ritz-Carlton, Kapalua

One Ritz-Carlton Drive
Kapalua
Maui 96761
Hawaii

✈ Kapalua 10km

tel +808 669 6200
fax +808 665 0026

Open all year

Member of:
Audobon Heritage Resort

Surrounded by century-old Cook pines and ironwood trees to the north of Lahaina on the Hawaiian island of Maui, is the beautiful Ritz-Carlton, Kapalua.

Private 'lanais' or terraces look out over the pacific, colourful tropical gardens, or the distant peaks of the West Maui Mountains. Shuttered doors welcome balmy breezes into rooms, which are gracefully decorated with soft muted colours and original Hawaiian artwork. White marble baths add a touch of luxury in which to unwind.

A wide array of international and regional dishes can be enjoyed at one of the hotel's many restaurants. The Anuenue Room exudes a relaxed ambience amid Pacific Ocean views and offers Hawaiian specialities. Pacific Rim dishes are showcased in The Terrace restaurant, while the Banyan Tree serves Mediterranean dishes for lunch with dramatic views of Honolua Bay.

Known for their startling beauty and challenging play, the golf courses at Kapalua are also home to a variety of rare wildlife species. Some of the world's most beautiful scenery can be found in the underwater sanctuary of Honolua Bay. Ancient lava formations and brilliant coral gardens are home to Hawaiian reef fish and sea turtles making this a paradise for snorkellers and scuba divers alike.

As the sun sets over the neighbouring islands, guests may choose to end the day with a romantic stroll along the secluded bay.

US$260–450 (548)
US$495–2700 (58)
from US$75
from US$25

Honeymoon specials
Champagne and chocolate-dipped strawberries in the room on arrival.

Sightseeing and leisure
Swimming pool, tennis, golf, professional croquet lawn and Fitness Centre available at the hotel for no extra charge. Wide range of watersports including kayaking, and deep-sea fishing available. Resident artist with workshops. Hikes in rainforest, to dormant volcano, helicopter tours can be arranged. Local town has shopping and nightlife.

New York

flying time
To: JFK/Newark
London: 7–8 hrs
LA: 5–6 hrs
Miami: 3 hrs

climate
Summers are sometimes
uncomfortably hot,
winters can be bitterly
cold with thick snow.
Spring and autumn/fall
are more pleasant.

when to go
The street parades are
quite a sight; St Patrick's
Day in March sees one of
the biggest. At weekends
business hotels may have
special rates.

getting around
The grid lay-out of the
streets makes travelling
on foot a viable option.
Yellow taxis and buses are
numerous and frequent
but daytime traffic is bad.
The tubes are dirty and
confusing, but very cheap.
Boston or Washington are
just an hour by away by
plane, 4–5 hours by train.

Yellow taxis, shimmering neon, the classic curves of the
Chrysler Building — images of New York are familiar to
us all. The city is one of the world's most popular tourist
destinations, yet it remains surprisingly un-touristy.

There are sights in abundance, of course: the Statue of
Liberty, Radio City Music Hall, the Guggenheim, even
the hectic, hustling street life itself. For most people,
however, the main attraction is in the doing rather than
the seeing: shopping like mad in the countless stores
and boutiques, enjoying a scintillating evening on
Broadway before a night to remember in one of the Big
Apple's innumerable bars and restaurants.

New York can justly lay claim to be Entertainment
Capital of the World. Life here is a distillation of the rest
of the planet's most exuberant entertainments played
double-time — with jazz, samba, cinema, dance, and
over five hundred galleries and nightclubs.

Nevertheless, there are still plenty of opportunities to
wind down. Pick the right spots and this can be an
extremely relaxing place. Take a stroll round the lake in
Central Park and finish up in one of the quiet, homely
diners that dot the city; or take a privileged view down
First Avenue from the spectacular vantage point offered
by the cable cars that trundle overhead. ●

Parades, baseball, hot dogs
and designer ice cream, the
sounds of jazz, house, rap,
Gershwin and Sinatra,
Greenwich Village coffee
bars, the glittering lights of
Times Square...

The Pierre

Fifth Ave at 61st St
New York
USA

✈ JFK 45km

tel +1 212 838 8000
fax +1 212 758 1615

Open all year

Member of:
The leading Hotels of the World

A landmark almost as famous as the city itself, The Pierre rises majestically above the greenery of New York's Central Park. Influenced by the graceful architecture of French chateaux, the hotel is an imposing structure of granite and cream-coloured brick, capped with a tall tower of gleaming copper. The splendour of the frescoed Rotunda, smooth Italian marble floors, and exquisite hand-woven carpets of the gloriously ornate interior evoke a golden age of opulence and refinement.

The Pierre's impeccable rooms are individually styled with most distinctive decor. Trompe l'oeil paintings, gold mouldings and wood panelling combine to create a welcoming, yet distinguished ambience. Festooned French windows look out over the famous expanse of Central Park, and the exclusive boutiques on Fifth Avenue.

The muraled Rotunda with its trompe l'oeil ceiling is the signature room of the hotel. Renowned for its afternoon tea service, it also offers light meals and cocktails. The celebrated Cafe Pierre is an intimate fine dining restaurant where patrons can enjoy romantic live piano music.

Set in the heart of the Big Apple, the hotel is conveniently located for New York's theatre district, some of the world's most distinctive museums and galleries, and a dizzying range of tourist attractions from the Statue of Liberty to the gospel choirs of Harlem.

The hotel offers all-inclusive wedding plans tailored to a client's specific requirements, which can include a butlered cocktail reception and a wedding cake designed by the 'Tiffany of cake makers'.

US$445–895 (149)
From US$695 (53)
US$50–70
US$20–25

Honeymoon specials
Honeymoon weekend rates range from US$315–595 per night.

Sightseeing and leisure
Located in the heart of New York. Shopping trips. Visits to museums, theatres, historic sights, concerts. The hotel is conveniently close to the exclusive boutiques of Fifth Avenue. Jogging and walks in Central Park.

Canada

flying time
To: Toronto
London: 8 hrs
Miami: 5hrs
NY: 2hrs
Pus 4 hrs to Vancouver.

climate/when to go
Summer averages 24°C.
Winter can be icy, but
Canada is geared for the
cold. Winter Carnival in
Quebec City in February
provides 11 days of
revelry. In Calgary, for ten
days in July there is a
showcase for cowboy
skills and showmanship
called Stampede.

currency
The Canadian dollar.

language
English is generally
spoken, although French
predominates in the
French territories.

getting around
Air travel is comparatively
cheap. Trains are a good
alternative, especially on
scenic routes. Buses
serve some locations that
railways do not. Car hire
is reasonably priced.

Canada is the second largest country in the world, with a stunning variety of locales, from the Rocky Mountains to Niagara Falls; from the glittering skyscrapers of Toronto to the lonely lakes and forests of the Algonquin Provincial Park.

There is a rainbow of nationalities and cultures too, producing a tantalising variety of cuisines and some unique shopping opportunities: Inuit and Native Indian crafts, textiles and furs; traditional patchwork quilting; woodcarving, cowboy outfits and pottery aplenty. Coastal waters provide oysters, scallops, lobster and salmon, as well as clams for the famous chowder. The prairies offer grain-fed beef and delicious breads, and in the French territories you find classic *haute cuisine* as well as hearty, herby French colonial nosh.

Nightlife in Toronto meets up to anything the USA has to offer. The lakes are great for sailing, and there is Alpine and cross-country skiing all winter. On the west coast, Vancouver is a vibrant city and a good starting point for jaunts into the wilds of British Columbia — like a trip on the *Rocky Mountaineer*, a splendid train that hugs

A breath of fresh air...

mountainsides and edges along lakes, past breathtaking scenery. Niagara Falls, one of the most popular honeymoon destinations, is a short hop away. The Algonquin Provincial Park, just three hours' drive from Toronto, offers 3,000 square miles of wilderness complete with wolves, vast lakes and primordial forests.

Quebec has a largely rugged terrain, and a distinctively French air. Experience the *joie de vivre* of the Winter Carnival, pop into a *croissanterie* for breakfast, or while away the afternoon with the chic clientelle at a Montreal pavement café. ●

La Pinsonnière

Cap-à-l'Aigle
Charlevoix
Quebec
Canada

✈ Montreal Dorval Int. 400km

Quebec City 150km

tel +1 418 665 4431
fax +1 418 665 7156

lapinsonniere@cite.net

Closed 1 Nov–15 Dec

Member of:
Relais & Chateaux

This exclusive family-run inn perches high above the broad St Lawrence River in the heart of Quebec's stunningly beautiful Charlevoix region.

Set on a rambling property in the picturesque village of Cap-à-l'Aigle, many of the inn's luxuriously appointed rooms feature a double whirlpool bath and private sauna. Canopy beds and fireplaces provide a welcoming, comfortable atmosphere. Elegant bay windows open out onto spacious private balconies looking out over the river. The refined interior is heightened by a stunning collection of artwork.

Award-winning cuisine is served in a sophisticated softly lit dining room decorated with the owner's impressive art collection, and is complemented by one of the country's most highly rated wine cellars.

A nature trail meanders through a cedar wood to a secluded unspoiled beach that is ideal for sunbathing and picnicking. In summer, guests can try out activities as diverse as whale-watching cruises, outdoor concerts with Sunday brunch and carriage rides. During the winter months, guests can ski, take a romantic sleigh ride, or try dog-sledding or snowmobiling. Daredevils can experience the thrills of white-water rafting or sea kayaking, or try their luck at the glamorous casino.

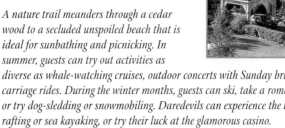

 CAD$130–400 (26)
 CAD$400 (1)
 from CAD$39
 from CAD$13

Honeymoon specials
Honeymoon package includes welcome cocktail, a celebratory five-course dinner, breakfast, champagne and a souvenir gift. The package is available for three and five nights at a cost of CAD$800–1,600 and CAD$1,250–2,600 per couple respectively.

Sightseeing and leisure
Outdoor concerts, boat cruises, wine tastings, art galleries and casino nearby. Whale-watching, skiing, sleigh rides, dog-sledding, snowmobiling, golf, horse-riding, white-water rafting and sea-kayaking can be arranged. Swimming and tennis. Sauna and massage by appointment.

Central America

climate/when to go
The weather varies greatly
with altitude and latitude.
All year the lowlands are
stiflingly hot at 25–30°C,
the highlands 10°C cooler.
The rainy season is Jun–Oct. In
winter conditions are still fine
but gentler and cooler.

currency
The US dollar dominates.
Traveller's cheques are
accepted in tourist areas,
credit cards only in cities
and exclusive venues.

language
Spanish predominates.
In Mexico and Belize
English-speakers abound.

health
Standard inoculations include
yellow fever, rabies, typhoid,
tetanus, polio, hepatitis, and
hepatitis B. Drink bottled
water. Take malaria pills for
tropical plains and jungle.

getting around
There are frequent flights
between major cities.

Remote Mayan ruins surrounded by jungle,
brash cities echoing to the lament of *mariachi*,
the peace of parched-white Caribbean beaches...

CARIBBEAN SEA

Panama

PANAMA

H ere at 'the sweet waist of America' a fantastic range of political, ethnic and environmental forces have collided, creating a magical hybrid.

In the big cites, a version of Coca-Cola culture moves to the rhythm of Colombian *salsa*. Deep in the forests, species of birds, beasts and plants from north and south live beside local species that are found nowhere else in the world.

There are places where it is not wise to travel, but the coral-fringed beaches of Belize, the beautiful bays and rainforests of Costa Rica, and the soaring, creeper-clad ruins of the ancient Mayan Indian civilisation in Guatemala, are truly unforgettable honeymoon locations. Neighbouring Mexico, a more cosmoplitan country with gorgeous beaches, pulsating resorts and magnificent monuments, is already a mainstream holiday destination.

The whole region is incredibly romantic: for its scenery of smouldering volcanoes rising above green and gold highland valleys; for its still, dark lakes and mysterious cloud forests shrouded in swirling mists; for its tropical jungles hiding ancient pyramids; for its crumbling, elegant colonial architecture; for its thrilling music and passionate people.

The great driving forces here are land, family and religion, and throughout the whole of Central America a fiery Latin heart beats just below the surface of all things.

Belize

Belize is a tiny strip of country bordering the Caribbean sea. Its coastline is sheltered by a huge barrier reef with hundreds of islands scattered along its length. Its almost uninhabited jungly interior harbours a rich collection of tropical flora and wildlife, including the endangered jaguar, as well as innumerable Mayan ruins.

The islands or cayes provide the main focus for visitors. The most developed resort island is Ambergris Caye, but there are plenty of hideaways, both exclusive and cheap. Life here is even more laidback than on the mainland, ruffled only by

Jungles teeming with wildlife,
easy-going, sandy Caribbean streets,
offshore islands fringed with palms,
spectacular living coral reefs and
flickering shoals of rainbow-coloured fish...

flying time
To: Belize City
via USA or Mexico.
London: 10–11 hrs
Miami: 2 1/2 hrs
NY: 6 1/2 hrs

climate/when to go
The rain stops and the seas are calm March–May, but temperatures soar. December brings the the finest weather of the year: fresh, clear and warm.

currency
The Belize dollar, fixed to the US dollar. Bring US dollars in cash and traveller's cheques.

getting around
By air to almost all main towns. The roads are the best in Central America. Car hire is recommended. High-clearance vehicles are needed when visiting the remote Mayan site of Caracol. Cycling is fun.

gentle sea breezes. The diving and snorkelling are excellent; beneath the surface of the sea you find a kaleidoscopic display of tropical fish, sharks, swordfish, marlin and ray.

The great reef is Belize's star attraction, but the tropical forests of the interior are equally exciting, especially if you travel along any of the rivers, where you may see giant iguanas sunning themselves on the shore, brilliant kingfishers and gorgeous butterflies, sleeping bats and lizards that walk on water.

To the south, the remote districts of Toledo and Stann Creek offer both tropical forests and rich wildlife, notably Cockscomb Basin, the only jaguar reserve in the world; also, highlands featuring Maya villages and ancient ruins; and some of the finest mainland beaches.

More accessible, the western Cayo district encompasses jungle lodges along the Rivers Mopan and Macal; Mountain Pine Ridge, a region of pine forests, meadows and waterfalls that is ideal for hiking and camping; and the huge ceremonial centre of Caracol, hidden deep in the jungle. Northern Belize is mostly flat, though it has some significant Maya ruins.

There are few festivals but the country's Caribbean culture ensures there is no lack of entertainment, with parties and discos almost every weekend.

Belize has an enormous variety of tropical luxury hotels, though only the best observe the highest service standards. Seafood is particularly fine on the cayes, where dishes include shark, snapper, wahoo, conch and shrimps. At Easter you may be offered iguana, which is surprisingly delicious, a bit like tender chicken. At any time of year, you will be offered delicious Belizean rum.

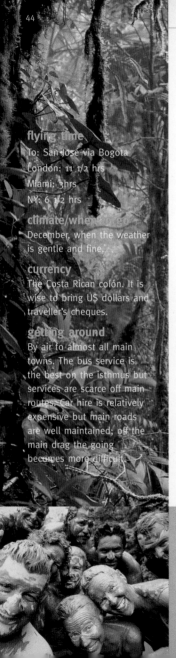

flying time
To: San José via Bogota
London: 11 1/2 hrs
Miami: 3hrs
NY: 6 1/2 hrs

climate/when to go
December, when the weather
is gentle and fine.

currency
The Costa Rican colón. It is
wise to bring US dollars and
traveller's cheques.

getting around
By air to almost all main
towns. The bus service is
the best on the isthmus but
services are scarce off main
routes. Car hire is relatively
expensive but main roads
are well maintained; off the
main drag the going
becomes more difficult.

Costa Rica

The second smallest of the Central American nations, Costa Rica is an increasingly popular destination with nature-lovers and sports enthusiasts in particular, but still relatively undiscovered — and cleaner, greener and more relaxed than its neighbours.

No less than 20 per cent of the country has been set aside for nature conservation in a superb network of national parks, all alive with the overwhelming fertility of the tropics, and offering a unique opportunity to see wildlife in the raw. The country is home to more than 750 species of bird — more than in the entire USA — and protected areas include steaming volcanic peaks, undisturbed tropical forests, lakes, islands, dry grassland, superb beaches, mountains and pre-Colombian ruins.

In this country of natural wonders and astonishing beauty highlights include Corcovado National Park, diving off the Cocos Islands, carnival in Puerto Limón, the Gold Museum in San José, Arenal Volcano — and a whole raft of sports. Pacific rollers pound the coast, attracting surfing enthusiasts. River rafting, also available in Belize and Guatemala, is a developing sport that requires no training. River and sea fishing are superb. Hiking encompasses a stroll along a beach, the gruelling ascent of a volcanic peak and wading through jungle mud. Wildlife viewing is in a league of its own. ●

Nimble spider monkeys
crashing through the trees,
massive sea turtles dragging
themselves ashore to deposit eggs,
surfing, white-water rafting, beaches...

Lapa Rios

Pto. Jiménez
Costa Rica

✈ 20km from local airstrip
50 min. local flight

Contact:
PO Box 025216, SJo-706
Miami, FL 33102-5216, USA

tel +506 735 5130
fax +506 735 5179
laparios@sol.racsa.co.cr

Open   Nov–Apr (High
Season)

May–Nov (Green

Set in a thousand acres of private rainforest, high up on the Osa Peninsula, overlooking the Pacific Ocean, owner-operated Lapa Rios is one of the most deluxe jungle and beach hideways in Costa Rica.

Fourteen luxury thatched bungalows are dotted throughout the jungle. Each has a private deck and patio garden with magnificent views over the ocean, showers with solar-heated water, and two queen-sized beds. The bungalows are furnished in wood and bamboo with tropical printed fabrics. Constant breezes pass through the screened window walls. Although isolated (no phones), service at Lapa Rios is sophisticated. Staff are outgoing and experienced. Electricity is provided 24 hours a day. The main lodge, soaring 50 feet into the air, has a full service bar and restaurant serving quality cuisine, with the accent on fresh fruits, vegetables and meat, and local seafood.

Visitors can relax on safe, unspoiled sandy beaches, watch the continuous parade of birds, butterflies and animals native to Costa Rica, and take part in adventurous organised activities – from jungle hikes to sea kayaking.

 US$164 (14)

 US$25

US$8

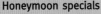

Honeymoon specials
Bouquet of flowers and welcome cocktail on arrival. The cost of US$164 includes all meals.

Leisure facilities
A romantic swimming pool set in tropical rainforest and a private tropical plant and orchid garden. Massage by appointment.

Local attractions
Resident naturalists give guided tours around the private reserve and the famous Corovado National Park nearby. Adventure activities include hiking deep into the rainforest, sea kayaking, horseriding, deep-sea, in-shore and on-shore fishing, mangrove river and gulf boat rides.

Mexico

Mexico's famous shimmering coastline along the Pacific, the Caribbean and the Gulf of Mexico is just one element of this vast country's extraordinary range of attractions.

The captivating landscape varies from snow-capped mountains to arid deserts, and lush, tropical forests to temperate valleys, while numerous archeological sites and historic cities inspire visitors with their mysticism and beauty.

Mexico City is cosmopolitan and modern, and a tribute to earlier civilisations with magnificent Aztec temples and the floating gardens of Xochimilco, where people still live on the canals, as the Aztecs did 500 years ago. The city is also an ideal base from which to visit the pyramids of Teotihuacan, one of the world's most impressive archeological sites, the temple of Tlahizcalpantecuhtli in Tula, with its gigantic Atlantes statues, and the colonial cities of Taxco, Toluca and Tepotzotlan.

Monuments of ancient civilisations, flamboyant fiestas, whales leaping from the deep blue water of the sea of Cortes, baroque churches, the lush colours of a patio garden glimpsed behind wrought iron gates...

flying time
To: Mexico City
London: 10–12 hrs
LA/Miami: 3 hrs
NY: 5 hrs

climate
Generally the northwest
coast, northern Baja
California and central
plateau are coolest. Overall,
the weather is temperate
and dry Nov–May, with
temperatures rising and
rainfall heavier June–Oct.

when to go
High season, with crowds
and action, is December,
February and July–August.
The quiet months are
April and May.

currency
The Mexican peso.

getting around
Frequent flights between
major cities, together with
a vast bus network and
rather slow rail system.

The south of Mexico was home to the Maya, one of the greatest civilisations dating from 3,000 years ago. Chichen-Itza is the most renowned of all Mayan cities, with some of the greatest monuments, including the great pyramid known as El Castillo.

Heading north, Guadalajara is hailed as the essence of Mexico, upholding traditions like the *charreadas* (rodeos) and *jaraba tapatio* (hat dance), while the famous *mariachis* create plenty of atmosphere in Plaza Tapatio. The region known as El Bajio, in central Mexico, features some of the country's most attractive cities.

Acapulco offers glittering nightlife and world-famous beaches surrounded by tropical mountains, with the famous divers of la Quebrada diving from a cliff 45 metres high.

Spectacular scenery, including pine forests, can be seen from the Chihuahua-Pacifico train which joins the *altiplano* of Mexico with the sea of Cortes. The train travels through historic towns such as Bahuichivo, a good base from which to explore the staggering Copper Canyon.

There are no fewer than 58 national parks and reserves. Among the rare animals to be spotted are jaguars, while whales swim through the sea of Cortes, where the islands are a refuge for sea lions and rare sea birds.

Good international food is readily available, as well as the native cuisine with its three indispensible elements: tortillas, beans and chillies. Ideal accompaniments are tequila, mezcal (the one with the worm in it) and pulque. Fiestas are a colourful spectacle, with some of the most important being Carnival (February or March), Independence Day (15–16 September) and the Day of the Dead (1–2 November). Despite its ominous sounding name, this last is actually a flamboyant celebration of ancestors.

You will find plenty of things to bring home — from shopping malls full of designer names, and markets with folk art and handicrafts.

Fiesta Americana Cancun

Bld Kukulcan Km 9.5
Cancun
Quintana Roo 77500
Mexico

 Cancun 10km

tel +52 98 85 1000
fax +52 98 85 1800
hbacelis@fiestaamericana.com.mx

Open all year

Tour operators/booking:
US: 1 800 Fiesta 1 (USA)

Set on one of the finest beaches on the narrow Cancun peninsula, the Fiesta Americana Cancun overlooks the smooth blue expanse of Mexico's Caribbean.

The Mediterranean inspiration of the hotel's design is reflected in the red-tiled roofs and stone balustrades of the private balconies. All rooms are sea-facing, decorated with airy Mexican modern elegance, and furnished with oak. Large picture windows lead out onto private balconies which afford views of the sun setting over the ocean.

A dining experience to suit all taste buds is assured by the range of restaurants and bars in the hotel. Friendly staff serve traditional Mexican dishes at Chulavista Café, while local seafood specialities are prepared by the pool at La Palapa. Fine Northern Italian cuisine is on offer in the relaxed atmosphere of Barolo Ristorante.

The hotel also offers a wide range of watersports including snorkelling, scuba diving, and waterskiing. Jungle and catamaran tours can be organised by the hotel. Visitors can venture further afield to archeological sites at Tulum and Chichen-Itza, take a boat to some of the surrounding islands, or explore the natural aquariums. There is a variety of nightlife in the area including discos and bars, and a jazz festival and carnivals.

The hotel is happy to organise flowers, table decorations, receptions and flower arrangements for weddings. Ceremonies can take place on the beach, at the poolside, or on a special deck situated by the ocean against a backdrop of spectacular Caribbean sunsets.

 US$143–402 (483)

 US$361–701 (19)

 from US$26

from US$17

Honeymoon specials
'Fiesta for Two' honeymoon package, costing from US$732 and based on a stay of 3 nights, includes deluxe ocean-facing room, flowers and champagne on arrival, daily buffet breakfast and one dinner. All taxes are included.

Sightseeing and leisure
Trips to eco-archeological park and archeological sites including Mayan ruins in the area. Shopping trips to the malls. Golf and tennis nearby.

Fiesta Americana
Condesa

Bld Kukulkan, Km 16.5
Hotel Zone, Cancun
Quintana Roo 77500
Mexico

 Cancun City 10km

tel +52 98 851000
fax +52 98 851800

ruriel@fiestaamericana.com.mx

Open all year

Member of:
The Leading Hotels of the World

Located on the powdery beaches overlooking the clear turquoise waters of Mexico's Caribbean, the Fiesta Americana Condesa Cancun features three horseshoe-shaped towers surrounded by lush tropical gardens and cascading waterfalls. The hotel has a distinctive architectural design beginning with the country's largest palapa which soars 35 metres into the air shading the main lobby.

The 502 rooms and suites have elegant marble bathrooms and are furnished with oak in light modern designs to create a relaxed and airy ambience. Each room has a private balcony overlooking the ocean or lagoon. Most suites have terraces draped with tropical plants to ensure romantic seclusion, and several are equipped with a jacuzzi.

The hotel has a number of restaurants and choosing where to dine can be difficult. From the Northern Italian specialities of the Rosato Ristorante to the international cuisine of the Kalmia, each restaurant has a unique atmosphere. The Kambu Palapa, overlooking the beach and pool, offers a delicious variety of local seafood for informal dining.

There are many fascinating archeological sites in the area, including Mayan ruins on the seashore. The hotel can also organise exciting jungle tours into the heart of Mexico. More closer to home, traditional thatch parasols shade bathers at the central lagoon-shaped swimming pool. The hotel spa and beauty centre provides a tranquil oasis where guests can unwind in luxury.

The hotel is pleased to take care of wedding arrangements from flowers to table decorations. The lower pool deck or the Patio Mexicano are ideal settings for private wedding ceremonies.

 US$160–450 (483)

 US$405–785 (19)

 from US$29

from US$18

Honeymoon specials
'Fiesta For Two' honeymoon package costs US$977 and includes 3 nights in a deluxe ocean view room, flowers and champagne in room on arrival, dinner, buffet breakfast in room. All taxes are included.

Sightseeing and leisure
Gym, tennis and watersports on site. Golf nearby. Trips to shopping mall and eco-archeological park nearby. Archeological sites including Mayan ruins in the area. Jungle and catamaran tours by arrangement.

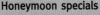

10

Las Brisas

Carretera Escénica 5255
39868 Acapulco
Mexico

✈ Acapulcao 15km

tel +52 74 841 580
fax +52 74 842 261

lasbrisas@infosel.net.mx

Open all year

Member of:
The Leading Hotels of the World

Tour operator/booking
US: Central Reservations

South of Mexico City, nestling high up into the hillside and overlooking Acapulco Bay, are the 300 pink and white casitas which make up Las Brisas. Palms and rich foliage tumble down to the water's edge, and stunning views rest the eye as the magnificent bay stretches into the distance.

Polished stone floors and rough-hewn walls keep the temperature comfortable in the spacious, open-plan luxury villas which are bleached to a brilliant white by the sun. Thatched summer houses offer shade beside elegant palmed pools, some of which have their own waterfall. Lush tropical plants in earthenware pots grace expansive patios and huge, comfortable beds and furniture make this an ideal place to lounge around during the endless summer.

Fresh fruit, sweet rolls and coffee are delivered daily to every casita. Gourmet cuisine of every description is prepared by an excellent cook and can be enjoyed in the intimacy of a private terrace.

Afternoons can be spent exploring the sights by jeep, watching divers dive from the heights of the La Quebrada cliffs into the crashing waves below, or simply sipping margaritas at the poolside. This is the place for would-be movie stars and oil tycoons.

Weddings can be arranged including music, flowers, priest, church, marriage officer and a trip to the beauty parlour. La Concha Beach Club can accommodate up to 450 guests and a torchlit ceremony is also available.

 US$170–790 (300)
 US$515–1,160 (29)
 US$35–50
 US$10–20

Honeymoon specials
Welcome cocktail and flower petals in the pool.
Upgrade subject to availability.

Leisure facilities
Private beach club, Jeeps for rental, most watersports and tennis. Golf courses available nearby.

Local attractions
Watching the La Quebrada divers. Trips to the famous Fortress of San Diego. Acapulco music festival in May. Speed boats and Shotover Jet Theme Park nearby.

The Ritz-Carlton, Cancun

Retorno Del Rey No. 36
Zona Hotelera Cancun
Q-ROO 77500
Mexico

 Cancun 16km

tel +52 98 810 808
fax +52 98 851 798

Open all year

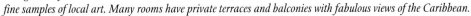

Magnificently positioned at the palm-fringed tip of the Mexican peninsula, the Ritz-Carlton, Cancun is surrounded by the pristine sands of the Caribbean and the ancient treasures of nearby Mayan ruins.

Designed to reflect a rich Spanish heritage, the tiled roofs and colonial fountains are reminiscent of a Mediterranean palace.

The spacious rooms and suites are decorated with simple colonial elegance and feature delicate wrought iron furniture, handcarved woodwork and fine samples of local art. Many rooms have private terraces and balconies with fabulous views of the Caribbean.

Guests can choose to dine in a number of formal and informal settings. The Fantino Restaurant, overlooking the sea, offers robust flavours of Tuscany and the Mediterranean. For al fresco dining, tasty American and Mexican specialities are served at the beachfront Caribe Bar and Grill.

There are a range of activities on offer including all watersports. Snorkelling and diving enthusiasts can discover the natural wonders of the world's second largest coral reef. Day trips can be organised to the recently discovered Mayan ruins at Xcaret allowing visitors a glimpse of Mexico's ancient heritage.

The hotel is happy to arrange wedding ceremonies and can organise everything from buttonholes to customised wedding cakes.

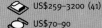 US$199–250 (365)
US$259–3200 (41)
US$70–90
US$20

Honeymoon specials
The Romance Package costs between US$1,500 and US$2,000 per night per couple and includes four nights accommodation, champagne and truffles in the room on arrival, private candlit dinner, aromatherapy massage and private airport transfers.

Sightseeing and leisure
Wide range of land and watersports including diving, fishing and tennis, fitness centre, beauty centre, boutiques and art gallery on site. Jungle tours and excursions to Mayan ruins can be arranged.

Caribbean Islands

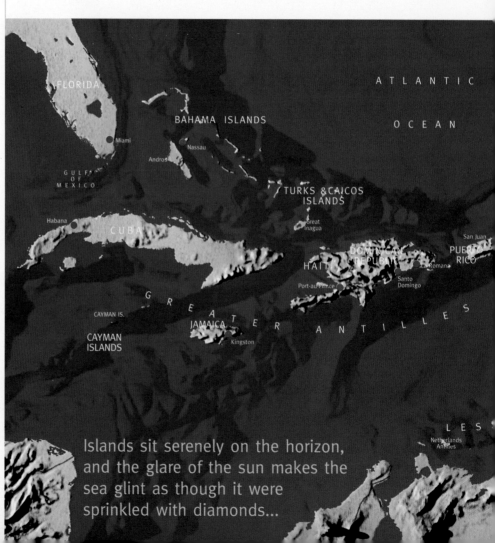

flying time
Most islands are reached via Antigua.
London: 10–12 hrs
Miami: 1–3 hrs
NY: 3–5 hrs

climate
Sunny and hot (21–28°C) with pleasant breezes. Summer (Jun–Oct) can be humid and still. The wet seasons are May/Jun, Oct/Nov. Hurricanes are most likely in September.

when to go
Any time, but the weather is at its best in the high season (mid Jan–mid April). February is carnival time.

language and currency
English, Spanish and French reflecting the islands' colonial past. The US dollar is in universal demand.

health
Malaria pills, and jabs against polio, typhoid and Hepatitis A are advisable. Tap water is generally safe to drink.

getting around
Boats and planes make island-hopping easy.

FLORIDA

ATLANTIC

OCEAN

BAHAMA ISLANDS

Miami

Nassau

Andros

GULF OF MEXICO

TURKS & CAICOS ISLANDS

Great Inagua

Habana

CUBA

DOMINICAN REPUBLIC

San Juan

PUERTO RICO

HAITI

La Romana

Port-au-Prince

Santo Domingo

G R E A T E R

CAYMAN IS.

JAMAICA

A N T I L L E S

CAYMAN ISLANDS

Kingston

L E S

Netherlands Antilles

Islands sit serenely on the horizon, and the glare of the sun makes the sea glint as though it were sprinkled with diamonds...

The Caribbean is the place for an all-over body holiday, and the world's most popular honeymoon destination by far.

Here you can dive in crystal seas to a glittering seascape of corals and tropical fish, take a trip on a catamaran, feel the surge of a windsurfer beneath you as you race off on the trade winds, or simply lie back and absorb the sun's warmth.

You will be bombarded by intense sensations — the sweet flavours of ripened fruits, the fragrance of jasmine on the night air, the impossibly bright plumage of a scarlet ibis and music played loudly, everywhere.

The region is an extraordinary melting pot of cultures including Parisian chic, English country churches, American-style cable television and large cruising cars, Hindu prayer flags, Moslem minarets and, of course, the spirit of Africa — in the islanders' faces, their spirit religions, and relentless drum-based rhythms.

These days, in places it can be difficult to find an isolated beach, and would-be island-hoppers should plan their route with care. Elsewhere, however, there are beaches from paradise, and some of the most exclusive places to stay in the world.

Try the Grenadines and Virgin Islands for isolated island settings, Barbados for grand, long-established hotels set in magnificent gardens, St Kitts and Nevis for plantation estate elegance, St Barts for chic and luxury, Anguilla for distinctive style and sumptuous, small-island charm and Jamaica for reliable luxury.

Western Caribbean

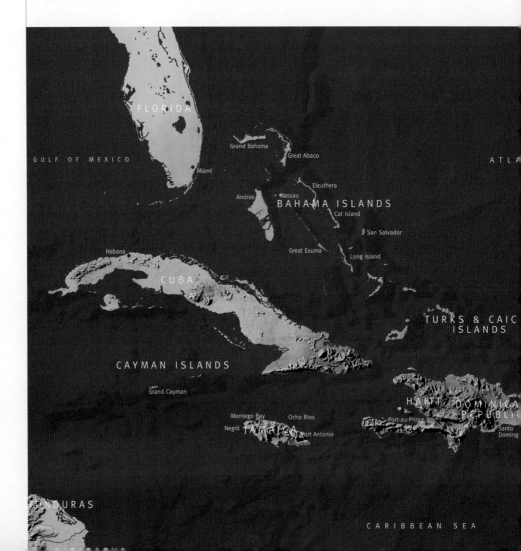

FLORIDA

GULF OF MEXICO

Grand Bahama

Great Abaco

Miami

Eleuthera

Andros

Nassau

BAHAMA ISLANDS

Cat Island

San Salvador

Habana

Great Exuma

Long Island

CUBA

ATLA

TURKS & CAIC
ISLANDS

CAYMAN ISLANDS

Grand Cayman

Montego Bay   Ocho Rios

Negril

JAMAICA

Port Antonio

Kingston

HAITI   DOMINICA
REPUBLI

Port-au-Prince

Santo
Doming

HONDURAS

CARIBBEAN SEA

One step to heaven...

OCEAN

VIRGIN
ISLANDS
PUERTO
RICO

The Bahamas

The Bahamas, 'the isles of perpetual June', are a favourite subject of satellite photographers; 700 low-lying emerald-green islands and cays scattered over 100,000 square miles.

The water is gin-clear and glistens over the banks of sand that stretch for miles; in places you must walk hundreds of yards into the sea before the water reaches your waist.

The fishing and sailing here are world renowned; the diving is something else, with superb reefs and many wrecks, and curious Blue holes that can grow to 200 feet across and descend up to 90 feet below the surface of the sea.

The islands divide into three groups. At the heart of the Bahamas is the the senior island of New Providence with the capital, Nassau, and the main resort areas of Paradise Island and Cable Beach — a place of pastel-painted palace hotels, cabarets and gambling halls with acres of slot machines.

To the north is Freeport/Lucaya on Grand Bahama island, an American-style resort, with suburbs and air-conditioned supermarkets, unlimited watersports by day, and gambling, glitz and cabaret by night.

Fantastic reef landscapes — bouquets of flower corals, layers of carpet anemones, gorgonians like vast fans, rays cruising, groupers loitering, luxuriously coloured angelfish twitching as they glide past...

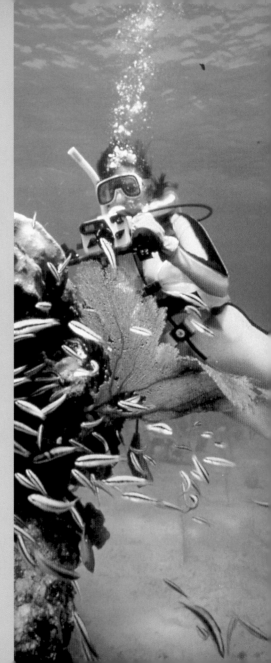

flying time
To: Nassau/Freeport
London: 10 hrs
Miami: 35 mins
NY: 3 hrs

climate/when to go
Fair and clement all year at
21–27°C, with festivals and
sailing regattas pretty much
year-round too.

currency
The Bahamian and the US
dollar, set at par with each
other. Traveller's cheques and
credit cards are widely
accepted, personal cheques
are not.

language
English.

getting around
There are frequent flights
from Nassau to most islands.
On the main islands you find
buses and taxis, or hire cars
and scooters (at a price).
On the Out Islands you can
hitch or cycle, or hail one of
the few taxi cars/boats.

The 697 other islands, known as the Out Islands, are less developed and offer a far gentler lifestyle, making them ideal for an isolated break.

If you feel like travelling, two weeks is sufficient to see a good variety of islands. You might start with a trip to one of the more developed Out Islands, perhaps Harbour Island or North Eleuthera, or to the lovely cays off the Abacos. Great Exuma is also worth a visit; from here you can reach the superb Exuma Cays, beloved of sailors. For a taste of small-island life, try Andros, Cat Island, Long Island or San Salvador.

The Bahamas were a colony of Britain until 1973. There is a large number of expatriate residents, but the USA is now the major influence on life, particularly in the main resorts. The cars are big American cruisers, food is fast, and good restaurants serve gourmet fare made with ingredients imported from the States.

Many hotels have private beaches and the major public beaches offer most watersports. Romantic options include hiring a boat for a day's snorkelling or a sunset cruise.

Diving lessons are available at all the main centres. There are some spectacular reefs right off Nassau that have been used in a number of film sets, where you can actually join in shark-feeding time. Further out, in the Out Islands, off the eastern coast of Andros is the third-largest barrier reef in the world. Off the Abacos and Eleuthera, dives include the wrecks of two trains that went down while they were being transported.

▶

Festivals include Junkanoo with masquerades in the streets on 26 December and 1 January. The festival of Goombay runs over the summer months, with a wide series of cultural events and carnival parades through the streets. In the summer, sailing regattas are amongst the liveliest occasions, with onshore parties and jump-ups.

The main resort islands attract over three million visitors a year, but even in the most developed areas it is easy to find bars where you can meet the islanders and eat delicious traditional Caribbean fare. Local markets, too, are a thriving, authentic part of West Indian life.

For the traditional Bahamian tropical idyll, nevertheless, you must go to the Out Islands, with their pretty waterfront towns and deserted beaches, where you can walk for miles and see no sign of human life.

Sandals Royal Bahamian and spa

Cable Beach
Nassau
Bahamas

 Nassau 5km

tel +1 242 327 6400
fax +1 242 327 6961

Open all year

Tour Operators
UK: Unique Vacations (UK) Ltd

This deluxe all-inclusive resort for couples only is located on Nassau's famed white-sand Cable Beach.

Classical gardens inspired by those at the Palace of Versailles, and magnificent statues reminiscent of ancient Greece, create an atmosphere of almost regal elegance.

All rooms and suites are stylishly furnished with classic mahogany furniture and king-size beds. Many have stunning views of the ocean. The Honeymoon One bedroom suite has a sumptuous four-poster and spacious sitting area.

There are a variety of sports on offer including all watersports, and swimming in the huge colonnaded pool. At the fully equipped fitness centre, guests can work up an appetite.

The resort's six restaurants serve dishes spanning the culinary globe. Guests can choose the intimacy of the Baccarat Restaurant, The Crystal Room for international à la carte dining, Spices, the Royal Café Grill, Café Goombay – the Bahamian Restaurant located on an offshore island or the Cricketers, an authentic English pub.

Weddings receptions can be arranged in the extensive grounds.

 US$660–780 (102)*
 US$830–950 (94)*
included
included

Honeymoon specials
A complimentary 20-piece Royal Doulton starter set for couples arriving between 19 Dec 1997 and 1 Dec 1998 and staying 13 nights or longer in a premium or higher category room. All meals, drinks, sports and snacks are included in the all-inclusive rate.

* prices are per person based on a stay of 2 nights

Sightseeing and leisure
All watersports, tennis, billiards, volleyball, croquet and golf are included in the all-inclusive rate. Golf carts are at an extra charge. Beauty and spa treatments cost extra.

Bermuda

A subtropical paradise set in the warm Atlantic some 600 miles off America's east coast, Bermuda actually comprises a 21-mile curve of linked islands blessed with a balmy climate, lush green countryside, a profusion of colourful flowering shrubs and beautiful beaches of fine coral-pink sand. With a wide range of quality accommodation, from American high-rise hotels to quaint country cottages, and plenty to see and do, it is a perfect holiday destination.

Discovered by Spanish mariner Juan de Bermudez in 1503, the islands were claimed in England's name in 1609 and they remain English-speaking and loyal to Britain to this day. Their proximity to North America has given them a New World feel and made them a popular cruise ship destination, while the mild climate, clean, safe environment and excellent sports facilities continue to attract many repeat visitors.

Bermuda offers all kinds of holiday. Those interested in history will love St George's Town, the islands' first capital, founded in 1612. A stroll through the narrow streets is a walk back in time — see the Town Hall, Old Rectory, St Peter's Church, several quaint museums and the *Deliverance*, a full-size replica of a 17th-century sailing ship.

At the other end of the island you can visit Gibbs Hill Lighthouse, which affords wonderful views over Great Sound and the whole archipelago. Then in Sandys parish you cross Somerset Bridge, the world's smallest drawbridge.

Do not miss Scaur Hill Fort Park with its 19th-century fortress, and the old Royal Naval Dockyard, beautifully restored and now one of Bermuda's premier attractions, with its Maritime Museum, Arts Centre, Craft Market and Pottery.

Pastel colours, whitewashed roofs, English bobbies, Bermuda shorts, pink-coral beaches, yachts bobbing at anchor, green rolling countryside, cricket and golf, sophisticated hotels and quaint country cottages...

flying time

To: Hamilton
London: 7 hrs
Miami: 3–4 hrs
New York: 2 hrs

climate

Summers (May–Oct) can
be hot and humid. Winters
are mild.

when to go

In summer for swimming,
boating, fishing and
watersports. In spring and
autumn for golf and riding.
In June of alternate
(even-numbered) years,
to enjoy the finish of the
great Newport to Bermuda
Ocean Yacht Race.

currency

The Bermuda dollar, at par
with the US dollar.

getting around

Distances are small, buses
and taxis are freely
available, although car
rental is not. Visitors hire
bicycles and mopeds.
Ferryboats are fun, and for
romantics there is no better
way to see Hamilton than
from a horse-drawn surrey
with a fringe on top.

In the capital, Hamilton, you find high-class shops
and stores facing the cruise ships which tie up right
alongside Front Street, and a number of interesting
buildings including Sessions House and the famous
Perot Post Office. The new Bermuda Underwater
Experimental Institute offers a unique insight into
marine life.

Other attractions include the Bermuda Aquarium,
Crystal Caves, the Botanical Gardens, and the dozens
of lovely beaches, bays and coves which dot the
coastline. Watersports enthusiasts will be in their
element. There is tennis, fishing and riding too, while
golfers have a choice of eight attractive and
challenging courses.

Nightlife tends to be limited to the larger hotels, but
that is not a problem. You can join in, or simply dine
al fresco on a restaurant terrace under the stars, then
stroll home in the warm scented air.

Cambridge Beaches

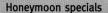

30 Kings Point
Sandys MA 02
Bermuda

✈ Bermuda Int. 35km

el +441 234 0331
fax +441 234 3352
cambeach@ibl.bm

Contact:

US: International Communications
    Consultants tel +1 203 431 0150
UK: Connect AB Ltd tel +44 1753 684 810

Open all year

This elegant cottage colony, situated at the western end of Bermuda on a 25-acre peninsula and surrounded by five private, soft pink, sandy beaches, is the perfect romantic getaway.

Individually decorated rooms and suites offer privacy and comfort and include balcony or terrace. Many have spectacular ocean views.

Award-winning gourmet cuisine can be enjoyed in a variety of indoor and outdoor settings including the privacy of guests' own cottage, the pool or beachside or the elegant Tamarisk Room. Afternoon tea is served daily at four o'clock in the Club House. For a truly magical evening guests, can dine al fresco beneath the stars on the beautiful Mangrove Bay Terrace.

The resort offers a wealth of activities including all watersports. Guests can choose to take a private shuttle to Bermuda's charming capital – Hamilton – for a day's shopping, or simply escape to the many beaches and coves which provide secluded locations for sunbathing, swimming and snorkelling.

This is an ideal setting for weddings and receptions for up to 50 guests can be arranged on the grass terraces or in the lounge overlooking Mangrove Bay.

 US$245–515 (62)
 US$370–595 (17)
 included
 included

Honeymoon specials

Deluxe accommodation, breakfast, afternoon tea and dinner, all taxes and gratuities, fruit basket and champagne on arrival. Massage, sailing trip, personalised photo and airport transfers. The package costs from US$3,200–4,350 per couple and is based on a stay of six nights. A wedding package is also available ranging from US$4,235–5,475.

Sightseeing and leisure

Ferry excursions to Hamilton. Visits to historic dockyard, maritime museum, arts and crafts centre and galleries. Private beaches, pool, croquet, tennis, fully equipped marina, reef snorkelling. Moped and bicycle hire. European solarium and spa with a range of treatments, sauna, steam room. Access to nearby golf courses, deep-sea fishing and scuba diving.

Pink Beach Club

Tuckers Town

Bermuda

✈ BDA Int. 7km

Contact:
Elite Hotels, 777 Boton Post Rd,
Darien, CT 08820 USA

tel: +1 800 355 6161
fax: +1 203 655 2797
elitehot@aol.com

Closed: 14 Dec 1997–1 Mar 1998

Tour operators:
UK:Prestige Holidays

Nestled in acres of rolling hills and lush gardens, overlooking two magnificent, pink coral beaches is the deluxe cottage colony – Pink Beach Club.

Soft pink-painted cottages dotted throughout the grounds house large rooms and suites, also decorated in light pastel shades, with wooden furniture and well-tended plants. Each room has two double beds, some king-size, and views of the ocean. Breakfast is served in the main Club House, or brought by a personal maid to the suite or private balcony.

Dinner is served by candlelight in the ocean-front restaurant, where international dishes are prepared by top European chefs.

Guests can discover the sights of Bermuda by moped, scooter, taxi or horse-drawn carriage; try scuba diving and experience the wonders of marine life; or simply sip cocktails by the pool.

For a relaxing evening in the bar or on the pool terrace, a pianist, jazz musicians and steel drum bands provide a range of live music from Calypso to Swing.

Couples can exchange their vows, in true Bermudian tradition, under the 'moongate' – a coral ring said to bring happiness and good fortune.

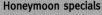

US$345–450 (+17.25%)

included

included

Honeymoon specials
Wine, cheese and fruit in the room on arrival, breakfast and dinner, and one day's complimentary snorkel gear and moped rental costs from US$2,287 per couple and is based on a stay of 5 nights.

Sightseeing and leisure
Moped rental, tennis and gym on site. Massage by appointment. All watersports, reef and deep-sea fishing, parasailing, sailing and golf nearby. Only 15 mins from the historic centre of Hamilton, and 5 mins from Crystal caves, nature reserve, aquarium and the Bermuda perfumery.

The Cayman Islands

Pink pastel palaces with cocktail bars, a plate of fresh lobster, conch or turtle, views over the sand to the lagoon where, deep in caves, fish dip and dart in your exhaled bubbles...

flying time
To: Grand Cayman
London: 10 1/2 hrs
Miami: 1 1/2 hrs
NY: 4 hrs

climate/when to go
It can be very hot and humid in high summer. The Batabano Carnival takes place in April. During Pirate Week in October there are choreographed invasions!

currency
Cayman Islands dollar, fixed to the US dollar.

language
English.

getting around
Via the extensive bus network, an abundance of taxis, or hire cars/mopeds/motorbikes.

These three English-speaking islands are a trendy, American-style idyll with large modern hotels, swish restaurants and a scintillating beach life. Scuba diving and snorkelling are cheap, readily available and huge fun; the coral grounds here are some of the finest in the Caribbean. You enter a world of peaceful wonder, a swirling kaleidoscope of light and colour featuring shoals of irridescent fish, sea horses and scuttling multi-hued shrimps. Uncle Sam's influence is palpable in the big cars, well-stocked shops and overwhelmingly friendly atmosphere. Yet, this being the Caribbean, life proceeds at a leisurely pace, and there are many isolated, Robinson Crusoe-style beaches. The main tourist action is centred around Seven-Mile Beach, a world-famous hot spot on the most southerly island of Grand Cayman, where the living is luxurious and unashamedly hedonistic. The beach is west-facing and enjoys some of the world's most beautiful sunsets.

From expensive and expansive to small, homely and cheerful, the Caymans have restaurants to suit every taste — Italian, French, Mexican, dial-a-pizza — in addition to the local cuisine, which is principally seafood. A multitude of cliff and beach bars fringe the island.

The Grand Pavilion

PO Box 30117 SMB
Grand Cayman
Cayman Islands

Owen Roberts 5km

tel +1 345 945 5656
fax +1 345 945 5353
absolute@candw.ky

Open all year

Just steps from a private, powdery sand beach, the Grand Pavilion on Grand Cayman Island combines European sophistication and Caribbean ambience in colonial-style surroundings.

Most of the 93 elegantly appointed rooms and suites are airily decorated in light pastel tones and feature king-size beds and a host of modern amenities. Guests are welcomed with champagne and traditional Caribbean hospitality.

The Waterfall Cafe offers an extensive breakfast buffet and casual lunches overlooking the delightful swimming pool which is set in a private courtyard with its own free-falling waterfall and jacuzzi. Ottmar's restaurant serves classic continental cuisine with an original Caribbean twist in the elegant dining room.

The famous coral reefs off the Cayman Islands are home to a stunning variety of marine life. Guests can swim with playful sting rays, scuba dive or snorkel among the underwater caverns and pinnacles, or simply stretch out on the beautiful white expanse of Seven Mile Beach.

The secluded courtyard set in tropical gardens or a private balcony are ideal locations for wedding ceremonies. Staff are happy to make all the arrangements necessary for a perfect wedding.

 US$160–575 (88)
 US$525–1200 (5)
US$45–65
US$18

Honeymoon specials
Champagne on arrival, room upgrade subject to availability and breakfast in bed. Package costs vary seasonally.

Sightseeing and leisure
Duty-free shopping, trips to Stingray City and Cayman Turtle Farm. Swimming pool with jacuzzi, beach and wide range of watersports at the hotel. Golf and full salon nearby.

The Dominican Republic

Follow in Columbus' footsteps and discover a Latin-Caribbean cocktail of delights — superb beaches, cool coastal towns and exhilarating nights...

The Spanish-speaking Dominican Republic is one of the Caribbean's largest countries and attracts over a million visitors a year. In parts it can be touristy, but the island is large enough, and vital enough, to remain both popular and genuinely attractive.

Picturesque colonial streets and buildings run alongside modern, fully equipped hotels. Various startling environments — rugged deserts, palm-clad mountains and lush green jungle — are all found in a country roughly the size of Scotland. Spanish-style resort towns offer the full range of traditional tourist facilities including golden sandy beaches, watersports, golf and riding, as well as some unique local pleasures — notably music and dancing. The swivel-hipped *meringue* is the unofficial national pastime, and joining in is practically compulsory. Beyond the tourist centres, however, in remote beaches, shimmering rainforests and quaint coastal towns, it is quiet, and you can be alone.

Living is lively and relatively cheap. There are bars and restaurants to suit every pocket, and fabulous shopping. ●

Casa de Campo

PO Box 140
La Romana
Dominican Republic

 La Romana 1km

tel +809 523 3333
fax +809 523 8548

Contact:
UK: Group Promotions Ltd
    tel +44 181 795 1718
US: Premier World Marketing
    tel +305 856 5405

Open all year

This 7,000-acre resort is located on the south eastern coast of the Dominican Republic in the quaint town of La Romana.

Luxurious villas with lush gardens and dramatic ocean views are dotted throughout the extensive grounds. Each has a large balcony and louvered shutters, allowing fresh air and cool breezes to pass throughout. Elegant hotel rooms, designed by Oscar de la Renta, capture the true Caribbean flavour.

As the sun sets, guests can toast the day's events in a gourmet restaurant while admiring the breathtaking cliff-side river views. There are a number of restaurants serving specialities ranging from traditional Italian fare to the treasures of Caribbean cuisine.

After dinner, guests can move to the rhythm of merengue in the open-air lounge, enjoy an evening's entertainment with folkloric ballet troupes, or dance the night away at the Genesis Discotheque.

There are a wide variety of sports activities to choose from, including the well-equipped La Terraza Tennis Centre and a fitness centre.

Weddings can be arranged in the village church. Receptions in the villas, restaurant or hotel grounds are fully catered for.

 US$125–200 (300)
 US$260–650 (150 villas)
 included*
 included*

Honeymoon specials
Champagne and flowers on arrival.

Leisure facilities
Golf, tennis, horseriding, clay pigeon shooting, windsurfing, sailing, snorkelling and squash. Aerobics, fully equipped gym. Massage by appointment.

Local attractions
Replica 16th-century village with art galleries and amphitheatre. Excursions and barbecues on an uninhabited island nearby. River cruises and fishing trips by arrangement.

*this is dependent on the package chosen

Jamaica

Jamaica is one of the liveliest islands, its allure the strongest of all the former British territories.

Physically the island is spectacular. Greenery bursts into life everywhere. You might almost expect a pencil to take root. And the scenery is fantastic; within a few hundred yards of the sea you can be at an altitude of 1,000 feet.

For the visitor, Jamaica has the most romantic allure of all the Caribbean islands. Neglected stone gateposts and decaying walls of abandoned plantation houses witness times when the island was the focus of British dreams, and source of fortunes for the planters. Noël Coward, Churchill and Errol Flynn all fell in love with the place.

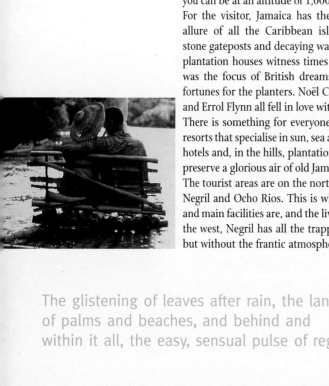

There is something for everyone here: humming resorts that specialise in sun, sea and sand, elegant hotels and, in the hills, plantation hideaways that preserve a glorious air of old Jamaica.

The tourist areas are on the north coast, between Negril and Ocho Rios. This is where the beaches and main facilities are, and the liveliest crowds. In the west, Negril has all the trappings of a resort, but without the frantic atmosphere. Ocho Rios is

The glistening of leaves after rain, the languor of palms and beaches, and behind and within it all, the easy, sensual pulse of reggae...

more developed, with some outstanding hotels. Close by, there are astonishingly exotic botanical gardens, and a genuine Jamaican countryside of steepsided valleys watered by numerous rivers and falls. Montego Bay, the tourist capital, is large and busy, with beaches and watersports, and a lively nightlife. The most famous great houses are here; and historic Falmouth, site of some of the finest Georgian architecture on the island.

Port Antonio is a charming, dozy town in the far east, the loveliest and most strikingly fertile part of the island. From here you can venture up into into the Blue Mountains, a region of spectacular natural beauty.

The capital, Kingston, is well worth a visit. Check out the mayhem and markets downtown, where limers loiter, chatting, amidst the constant calls of 'Bag-juice!' and the pulse of dancehall music. This is the Jamaicans' Jamaica — energetic, lively, noisy and sometimes tricky. ●

flying time
To: Montego Bay/Kingston
London: 11 hrs
Miami: 1 1/2 hrs
NY: 3 1/2 hrs

climate/when to go
The weather is pretty well perfect (27°C at sea level, 13°C in the mountains), with overcast periods in winter and rainfall all year. April is carnival, the big reggae festivals happen in February and August.

currency
The Jamaican dollar, US dollars, credit cards and traveller's cheques are widely accepted, personal cheques are not.

language
English.

getting around
There are regular internal flights, frequent if chaotic buses; taxis, and minivans. Hire cars are expensive.

Couples Resort

PO Box 330
Ocho Rios
Jamaica

 Montego Bay 100km

tel +1 876 975 4271
fax +1 876 975 4439

Contact:
UK: Group Promotions Ltd
tel +44 181 795 1718
US: Couples Resort
tel +305 668 0008

Open all year

Set along a romantic coast bordered by the lush green mountains of Jamaica's Ocho Rios, this all-inclusive resort provides an essential getaway for couples wishing to spend time alone.

Accommodation is in luxurious rooms designed in traditional Caribbean style, with large balconies overlooking exotic gardens to the sea beyond. Some rooms have jacuzzis and king-size four-poster beds.

There are secluded whirlpools as well as jacuzzis in which to while away lazy afternoons whilst enjoying your partner's company. The more adventurous can explore the island on horseback, and work up a healthy appetite in the gym.

Lavish breakfasts and buffet lunches are served at the beachside Patio Restaurant, and snacks and sandwiches can be enjoyed at the Beach Grill beside the beach. For gourmet dining, there are three award-winning restaurants to choose from, together offering a vast array of culinary experiences. After dinner, guests can relax to the sounds of a professional pianist at the elegant piano bar.

Couples is the perfect place to have a wedding. The romantic beachfront and tropical jungle gazebos provide beautiful locations in which to exchange vows, and hotel staff can arrange everythingfrom the bouquet to the champagne, at no extra charge.

 US$205–245 (212)
 US$270–305 (11)
 included
 included

Honeymoon specials
Champagne in room on arrival. Room upgrade subject to availability. Half-hour massage.

Leisure facilities
All watersports, and horseriding, tennis, squash, golf and volleyball are included. Rafting extra. Beauty salon, gym, massage room, jacuzzi and sauna.

Local attractions
Excursions to spectacular Dunn's River Falls, Prospect Plantations, shopping in Ocho Rios and sunset catamaran cruises are included in the price. Trips in glass-bottomed boats, bicycle tours and horseback excursions are available at no extra charge.

18

Grand Lido Negril

Po Box 88
Negril
Jamaica

 Montego Bay 88km

tel +1 876 957 5010
fax +1 876 957 5517

Open all year

Tour Operators:
UK: SuperClubs
US: International Lifestyles

This luxury super-inclusive resort hotel is tucked into a protected cove at Negril, along Jamaica's popular west coast.

Stunning marble and glass architecture and cool, elegant interiors blend into the natural contours of the landscape. Luxurious suites have king-size beds, large private bathrooms and 24-hour room service.

There are a number of award-winning restaurants, all serving an array of dishes from around the world, including traditional Jamaican fare such as jerk chicken.

Secluded hammocks and jacuzzis are scattered throughout acres of tropical gardens where couples can while away lazy afternoons in peace and privacy. Sports facilities are unusually comprehensive.

Evenings can be spent enjoying live entertainment featuring Jamaican artists, perhaps dancing the night away in the disco, and ending the evening with a romantic stroll along the edge of the Caribbean.

Wedding ceremonies are free and can be arranged in a romantic gazebo by the water or aboard the yacht where Prince Rainier and Princess Grace spent their honeymoon.

 US$260–360 (210)
 US$380–440 (24)
included
included

Honeymoon specials
Rose for the bride and champagne in room on arrival. Dinner in Piacere on wedding night. Manicure and pedicure for the bride. Weddings, including marriage officer, licence, cake, champagne, flowers and decorated location within hotel's grounds or aboard the M/Y Zein yacht.

Sightseeing and leisure
Glass-bottom boat rides, waterskiing, scuba diving, tennis, golf, volleyball, fully equipped fitness centre, cycling and croquet are some of the activities available at the hotel at no extra cost. Trips to Dunn's River Falls, shopping excursions, river rafting, plantation tours, horseriding and other excursions can also be arranged.

Half Moon
Golf, Tennis & Beach Club

PO Box 80
Jamaica

🛬 Montego Bay 6km

tel +876 953 2953
fax +876 953 3244
hmoonmvd@infochan.com

Open all year

Member of: Elegant Resorts

Tour operators:
UK: Elegant Resorts, UK
UK: Caribbean Connections
US: Gogo Tours

Located on the northern coast and within easy reach of Montego Bay – the tourism capital of Jamaica – is the Half Moon Golf, Tennis and Beach Club. This self-contained estate is set amid green hills, nestling behind a mile of crescent-shaped beach.

All rooms and suites are individually decorated and have splendid sea views. Luxury rooms at the eastern end of the estate make for a charming hideaway. For those getting married at the resort, the newly built villas, with their canopied beds, grand colonial-style staircases, private pools, and their own gardeners, maids and cooks, are ideal for larger groups.

A shuttle bus links the villas to the main resort where guests can chose from six gourmet restaurants serving a variety of Caribbean and international dishes with the accent on fresh fruit and vegetables. After dinner, guests can relax to the sounds of calypso bands, sip Jamaican rum at the terrace bar, and end a perfect day with a moonlit stroll through the gardens.

The full range of sports and beauty treatments is available.

Wedding ceremonies can be arranged in the lush tropical gardens or a magnificent gazebo on the edge of the Caribbean. Parties of all kinds are fully catered for at every stage – from the provision of a marriage officer and photographer, to the entertainment and floral decorations.

 US$330–480 (238)
 US$530–1100 (180)
 US$40–60
US$20

Honeymoon specials

Flowers and champagne on arrival. Use of tennis courts, watersports, all drinks at the hotel's bars and dinner at all of the hotel's restaurants. The package costs from US$480 per couple per day.

Sightseeing and leisure

Historic landmarks in Jamaica's thriving capital – Kingston. Boat cruises along the coast to Montego Bay, tropical bird sanctuary and Reggae festivals. Sunset tours to Negril. Tennis, squash, riding, all watersports, deep-sea fishing, swimming and an 18-hole golf course. Health and fitness centre with massage, sauna and herbal body wraps.

Sandals Negril

PO Box 12
Negril
Jamaica

✈ Montego Bay 70km

tel +1 876 957 5216
fax +1 876 957 5338

Open all year

Tour Operators
UK: Unique Vacations (UK) Ltd

The resort area of Negril consists of 7 miles of spectacular palm-backed, white-sand beach stretching along the lively north western coast of the island of Jamaica. Since the end of the sixties the area has been renowned for its pleasure-seeking, laid back way, and in keeping with this history the all-inclusive resort of Sandals Negril has been created as place where couples can relax together in style.

All rooms have king-size beds and many overlook the ocean. Some, such as the beachfront Honeymoon Loft Suite, have spiral staircases leading to mahogany four-poster beds and deluxe marble bathrooms.

There are four restaurants serving a delicious selection of Caribbean, oriental, international and even low-calorie dishes.

There is a wealth of activities including a fully equipped fitness centre and all watersports, not least some of the best scuba diving in the Caribbean.

After an exhilarating game of tennis, guests can wind down with a deep sea-mud bath or Swedish massage in the European Spa, relax in the whirlpools, or watch the sun set over the Caribbean from a hammock made for two.

The hotel's wedding coordinator is happy to help with the organisation of every aspect of wedding ceremonies and receptions.

US$550–740 (187)*
US$780–860 (28)*
included
included

Honeymoon specials
A complimentary 20-piece Royal Doulton starter set for couples arriving between 19 Dec 1997 and 1 Dec 1998 and staying 13 nights or longer in a premium or higher category room. All meals, drinks, sports and snacks are included in the all-inclusive rate.

* prices are per person based on a stay of 3 nights

Sightseeing and leisure
Watching Negril's famous sunsets, and cliff diving nearby. Visits to the 'YS' Falls, Jamaica's most beautiful. All water-based activities, including reef diving, snorkelling and sailing, plus kneeboarding, tennis, racquetball, volleyball, billiards and croquet are included in the all-inclusive rate. Beauty and spa treatments cost extra.

  VISA

Eastern Caribbean

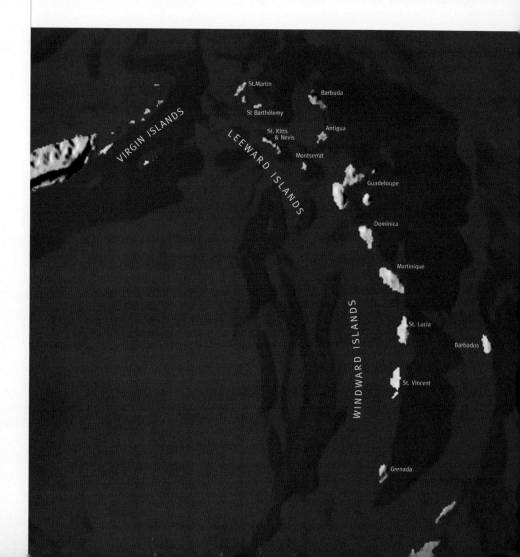

VIRGIN ISLANDS

St.Martin

St Barthélemy

Barbuda

St. Kitts
& Nevis

Antigua

LEEWARD ISLANDS

Montserrat

Guadeloupe

Domínica

Martinique

WINDWARD ISLANDS

St. Lucia

Barbados

St. Vincent

Grenada

Wickedly relaxed...

Barbados

Barbados stands alone, out in the Atlantic, about a hundred miles beyond the rest of the Eastern Caribbean, a small coral island with some of the finest golden sandy beaches anywhere and a most agreeable climate. The island is long established as a winter getaway, and its famous west coast, second home to a crowd of international sophisticates, has given it the nickname 'millionaires' playground'.

At just 21 miles by 14 miles, the island can get fairly crowded, but it is easy to have an extremely good holiday here. As well as some of the smartest, most expensive hotels in the Caribbean, Barbados has a steadily growing tradition of fine food. The Bajans handle service well too, which can be a problem elsewhere. The result is a string of excellent restaurants, wine bars and lively beach bars where you can eat well in charming locations.

Bajan fare includes plenty of seafood, especially flying fish, and sea egg, the roe of the white sea-urchin, which is supposedly an aphrodisiac. As well as the ubiquitous

Gardens, all impeccable, festooned with plants, palms and flowering trees, verandahs threatened by explosive tropical flora...

flying time
London: 3 1/2 hrs by
Concorde, 8 hrs by jet.
LA: via Miami 9 1/2 hrs
Miami: 3 1/2 hrs
NY: 4 1/2 hrs

climate/when to go
You can visit the island
any time, but May/Jun
and Oct/Nov are wet
seasons, with fewer
festivals and regattas.

currency
The Barbados dollar,
fixed to the US dollar.
Credit cards and
US dollars are very
widely accepted.

language
English.

getting around
There are relatively
frequent air and sea
services to the other
islands. On Barbados
use the friendly local
buses or plentiful,
un-metered taxis.
Car hire is expensive.

cocktails, fruit punches are particularly good.
The island's British heritage has left a delightful and often old-fashioned charm in its manners, buildings and even its language. (You can hear distinct traces of a West Country accent in Bajan speech.) Classically beautiful plantation houses stand in swathes of sugar-cane, cricketers in whites play beneath palm trees. In the thriving capital, Bridgetown, grand old colonial structures with filigree metal balconies jostle with purposeful glass-fronted shops and offices .

Also courtesy of the island's colonial past, perhaps, many hotels, clubs and restaurants enforce a fairly formal dress code (jacket and tie). Evenings are, however, less than sedate in the many clubs, rum shops and bars — often with excellent live bands, that pepper the areas around Bridgetown and the south coast.
Spectator sports include horse racing and polo, but cricket is the national sport, with weekend matches all over the island and less formal games being played by children in the backstreets. ▶

Top-class hotels provide most sports including riding, deep-sea fishing and golf. Watersports operators on the main beaches on the west and south coasts can fix you up with a kayak, small sailing boat, windsurfer or jetski; arrange a ride in a glass-bottom boat or on a bouncy banana. Windsurfing is excellent on the south coast. The east coast boasts big surfing waves, and an excellent hiking district known as Scotland.

The highlight of the festival year is Cropover, which culminates in early August (the crop referred to is the sugar-cane harvest). This is a major blow-out along Carnival lines, with calypso-singing competitions, steel band music and carnival bands made up of hundreds of costumed players who strut through the streets to *soca* music. You can 'play mas' by buying a costume and joining the masquerade, or just dance on the sidelines.

There is a jazz festival in early January, attracting the likes (in 1997) of Patti LaBelle and Grover Washington, and in the middle of the month there is an international regatta. In February, the Holetown Festival commemorates the first settlement of the island in 1627 with a week of exhibitions, tattoos and a general jamboree. Around Easter-time, there is a round of open-air opera and Shakespeare plays for which, in 1997, Pavarotti was the star attraction.

Cobblers Cove

St Peter
Barbados

Grantley Adams 28km

tel +246 422 2291
fax +246 422 1460
cobblers@caribshaf.com

Closed September

Member of:
Relais and Chateaux

Situated on the beautiful coral island of Barbados with its fine golden sandy beaches, Cobblers Cove provides an intimate and comfortable retreat with a tranquil ambience, blending the elegance and charm of an English country estate with the tropical beauty of the Caribbean.

The forty suites are the epitome of Caribbean-style comfort with an attractive combination of rattan furnishings, pretty fabrics and terracotta tiles to make every guest feel pampered and at home. Each suite is arranged around vibrantly coloured tropical gardens, and the breeze-cooled sitting rooms open onto private terraces or balconies. For the ultimate in luxury, the Camelot and Colleton suites feature four-poster beds, private plunge pool and a roof-top terrace with fabulous views of the Caribbean Sea.

Days can be spent trying out the range of watersports and leisure activities on offer, relaxing by the pool with a cocktail from the poolside bar or discovering the charming old buildings and easy-going air in nearby Speightstown.

At the elegant beachfront restaurant French-trained chefs specialise in dishes that take full advantage of the local produce. The cuisine is complemented by an extensive list of fine wines. Efficient yet friendly staff are always on hand to ensure that every whim is catered for. After dinner, guests can enjoy a romantic stroll along the pristine shoreline of the bay.

The resort is delighted to arrange wedding ceremonies. Popular locations include tropical gardens and 'castle' courtyards.

 US$220–1500
 US$60
 US$25

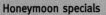

Honeymoon specials
Fruit, flowers and sparkling wine in the room on arrival. Room upgrade subject to availability.

Sightseeing and leisure
Tennis, waterskiing, windsurfing, sailing and snorkelling are complimentary. Scuba diving, deep-sea fishing, island excursions, cocktail cruises, private yacht hire and golf on a championship course can be arranged for a fee. Beauty centre nearby.

The French Caribbean

From a romantic beginning as a base for 16th-century pirates, the French Caribbean has developed into a thoroughly modern, chic and, above all, thoroughly French tropical playground. Sun, sea, surf and champagne combine deliciously in these extravagant fantasy islands.

The Gallic influence is overt: shops are filled with Lacroix and Givenchy, *boules* is played in dusty town squares, and bakeries provide a daily supply of baguettes and croissants. Underpinning all this, however, is a Caribbean sensibility. Leisure and pleasure are assiduously pursued — sunbathing, snorkelling and windsurfing all day, dining and dancing all night.

The exclusive and very French St Barts provides an idyllic environment for transient millionaires and glamour-seekers, with glorious sandy beaches and luxury riviera-style hotels.

On Guadeloupe, the Caribbean influence is stronger. Its two islands provide combine luxury, crystal-blue waters, and a multitude of cafés and restaurants, with tropical splendour — volcanoes, hot springs, mangroves and waterfalls.

St Martin has much the same Gallic-style luxury as St Barts, albeit at more affordable prices, whilst the food on Martinique is reputed to be the best in the Caribbean.

Throughout the islands, festivals and carnivals, especially those that take place around Bastille Day and during Lent, are loud, colourful and enormous fun.

flying time
To: St Barts/St Martin
via Antigua.
London: 13–14 hrs via Miami
Miami: 3 1/2 hrs
NY: 4 1/2 hrs

climate/when to go
There are festivals during spring and summer at Mardi Gras and on Bastille Day. There is also a music festival on St Barts in January.

currency
The French franc.

language
French, some English in tourist areas.

getting around
There are good public bus services between major towns. Taxis and hire cars are reasonably priced.

French flair
with Caribbean cool..

La Cocoteraie

Avenue de L'Europe
97118 St Francois
Guadeloupe

✈ Pôle Caraïbes 30km

tel +590 887 981
fax +590 887 833

Closed 24 Aug–23 Oct 1998

Managed by:
Le Meridien

Nestled between one of the most beautiful lagoons on Guadeloupe and the impressive golf course designed by Robert Trent-Jones, La Cocoteraie combines the charm of a colonial habitation with the luxury of a first class hotel.

Each of the 50 personalised suites is exquisitely decorated in typical Creole style. Spacious bathrooms with hexagonal-shape raised baths provide magnificent views of the sun setting over the lagoon. Each has a colourful and comfortable living room and flowered terraces overlooking the pool and sea beyond.

At La Varangue chefs prepare refined and imaginative local specialities based on local produce, such as fish and shellfish freshly landed at the port of Saint François.

Guests can sail away in a catamaran, play a round of golf on one of the neighbouring islands or simply relax in the magnificent swimming pool decorated with Chinese vases whilst enjoying colourful rum-based cocktails at the Indigo Bar.

The hotel is happy to organise anything from a Corsair party with a steel band or a full-blown carnival party to the rhythm of a zouk band, complete with Limbo dancers.

A one-day excursion on board a fully-equipped sailboat discovering the small neighbouring island of Petite Terre will add the finishing touch to a truly unforgettable honeymoon.

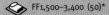

📖 FF1,500–3,400 (50)*

🍽 à la carte

☕ FF95

Honeymoon specials

Welcome gift, champagne in room on arrival. Candlelit dinner. The package is available from the 1 April–30 June 1998 and is based on a stay of 5 nights.

Sightseeing and leisure

Golf course designed by Robert Trent Jones, parachuting, windsurfing, swimming and tennis. The hotel has its own private beach.

*These prices are for the period 1 April–18 December 1998

Hotel Guanahani

Anse De Grand Cul de Sac
St Barthélémy

 St Barthélémy 5km

tel +590 276 660

fax +590 277 070

guana@outremer.com

Open all year

Member of:
The Leading Hotels of the World

Resting amongst the lush grounds of a 16-hectare peninsula, set between two white sandy beaches and clear aquamarine seas, the Guanahani is the only full-service hotel on the tropical island of St Barthélémy.

Bungalows painted in cheerful colours, with terracotta floors and wooden-rafted ceilings, reproduce the genteel ambience of the island's colonial past. Most of the bedrooms offer panoramic views of the Atlantic on one side, or, on the other, wide expanses of deep ocean bordered by picturesque coconut groves.

The hotel has two clear, fresh-water swimming pools and a large jacuzzi – a wonderful place to unwind. For tennis enthusiasts, there are two floodlit courts with a professional instructor on hand to help guests improve their game. Alternatively, down on the beach, the hotel provides complimentary use of all non-motorised watersports.

Guests are invited to experience light salads and fresh seafood at The Indigo, an al fresco beach restaurant. The Bartolomeo, an impressive French restaurant, offers delicious Spanish, Tuscan, and Italian specialities to the romantic accompaniment of the resident jazz pianist.

 FF1,300–3,670 (54)

 FF2,810–5,510 (21)

 FF250–375

 included

Honeymoon specials

All newlyweds receive champagne and chocolates in room on arrival. Those booking the Honeymoon Package receive welcome gift, full American buffet breakfast daily, one lunch for two, one dinner for two, round trip airport transfers. This 7-night package costs FF9,660–25,760 per couple, and includes tax and service charges.

Sightseeing and leisure

Exclusive boutiques and restaurants. Cruises in a private boat or yacht and island-hopping excursions. Range of watersports including windsurfing and snorkelling. Tennis, volleyball, table tennis, and fitness centre with exercise classes. Sailing, deep-sea fishing and horseriding nearby.

Le Toiny

Saint Barthélémy

✈ Saint Jean 6km

tel +590 278 888

fax +590 278 930

letoiny@saint-barths.com

Closed 1 Sept–20 Oct

Member of: Relais & Chateaux

Tour operators:

UK: Caribbean Connection;
    Elegant Resorts

US: Wimco

Tucked into the hillside of St Barts, a tiny outpost in the Caribbean, is the stylish hotel hideaway of Le Toiny.

The hotel's architecture is influenced by the old plantation houses of Guadeloupe and Martinique. There are 12 cottages decorated in typically Caribbean pastel shades. All have handmade terracotta and mahogany furnishings and four-poster beds. Each has a private swimming pool and terrace with teak chaises longues where guests can contemplate the views of a lagoon fringed with coconut palms, and the vast blue sea beyond.

French chef Maximé Déschamps prepares a harmonious blend of traditional French and innovative Caribbean cuisine in the Le Gaiac restaurant.

Nightlife on the island is centred around the many restaurants with their well-stocked wine cellars. After a gourmet meal, guests can enjoy a nightcap on the lovely terrace of the main pool with chirping tree frogs and songs of cicadas for entertainment.

Days can be spent trying out the many sporting activities or touring the small villages across from the island, where women, still dressed in traditional costume, braid handicrafts in straw and latanier.

 FF2,920–4,730

 à la carte

 FF120

Honeymoon specials

Champagne welcome on arrival. Fresh flowers daily. Transfers to/from airport. Candlelit dinner at Le Gaiac, use of car during stay, sunset cruise, mementos. This package is based on a stay of 4 nights.

Sightseeing and leisure

Tours by Jeep around the island. Shopping excursions to nearby Gustavia, sightseeing around the harbour, and yacht trips to neighbouring islands. Tennis, horseriding, scuba diving, sailing, deep-sea fishing, windsurfing and snorkelling (the hotel provides flippers and diving masks).

Leeward Islands

Bays where coconut palms bend and brush the beach, reefs close to the surface, ruined forts and gracious plantation houses...

flying time

To: Antigua
London: 8 hrs
Miami: 3 hrs
NY: 4 hrs

climate

Warm year round, with the notable exception of Kitts and Nevis, and slightly less rainy than the soaring Windwards which complete this easterly arc of islands.

when to go

As elsewhere in the region, the summer months (Jun–Aug) are the best time but things do get booked up.

currency

The US dollar dominates. Local currencies are necessary if you intend to venture out of tourist areas.

language

English

getting around

Antigua is the hub for the northeastern Caribbean, with connections to Europe and North America, and daily flights to all other Windward and Leeward Islands.

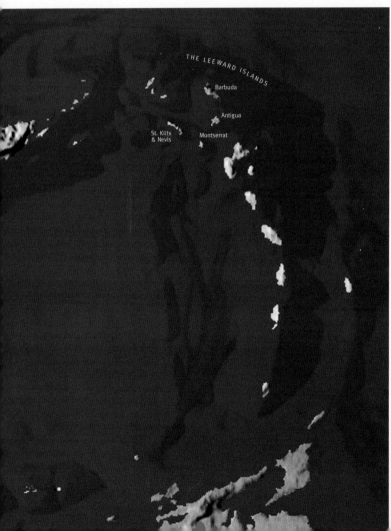

THE LEEWARD ISLANDS

Barbuda

Antigua

St. Kitts
& Nevis

Montserrat

The Leeward Islands lie scattered over 150 miles in the eastern Caribbean, between the Atlantic Ocean and the Caribbean Sea, forming an arc above the mountainous Windwards to the south.

This is an attractive part of the Caribbean; the horizon is studded with the shapes of islands that rise majestcially from the sea.

Montserrat and the twin islands of St Kitts and Nevis stand in the west, invariably capped in cloud, soaring from the water. They have many of the features of the Windwards — rainfall, stunning, luxuriant vegetation and a massive, majestic beauty. They are the peaks of a submarine mountain range, volcanic in origin, which until recently was thought to have quietened down. Sadly, the recent activity on Montserrat has shown that belief to be misfounded.

Antigua, Barbuda and Anguilla, by contrast, are coral-based and lie lower in the sea. Their climates are milder, which is an advantage in the rainy season when the other islands are often shrouded in cloud. Physically, they may not be impressive, with their mantles of sparse vegetation, but between them they boast the finest beaches in the Caribbean.

Antigua and Barbuda

Cricket matches, yachting parties and rum punch,
soft manners, gentle shores and soaring frigate birds...

when to go
Antigua: April for regattas,
July for carnival, October for
the jazz festival.
Barbuda: Take is as it
comes. Life's a beach.

currency
The Eastern Caribbean
dollar, fixed to the US
dollar. Life can be
expensive on both islands.
The Antiguan government
raises taxes through sales
of food and goods, and in
Barbuda most goods and
essentials are imported.

language
English.

getting around
Angua: Daily flights to the
other islands. No scheduled
boat services and few local
buses, but an abundance of
taxis, bicycles, hire cars.
Roads are poor. Hire a four-
wheel-drive if you intend to
venture off main routes.
Barbuda: A few hire cars for
which you must bargain.

Antigua is one of the Caribbean's most popular destinations, the largest of the Leeward Islands, a hub for local transport and the proud possessor of an international test cricket ground.

There is something here for everyone. Within the sweeping curves of bays on the protected shores of the Caribbean Sea, gentle wave action on the reefs has pushed up miles of blinding white sand. Between the main beaches there are any number of small coves, and reefs on all sides with plenty of wrecks to dive.

In Antigua's capital, St John's, many of the old wood and stone buildings with overhanging balconies remain, and traditional West Indian life can be still be seen — in the chaos of the market, and by the water where fishermen mend their nets.

At English Harbour, a pretty enclave in the southeast, Nelson's Dockyard is a centre for tourism and yachting that is touristy but nevertheless charming, with restored 18th-century warehouses, shops, hotels, restaurants and bars.

In the 18th century the island bristled with forts and fortlets, and today many visitors enjoy rootling around the ruins, now 15 feet deep in scrub, and taking in the glorious views for which the forts were built in the first place .

Yachting is a big activity, with a major regatta at the end of the winter season that attracts sailors from everywhere, and is a good excuse for a 'jump-up'. There are a few fine hotels tucked away in their own coves; one or two sit in splendour in the historical setting of English Harbour. In a few you get good

food in the best Caribbean settings, and independent restaurants serve French, Italian, even Argentinian, as well as West Indian food. There are some buzzing local and tourist haunts, and it can be lively around English Harbour.

Barbuda's great attractions are marine life and beaches. The contours of the island are even gentler than Antigua's, and the pace of life considerably slower. Tourism amounts to two extremely exclusive hotels, a small resort and local guest houses. There are few sights, but a visit to Codrington Lagoon to see thousands of frigate birds from a boat in amongst the mangroves is quite an experience.

Barbuda is a wonderful place to be alone, but that's not to say the people are unfriendly. Far from it. A couple were greeted at the airport recently with the words: 'But nobody said you were coming...'

Sandals Antigua

Dickenson Bay
St John
Antigua

✈ de Vere Bird 8km

tel +1 268 462 0267
fax +1 268 462 4135

Open all year

Tour Operators
UK: Unique Vacations (UK) Ltd

Antigua, which has 365 beaches, is one of the most popular destinations in the Caribbean. Located on the west coast along the beautiful white-sand beach of Dickenson Bay – one of the best beaches on the island – is the popular Sandals Antigua.

This all-inclusive resort has been designed to recreate the feel of a Caribbean Village. Low-rise buildings, scattered throughout lush green gardens, house luxurious accommodation including elegant honeymoon suites, and unique suites in the romantic seaside rondovals. All are decorated in bright Caribbean fabrics and have delightful four-poster beds.

There are four gourmet restaurants. Guests can dine by candlelight overlooking the moonlit sea, be entertained by the chefs at Teppanyaki Restaurant as they cook at table, sample delicious Italian dishes at Il Palio, or tuck into South Western fare at the OK Corral with its ocean views.

Sports and leisure facilities are unusually comprehensive.

For those couples wishing to marry on the island, the resort's own wedding coordinator is happy to arrange every detail – from ceremony to candlelit dinner to day passes for guests.

US$860–1,050 (98)*
US$1,080–1,310 (91)*
included
included

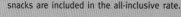

Honeymoon specials
A complimentary 20-piece Royal Doulton starter set for couples arriving between 19 Dec 1997 and 1 Dec 1998 and staying 13 nights or longer in a premium or higher category room. All meals, drinks, sports and snacks are included in the all-inclusive rate.

* prices are per person based on a stay of 3 nights

Sightseeing and leisure
Trips to forts and 18th-century ruins. The lively capital of St John, dotted with cafés and restaurants, is a short drive away. All watersports, tennis, volleyball, billiards, croquet and shuffleboard are included in the all-inclusive rate. Beauty and spa treatments incur an extra charge.

Siboney Beach Club

PO Box 222
St John's
Antigua

✈ VC Bird Int. 10km

tel +1 268 462 0806
fax +1 268 462 3356
siboney@candw:ag

Open all year

Tour operators:
UK: Unique Hotels, Thomas Cook,
   Silkcut Travel

'How pleasant it would be,' wrote the naturalist Charles Darwin, 'to pass one's life in such quiet abodes.' In Antigua, it is not only the fittest which have survived but the most beautiful as well. Brightly-coloured papaya, mangoes and guava abound, growing under flamboyant trees and palms and amidst this miniature jungle beside a sheltered mile of white sand and emerald waters is the intimate Siboney Beach Club.

The suites are individually decorated in rich, earthy colours and furnished with tropical prints, comfortable sofas and king-size beds. Twin double doors open onto balconies affording glimpses of the Caribbean through a profusion of palm fronds and bougainvillea.

The food is a riot of colour and taste and attests to the Antiguan proverb 'Better man belly bus' than good food waste'. Delicious concoctions of fresh lobster and seafood, spicy curries, thick steaks, bright salads, barbecues, baby back ribs and even Conch Fritters are all available nearby.

Weddings are easily arranged. Couples can exchange vows barefoot in the sand or, more formally, at the Siboney Beach Club itself. Wedding extras can include anything from cake and champagne to steel pan soloist.

 US$130–190 (1) +18.5%tax
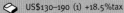 US$155–290 (12) +18.5%tax
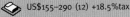 US$15–35
US$5.50–8.95

Honeymoon specials
Cocktail, wine, fresh flowers, use of snorkels, masks, beach lounges and towels. Honeymoon packages cost from US$695 based on a stay of 4 nights.

Leisure facilities
Sailing, scuba diving, snorkelling, golf, tennis, windsurfing, fitness club, bicycling.

Local attractions
Trips to Nelson's Dockyard, wind-powered sugar mill, historic naval buildings, Redcliffe Quay, Museum of Antigua and Barbuda, St. John's Cathedral, Jolly Harbour, Indian Town and Devil's Bridge. Antigua sailing week in April, Carnival in July.

27

St Kitts and Nevis

St Kitts and Nevis stand side by with strikingly beautiful views of one another across a channel just two miles wide. Both are welcoming and laid-back in classic old-Caribbean style. There is a strong and vibrant West Indian culture here and, unfortunately, some poverty.

The islands share far and away the finest collection of plantation house hotels in the Caribbean. Many are surrounded by sugar cane as they were 200 years ago, and they retain the grace and hospitality of the era — being relatively small and run in the style of a private house, with guests meeting informally for drinks before dinner. As former estate houses, most of these hotels are not on the beach; but if being right on the sand is the important thing, there is an increasing number of nice beach hotels.

St Kitts is the larger of the two islands. In the mountainous northern areas, beaches are mostly of black sand, but in the southern peninsula the there are a number of good strips of golden-brown sand, usually deserted.

Nevis was once so illustrious it was known as the Queen of the Caribbees. The 'old-time' elegance of the West Indies is still just about visible in the finely crafted bridges and dark stone walls that poke out of the ever-encroaching jungle.

The Nevisians themselves are extremely polite, and the island has oodles more charm than many other islands that pretend to be undiscovered. ▶

Concave slopes rising gracefully through shoreside flatlands to rainforested, cloud-capped summits...

code number

There is the normal range of watersports on both islands, though you may have to travel a little further than on some of the other islands to find the right facilities and conditions. Most of the diving takes place off Nevis, where there are submarine volcanic vents for explorations as well as the usual reefs.

On land, there are excellent hikes into the jungle which take a look at the islands' more exotic flora, follow rivers to hidden pools and waterfalls high in the rainforest, and visit the old plantation estates.

Ottleys Plantation Inn

PO Box 345
St Kitts

 St Kitt's 10km

tel +1 869 465 7234
fax +1 869 465 4760

ottleys@caribsurf.com

Open all year

Tour operators
UK: Caribtours
    Harlequin
    Kuoni
    Caribbean Connection

Lovingly transformed from the ruins of an old 18th-century sugar plantation, Ottley's Plantation Inn has risen from the depths of neglect to the heights of beauty. Family run, it snuggles in the foothills of Mount Liamuiga, a dormant volcano surrounded by acres of lush unspoilt rainforest, bright tropical gardens and rolling green lawns.

Accommodation is in the majestic Great House or one of the nearby stone cottages, in which HRH Princess Margaret herself once stayed. The rooms are sensual and cool, decorated in colourful chintzes and tropical prints with polished wooden and wicker furniture. All have a balcony or private patio with spectacular ocean and mountain views.

The award-winning restaurant, The Royal Palm, is set into the old stone walls of the sugar mill house. and guests can discover the delightful New Island-style cuisine, cooked and prepared with particular accomplishment and served in an al fresco setting.

Guests can while away time at the spring-fed swimming pool, sipping rum punches and enjoying the peaceful view of the surrounding tropical gardens, or venture out onto the cobbled trails of the property's own rainforest ravine – home to some of the island's green vervet monkeys. The hotel provides daily shuttles to the beach and the historic city of Basseterre.

 US$220–425 (11)

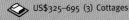 US$325–695 (3) Cottages

 from US$55

 included

Honeymoon specials

For direct bookings a package costing from US$2,195 for a stay of 7 nights is available. The package includes airport transfers, champagne and flowers on arrival, all breakfasts, five dinners, Sunday brunch, deluxe island tour and a catamaran trip. A wedding package is also available, please enquire.

Sightseeing and leisure

Visits to Independence Square, where slaves were once sold in the days of the working sugar plantation, Brimstone Hill and the capital with its West Indian architecture. Batik demonstrations, carnival in December and music festival end June. Rainforest, volcano and historic tours and hikes. Spa services, swimming and watersports.

Virgin Islands

These islands, more than a hundred of which are scattered over a thousand square miles, are a glorious sight — forested volcanic colossi soar from the water, tiny cays barely make it above the surf. Five hundred years ago, when Columbus passed through, he was so awestruck by their beauty that he compared them to Saint Ursula and her 11,000 virgins; a name that has remained ever since.

Most people who come here spend time on the water; the sailing is some of the best the Caribbean can offer. You can moor in coves where headlands enclose a horseshoe of white sand and a few palms, and where the water is so clear the boat seems to be suspended in the air. If it gets too hot on board, you can dive into the water and collapse on the beach. In the cool of the evening, you can sip a rum punch and watch for the Green Flash as the sun disappears below the horizon.

Yachts of all types are available for hire, and most hotels have small boats. If you are not sure you want to do some actual sailing, there are plenty of options for trips including visits to offshore islands with picnic and snorkelling stops.

The United States Virgin Islands are more developed than the smaller British Virgin Islands, but the setting is wonderful, the towns are as pretty as any in the West Indies and, of course, the sea, sand and sailing are impeccable.

Islands like sleeping animals all around,
classic beach bars, fantastic shops,
endless coral reefs, hundreds of wrecks,
and treasure worth a billion dollars...

flying time

To: Beef Island (BVI) via
Puerto Rico or Antigua.
St Thomas/St Croix (USVI)
direct from the USA.
London: 9–10 hrs
Miami: 3–4 hrs
NY: 4–5 hrs

when to go

Carnival culminates early
Aug. New Year's Eve at
Foxy's, Jost van Dyke,
attracts up to 2,500
people from 300 yachts,
with drinking and
jumping-up 'til dawn.

language

English.

money

The US dollar. Major credit
cards are accepted.

getting around

There are frequent ferries
and scheduled flights
between islands, and
reliable but expensive
taxis, sightseeing by
plane, and hire cars.

There is considerable variety in the islands, and it is worth travelling between them. St Thomas, the capital island, is one of the most developed in the Caribbean, but attractive for its good hotels and upbeat tempo. Cruise ships crowd the harbour at Charlotte Amalie; top entertainment acts maintain the island's reputation as 'the nightclub of the Virgin Islands'; restaurants offer 'contemporary exotic' and even 'passionate' cuisine; and life is clearly American, with big cruising cars, drive-through banks and fast-food joints. The shopping here is some of the best in the Caribbean.

St Croix, the largest island, is a little less developed and has a more pastoral air. St John is almost entirely given over to the National Park; Cruz Bay is the one small pocket of real development and has a quiet charm.

Life on the smaller BVI is more gentle and slow., but can be expensive. The islands are a sophisticated Caribbean playground, mostly easy-going, with a low hustle factor.

Tortola (Turtle Dove) is the largest of the British Virgins, with some fine beaches and an increasingly upbeat air. Virgin Gorda (the fat virgin) is gradually being developed; in the whiplashes and switchbacks of her coastline there are some classic Caribbean coves. The other islands are pretty much undeveloped.

The little island of Jost van Dyke lies a short distance off Tortola. It is a perfect place to be marooned — just a couple of square miles of scrub, and idyllic beaches and bars to retreat to. Anegada (drowned one) lies on its own about 15 miles off the main group of islands; a coral cap that supports about four hundred 5-foot iguanas, and little else. The underwater life, however, is superb, with hundreds of wrecks and, allegedly, treasure worth a billion dollars.

Finally, the BVI have classic beach bars, many with charming settings and a waterfront deck, where you can retreat for a beer and a fish platter in the heat of the day. At night, there are often live bands and big crowds. ●

Long Bay Beach Resort

Tortola
British Virgin Islands

 Beef Island 19km

Contact:
British Virgin Islands Club
tel +44 1932 220 477

Open all year

Tour operators:
UK: BVI Club

Above the beautiful sandy beach from which this resort takes its name, Long Bay Beach Resort boasts lovely gardens of oleander, bougainvillea and frangipani, which slope down to white sands bordered by sea grape.

Rooms are comfortably furnished and spacious, with king-size beds and private patios. Special honeymoon suites have private outdoor hot tubs.

The resort also has twenty luxurious villas, some with private swimming pools, tucked into the hillside overlooking the extensive grounds, and enjoying magnificent views across beach palms and turquoise seas to the island of Jost van Dyke beyond.

The atmosphere at Long Bay is informal, providing the ideal place to unwind and enjoy one of the most enticing beaches in the Caribbean.

The poolside restaurant and bar, converted from an old stone mill, serves as an attractive alternative to the more formal setting of the Garden Restaurant, which offers an excellent choice of gourmet cuisine and fine wines.

Weddings can be arranged on Long Bay Beach or the balcony of the Garden Restaurant, where receptions for up to 80 guests can also be held. Hotel staff are happy to arrange every detail.

 US$312–432 (72)
 US$660–930 (20)
 US$26–60
 US$5–14

Honeymoon specials
Champagne and flowers on arrival. A day's sailing aboard the resort's yacht.

Local attractions
Carnival week in August. Trips to Folk Museum, bustling markets, Mount Sage National Park and Botanical Gardens.

Leisure facilities
Tennis, sailing, yacht charter, two pools and sea kayaking. Beauty salon, massage by appointment, manicure, sauna and fully-equipped gym.

The Ritz-Carlton, St. Thomas

6900 Great Bay
St Thomas
US Virgin Islands

Cyril King Int. 4km

tel +340 775 3333
fax +340 775 4444

Open all year

Resting on the eastern tip of St Thomas – the second largest of the US Virgin Islands – this Ritz-Carlton hotel is set in a secluded expanse of manicured grounds overlooking the Caribbean sea. Cool stone arches, tiled roofs and towers revealing the classic Mediterranean influence of the island's rich past, combined with the relaxed ambience of the Caribbean, create an idyllic setting for a honeymoon.

Wide-arched windows frame ocean views in the luxurious rooms, where tropical plants, pretty cotton fabrics and cool rattan and wicker furniture add a touch of Caribbean comfort. All rooms have delicate wrought iron balconies, reminiscent of southern Europe.

The Cafe features inventive menus of Caribbean and American favourites. The elegant surroundings of the Dining Room offer nightly entertainment and classic European cuisine. A relaxed and breezy ambience prevails at the informal Pool and Beach Pavilion, where light snacks and cooling drinks are served on the beach front.

Almost a kilometre of private beach fringed with palm trees is the perfect spot for snorkelling or trying one of the wide range of watersports on offer. The resort's luxury catamaran, the Lady Lynsey, makes daily excursions to the surrounding islands.

The resort is happy to organise flowers and catering arrangements for marriage ceremonies, and has an on-site coordinator to ensure that wedding preparations run smoothly.

US$195–695
US$550–1,325
US$60–80
US$16–24 pp

Honeymoon specials

The hotel offers three wedding packages costing from US$1,350, which are available from 15 April to 18 December 1998. Please enquire.

Sightseeing and leisure

Tennis, golf, freshwater swimming pool, fitness and recreation centre, range of watersports available at hotel. Visits to nearby British Virgin Islands and diving trips can be arranged. Botanical gardens and underwater caves nearby.

Windward Islands

flying time

To: St Lucia, Grenada or via the main islands such as Antigua, Barbados or Trinidad.
London: 8–9 hrs
Miami: 4–5 hrs
NY: 4–5 hrs

climate

The Windwards are in the middle of the hurricane belt. Season: Jul–Nov. On their upper slopes, the rainfall is measured in feet. Lower down, expect sunshine year round, tropical rainstorms, and a pretty steady 27°C.

when to go

Throughout the region, Jun–Aug sees the greatest density of regattas and excuses for a 'jump-up'.

currency/language

The US dollar dominates although you will need the local currency outside the tourist areas. English is spoken everywhere.

getting around

Buses, taxis and motor bikes are all readily available and cheap. You will need to a local driving license, however, if you want to hire a car.

Domínica

THE WINDWARD ISLANDS

St. Lucia

St. Vincent

Grenada

Towering mountains mantled in explosive rainforest, swathes of banana trees, volcanoes, coastal inlets and bays of white sand beaches furred with palms...

These islands in the southeastern Caribbean are among the most fertile and dramatically beautiful in the region.

They rise sheer from the water to serrated volcanic peaks, usually stacked with rainclouds as the Altantic winds are forced up their slopes. Up on the heights, the rainfall is measured in feet rather than inches, and it crashes down the hills in torrents and waterfallls.

The land is incredibly fertile. Much of the interior is wild and remote, with large tracts of rainforest where huge trees are grappled by creeping vines and clumps of creaking bamboo can grow to over 6o feet.

The largest industry now is tourism, and the face of the islands is changing, but the one thing that does not change is the friendliness of the islanders. If ever you want to talk, you simply stop anyone you come across in the street.

Grenada

Grenada in the far south of the Windwards is typical of this chain of islands in its tropical beauty.

It has excellent beaches and the capital, St George's, is the prettiest harbour town in the whole Caribbean, being set in a massive volcanic bowl, its slopes lined with red-tiled roofs that descend to the edge of the bay, where yachts and old-fashioned schooners have long lined the waterfront. In the valleys of the interior there are fruit and spice plantations.

Grenada is less developed than St Lucia, but it sees a steady stream of tourists to its broad range of hotels. The nightlife is generally pretty quiet, but most hotels and restaurants have bars, and there are clubs that attract a young crowd. The island is also well positioned for exploring the Grenadines, by yacht, ferry and island-hopping plane.

Volcanic peaks and rainforests,
fruit and spice plantations,
great beaches, easy islanders...

flying time
To: Direct to Port Salines or via St Lucia, Trinidad or the Bahamas.
London: 8–9 hrs
Miami: 3–4 hrs
New York: 4–5 hrs

when to go
August for Carnival and the island's most lively sailing regatta.

currency
The Eastern Caribbean dollar, fixed to the US dollar. US dollar cash, traveller's cheques and credit cards are very widely accepted.

language
English.

getting around
Local buses, taxis, ferries and island-hopping planes all offer their services. Hiring a car is a good way to see the island if you are prepared to brave the somewhat erratic roads.

Secret Harbour Resort

Lance aux Epines
St George's
Grenada

Point Salines 10 km

tel +473 444 4549
fax +473 444 4819

secret@caribsurf.com

Open all year

Tour operators:
UK: The Moorings

The intimate hideaway resort of Secret Harbour is tucked into a tropical hillside overlooking Mount Hartman Bay on the island of Grenada. This is an island of outstanding natural beauty with stunning mountain vistas, cascading waterfalls that invite bathers, palm-fringed beaches and picturesque harbours.

The rooms retain the Mediterranean influence of the early explorers and feature carved four-poster beds, sunken sitting rooms, vaulted brick ceilings, and sumptuously oversized bathrooms with Italian-tiled tubs. French windows lead out onto private balconies with views encompassing the ocean, dotted with sailing boats, and the busy little harbour.

Guests can dine al fresco at the elegant restaurant, with Moorish arches framing the ocean views, or relax in the casual atmosphere of the poolside terrace restaurant.

There are a wealth of activities on offer from swimming in the freshwater pool to windsurfing along the shores of the private beach. The resort also offers excursions to local islands on skippered or self-skippered yachts, and can arrange 'Sail and Stay' packages combining three days on a yacht with four days at the resort.

Wedding ceremonies are staged under a rustically tiled archway with a canopy of local flowers, or at one of the village churches.

US$130–250 (20)

US$10–40

US$7–20

Honeymoon specials
Flowers, fruit and champagne in room on arrival. Champagne breakfast on request. Full day's sailing along the Southern Coast of Grenada. Honeymoon suite with canopied bed and all inclusions can be booked as part of honeymoon package, priced from US$899–1,199.

Sightseeing and leisure
Waterfalls, mountains and beaches. Annual carnival and sailing festivals. Trips to daily farmer's market. Complimentary tennis and watersports including kayaking and windsurfing. Fitness centre and beauty salon nearby. Extensive sailing facilities. Private beach and swimming area. 'Sail and Stay' package offered, combining a 3-day sail aboard a 50-foot yacht.

Spice Island
Beach Resort

PO Box 6
St George's
Grenada

 Pointe Saline 5km

tel +1 809 444 4258
fax +1 809 444 4807

Open all year

Tour operators:
UK: British Airways Holidays

Along Grenada's southern coastline is the palm-studded, satin-soft sand of Grand Anse Beach, home to the elegant Spice Island Beach Resort.

There are 56 rooms including a number of individual suites, many surrounded by landscaped gardens. All rooms are decorated in a stylishly Caribbean motif with soft pastel hues, light-coloured wood furniture and paintings by local artists. For the ultimate in luxury, the Royal Private Pool Suites offer king-size beds, marble bathrooms, sun deck and personal fitness area with sauna.

Dining can be a delightful experience at the open-air beachside restaurant, which serves lavish buffets, continental cuisine, local and seafood specialities. Room service is available for more intimate dining.

Guests can choose to be as active as they wish. A host of activities are on offer including most watersports. Or they may simply enjoy lounging on the beach.

For those seeking to wed in paradise, the resort is happy to make all the arrangements. Wedding receptions for up to 250 are catered for on the patio or beach, or in the bar area.

US$315–750 (56)
included*
included

Honeymoon specials
Flowers, tropical fruit and champagne in room on arrival.

Leisure activities
Watersports, horseriding, diving and tennis. Use of bicycles and fitness centre. Complimentary green fees at golf club nearby.

Local attractions
Island cruises, walks through tropical rainforests, Spice plantations. Grenada festival in August. Trips to sister island Carriacou, the oldest rum distillery in the Caribbean, picturesque waterfalls, botanical gardens and local markets.

* This is half-board and does not include lunch

St Lucia, St Vincent & the Grenadines

flying time
To: Direct to Hewanorra Int, St Lucia, or via Barbados or Grenada.
London: 8–9 hrs
Miami: 3–4 hrs
NY: 4–5 hrs

when to go
St Lucia: February for Independence Day and a real Carnival blast;
May for the jazz festival;
December for National Day.
St Vincent: June for Vincie Mas.

currency
The Eastern Caribbean dollar, fixed to the US dollar. US dollar cash and traveller's cheques, and credit cards are widely accepted.

language
English.

getting around
By local bus, taxi or hire car. Ferries and hopping planes connect islands. Yacht charters are especially popular around the Grenadines. Hiking.

One of the Caribbean's most popular destinations, St Lucia is a charmed isle — for her people, among the friendliest anywhere, the natural beauty of her hidden coves, her tropical abundance and her twin volcanic pyramids or Pitons.

The majority of hotels are on the leeward coast facing the calm Caribbean sea and the sunset. Some charming smaller hotels offer seclusion in dramatic settings, tucked away in coves or in view of the Pitons. Many hotels including a number of luxury resorts follow an all-inclusive plan.

The French heritage extends to the food, and West Indian ingredients take on a new life here in such creole dishes as treacle and coconut chicken stew. Nightlife is lively. The best-known party is the weekly jump-up on Friday nights, when four or five clubs spill out onto the street, speakers turned into the road.

St Vincent and the Grenadines offer a classic Caribbean combination: the staggering lushness and friendly way of the Windward Islands, and the slow-time, easy life of the tiny Grenadines.

The Grenadines are 30 islands strung out over 60 miles of strikingly blue sea, each a short hop from the next — a sailor's paradise. The islands are not as developed nor as expensive as the other sailing heaven, the British Virgin Islands, and there are some charming places to stay: island resorts comprising just a few rooms on an isolated cove; luxury villas on more developed islands like Mustique; rooms in fine old buildings and small hotels, like those strung out along the waterfront in pretty Bequia.

St Vincent is dominated by the mighty Soufrière, a volcano which last blew in 1979. There are comparatively few many tourists, probably because the island is not known for its beaches. The capital, Kingstown, sits on a sweeping bay, surrounded by deep ridges, from where Fort Charlotte commands a magnificent view of the 60-mile string of Grenadines. Downtown, modern shops stand out against old stone warehouses. On higher ground, colonial houses, once majestic, stand in open tropical gardens. ●

White triangles of yachts plying from island to island, pretty waterfronts, isolated beaches and swim-up bars, luxurious hideaways, tropical abundance...

Sandals St Lucia

PO Box 399
Castries
St Lucia

 Vigie airport 5km
Hewanorra 70km

tel +1 758 452 3081
fax +1 758 452 1012

Open all year

Tour Operators:
UK: Unique Vacations (UK) Ltd

This striking pink hotel is framed by pastel-hued villas which dot the lush green hillside along a half-crescent-shaped beach.

Luxurious suites are located on a bluff overlooking the ocean. Many have their own private plunge pools and sumptuous mahogany four-poster beds.

There are five restaurants to choose from including The Pavilion, which overlooks the Caribbean, and the Kimonos Teppanyaki restaurant serving delightful oriental dishes cooked at the table.

The resort boasts the largest pool on the island, incorporating a dramatic waterfall, swim-up bar and romantic bridges. Sailing, waterskiing, scuba diving, tennis, volleyball and golf are just a few of the sports included in the all-inclusive rate.

Following an exhilarating game, guests can cool down with an exotic cocktail then relax in one of the resort's three whirlpools. The European Spa offers an array of treatments from massages and reflexology to body wraps.

Weddings receptions are arranged in the extensive grounds, and may include a candlelit dinner. The resort's wedding coordinator can advise on popular locations for wedding ceremonies.

US$940–1,770 (210)*
US$900–1,720 (52)*
included
included

Honeymoon specials

A complimentary 20-piece Royal Doulton starter set for couples arriving between 19 Dec 1997 and 1 Dec 1998 and staying 13 nights or longer in a premium or higher category room. All meals, drinks, sports and snacks are included in the all-inclusive rate.

* prices are per person based on a stay of 3 nights

Sightseeing and leisure

Paddle boating, scuba diving, snorkelling, sailing in hobie cats and kayaks, waterskiing, windsurfing and golf are included in the all-inclusive rate. Caddies and treatments in the beauty salon cost extra. Romantic expeditions to hidden coves and the dramatic pitons (twin volcanic pyramids) can be organised at a cost.

LeSPORT

Cariblue Beach
PO Box 437
Castries
St Lucia

 Hewanorra 90km

tel +1 758 450 8551

fax +1 758 450 0368

tropichol@aol.com

Open all year

Situated on the north-western tip of the jewelled Caribbean island of St Lucia, LeSPORT enjoys a crescent shaped beach of soft sand on its doorstep. This all-inclusive resort is surrounded by lush tropical gardens of cascading bougainvillaea, sweet-scented ylang-ylang and beautiful gardenia. Here, the accent is on body and mind in harmony, and while the senses soak up the natural beauty, every opportunity is afforded to shed the stresses and strains of the outside world.

The rooms are decorated in soothing pastel shades with white wicker furniture, king-size four-poster beds draped Caribbean-style, and cool marbled bathrooms. Soft, bright and clean, the rooms complement the surrounding environment.

The cuisine at LeSPORT is an experience that will tempt the gourmet. An abundance of regional and international dishes are served at the extensive breakfast and lunch buffets. The wonderful à la carte dinner menu features dishes such as grilled dorado with callaloo and crab risotto, followed by a dessert of chocolate and mango tart with meringue glaze. Afterwards, spectacular nightly entertainment can be enjoyed, such as limbo dancing, fire-eating or steel bands. The staff at LeSPORT have also become famous for putting on their own shows.

The romantic wedding gazebo is an ideal location to exchange vows, and for a nominal fee, staff are happy to arrange everything from bouquets to champagne receptions. They will even provide a best man and maid of honour if required.

 US$215–275 (100)

US$265–325 (2)

included

included

Honeymoon specials
Sparkling wine, fresh fruit basket, tropical flower arrangement, honeymoon massage by appointment.

Local attractions
Local markets, shops and restaurants at nearby Castries, jazz festival in May, carnival in Feb. Lessons on cocktail mixing.

Leisure facilities
Watersports, diving and snorkelling, tennis, golf, archery, fencing, cycling, gym with personal trainer, health and relaxation treatments (such as facials, salt loofah body buffs, aromatherapy, reflexology, T'ai Chi, yoga, meditation, stress management and much more), fitness classes, board games are among the activities on offer.

Windjammer Landing

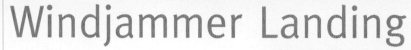

PO Box 1504
Labrelotte Bay
Castries
St Lucia

 Vigie Airport 8km

tel +1 758 452 0907
fax +1 758 452 9454
windjammer@candwi.lc

Open all year

This resort was built to look and feel just like a village. White adobe turrets and red-tile roofs nestle on a lush green hillside overlooking Labrelote Bay. Brick paths meander through hectares of lush landscaping, scented gardens, waterfalls and sparkling pools, all in perfect keeping with one of the last unspoiled islands in the Caribbean.

The villas are impressive. Each is hidden from its neighbours by magnificent trees and flowering bushes to offer a high level of privacy. A casual and spacious open-plan design incorporating sunny prints, rattan, warm ceramic tiles, vibrant art pieces and green plants give them a fresh and homely feel. French windows open onto well-proportioned balconies enjoying magnificent views, while most villas boast their own splash pool.

Gourmet meals can be prepared in the villa's own kitchen, delicious picnics can be packed for excursions or residents can dine under the stars beside the lapping waves, feel the warm sand between their toes and savour the local specialities and lively West Indian atmosphere.

Weddings can be held at the resort and the wedding coordinator is happy to take care of the details from ordering the flowers and cake to arranging a mariage officer. Receptions for up to 100 guests are catered for in a choice of locations.

 US$150–280* (74) (+18% tax)
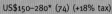 US$235–450 (91) (+18% tax)
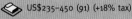 US$35
US$14

Honeymoon specials

Champagne, tropical fruit and flowers, complimentary sunset cruise and a souvenir photograph for couples staying 7 nights or longer. Couples booking half board receive a candlelit dinner in the restaurant or villa. Room upgrade subject to time and availability.

*Superior & Deluxe rooms available without pools or kitchens.

Sightseeing and leisure

Jeep safari tours, rainforest walks, bush expeditions. Excursions and boat trips by arrangement. Trips to Marquis Plantation, Pigeon Island, nearby Castries and shopping. Annual carnival in February and St Lucia Jazz Festival in May. Fitness and beauty centre, tennis and watersports free on site. Golf, horseriding, fishing and diving available nearby.

Europe

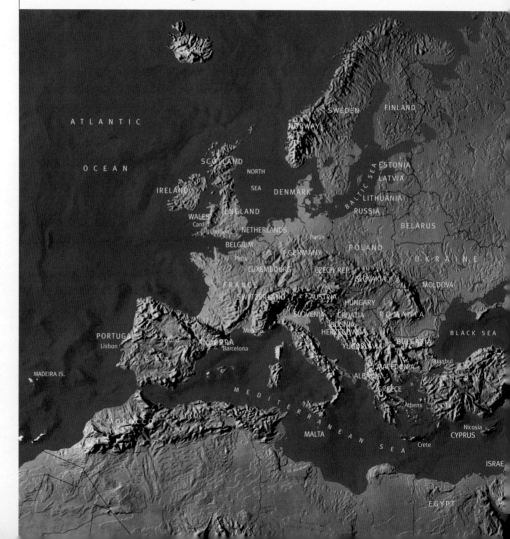

RUSSIA

The crazy quilt of countries that comprises Europe fairly bursts with romantic honeymoon destinations for every taste. Here, dramatic landscapes have been softened by a patina of centuries: only in Europe will your wanderings uncover a perfect hill town amidst rolling vineyards, or perhaps a medieval abbey cloaked in ivy, or a cosy 300-year-old thatched inn, or a Renaissance palace with gardens shimmering under the moon.

The rest is fine tuning. Looking for something hot, ancient and exotic? There's Turkey and Greece. Unspoiled green landscapes and a warm welcome? Try Scotland or Ireland. Italy and France combine matured beauty, marvellous food, wine and art; Austria and Switzerland offer alpine scenery and picture-postcard villages. Eastern Europe adds a hundred, long-forbidden surprises and delightful cities, while Scandinavia with its deep forests offers a retreat into nature.

Austria

Snatches of Mozart drifting from elaborate Baroque facades, crystal chandeliers glittering in gold-leafed ballrooms, aromas of coffee and croissants wafting past shop windows piled high with foil-wrapped chocolate...

If you are seeking a perfectly romantic setting for a winter honeymoon, Austria will fit the bill.

In the weeks before Christmas the streets come to life, bright with the lights of the Christkindl — Christmas markets that sell gifts and Christmas decorations, fresh local produce for the festive season, and hand-warming cups of spicy *gluhwein*. And on New Year's Eve in Vienna, the grand Imperial Ball kicks off a season of hundreds of lavish, glittering, full-dress balls that lasts through January and February.

On a snowy winter's day, you can escape the cold and join the locals over their coffee and cake in a *gemütlich* Viennese coffeehouse such as the Café Sacher, which gave its name to the wickedly rich chocolate confection. Forget calorie-counting and fuel up on a hearty lunch of paprika-peppered goulash, and apple strudel with lashings of cream. Try the Austrian wines, too, which are as praiseworthy as many French or German varieties but lesser known.

Austrian ski resorts are renowned for their village charm, picturesqueness and apres-ski jollity. Most have as their centrepiece a pretty onion-domed church and a lattice of old-world streets lined with enticing shops and snug cafés. In the late afternoon, still in your ski-gear, you can party to the music at a tea-dance and, after an ample dinner, try a sleigh ride or toboggan racing by moonlight. There are resorts to suit everyone, from fashionable Kitzbühel, St Anton and Lech, to lively but less expensive Söll and Schladming.

flying time

To: Vienna/Salzburg
London: 2 hrs
LA: 13 hrs (Vienna only;
no direct flights)
Miami: 10 hrs
NY: 9 hrs (Vienna only)

climate

There are four distinct
seasons, with warm
summers and cold winters
with widespread snow.

when to go

Tourist areas are very
busy in July and August.
Ski resorts operate
December to April.
The months May/Jun,
and Sept/Oct are quieter
and good for touring.

currency

The Austrian Schilling.
Credit cards, Eurocheques
and traveller's cheques
are very widely accepted

language

German. Many Austrians
also speak some English,
French or Italian.

getting around

By efficient train, bus and
tram systems. Scenic boat
trips on the lakes and the
River Danube.

Skiing, snowboarding and tobogganing are not the only sports. In summer the resorts attract visitors wanting to go walking on carpets of alpine flowers or to try relatively challenging activity holidays. Hiking and climbing, hang-gliding, mountain-biking, horse riding, sailing, windsurfing and fishing are all popular, amid the spectacular mountain scenery of Austria's lakes and rivers.

While Vienna and Innsbruck are attractive, Salzburg is irresistible; a treasure trove of opulent, magnificently preserved Baroque buildings, splendidly situated between mountain peaks. It was in and around Salzburg that 'The Sound of Music' was filmed in 1964 and a half-day tour takes you round the locations where Julie Andrews and the children belted out those familiar songs.

But while some visitors might be humming' Do Re Mi' and 'Eidelweiss', others are focused on 'The Magic Flute' or 'The Marriage of Figaro'. For Salzburg was, and still is Mozart's city. You can visit the house where he was born in 1756, see the font in the cathedral where he was christened and hear his music in palaces, churches and concert halls. Several times a year the city revels in classical music festivals like the Mozart Week (January/February), the Easter Festival and the famous summer opera festival (July/August), which is always a sell-out. If you want to be part of it, book well in advance.

Hotel Kobenzl

Gaisberg 11
A-5020 Salzburg
Austria

✈ Salzburg 20km

tel +43 662 541 510
fax +43 662 642 238
kobenzl@salzburginfo.or.at

Open all year

Member of:
Small Luxury Hotels of the World

The deluxe hotel and vital centre Kobenzl is set in 15 acres of landscaped gardens and coniferous forest high above Salzburg, enjoying unparalled views of the beautiful baroque city and mountains beyond.

Built in 1864 and recently renovated, this family-run hotel is furnished in wood and gold fittings, creating a setting of elegance and charm.

The bedrooms are especially romantic, with candelabra, mirrors, delicate, gilt-painted furniture and pretty drapes over the beds.

All rooms have radio, satellite television and minibar.

In the award-winning restaurant, guests are offered simple, good Austrian fare and fine wines — roast suckling pig, fresh fruit, delicate pastries. In the spa or Vital Centre, a range of natural treatments help visitors relax and unwind.

The von Buseck family welcome visitors as members of the family, and are delighted to arrange weddings, with music and fireworks, in the unforgettable settings of the Marble Hall of Schloss Mirabell or the baroque church of Maria Plain.

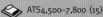 ATS1,900–5,900 (40)

 ATS4,500–7,800 (15)

 ATS300–1,000

 ATS415

Honeymoon specials

Champagne on arrival. Bed and breakfast accommodation in double room, candlelit dinner, concert visit, guided tour of Salzburg and optional one-day vitality treatment costs from ATS9,950 and is based on a stay of 3 nights.

Sightseeing and leisure

The beautiful, historic city of Salzburg. Specialised fitness and training programmes, swimming, body-shape gymnastics, thalosso therapy, aromotherapy and a range of massage treatments. Walking, hiking, river-rafting and hot-air balloon trips in the surrounding countryside. Golf, tennis and horseriding nearby.

Hotel Schloss Mönchstein

Mönchsberg Park 26
A-5020 Salzburg City Centre
Austria

Salzburg Int. 5km

tel +43 662 848 5550
fax +43 662 848 559
moenchstein@salzburginfo.or.at

Open all year

Member of:
Relais & Châteaux
European Castle Hotels &
Restaurants Johansens

This enchanting castle hotel, above the rooftops of Salzburg in Mönchsberg Park, was originally built in 1358 to house the guests of archbishops and later became a popular venue for musical soirées by Haydn and Mozart. Today, Hotel Schloss Mönchstein has the reputation of being the 'Urban Sanctuary of the World' (Hideaway Report, USA).

Towers and turrets cloaked with ivy in summer and sparkling with snow in winter, renaissance-style furnishings and precious paintings characterise this splendid building. Most rooms are spacious and decorated in pastel shades with gilt-framed mirrors.

A variety of authentic Austrian and international dishes are served in the award-winning Paris-Lodron restaurant, which has outstanding views of the city below. Harp concerts take place every week in the castle café, Maria Theresia, or on the garden terrace, Apollo.

A lift and a romantic 7-minute walk through the park links the hotel to the beautiful baroque buildings of the old town, and a rich and varied cultural programme of concerts and entertainment.

The castle chapel, where brides and grooms have exchanged their vows since 1531, still provides a perfect setting for a fairytale wedding. The 'Salzburger Wedding Wall' in front of the chapel is covered in brass plates bearing the names of all couples married inside. Receptions of up to 80 guests are catered for in the restaurant, café or castle grounds and staff will be delighted to arrange cocktail parties and concerts.

ATS2,400–6,500

ATS4,900–28,000

ATS530–1,300

included

Honeymoon specials
Wine and fruit on arrival. A generous extended castle breakfast, candlelit gala dinner and palace concert. Room upgrade subject to availability. The package costs from ATS7,000 per couple and is based on a stay of 2 nights.

Sightseeing and leisure
The historic city of Salzburg, castles, lakes mountains. Visits to Mozart's birthplace, Castle Mirabell and an underground glacier. Music festivals and events in the castle grounds and the city. Beauty treatments and massage by appointment. Tennis, golf and jogging. A full range of summer and winter sports nearby.

Cyprus

Often in the news, Cyprus is one of those islands that is well known and little known at the same time. Visitors pour through the airports at Larnaca and Paphos, yet few take the time and trouble to explore the real Cyprus behind the brash development of some coastal resorts.

That is a pity, for this is a most interesting island with a long and thrilling history of colonisation, invasion and conquest on account of its natural riches and strategic location in the Eastern Mediterranean. Sadly, since 1974 the island has been partitioned, with the northern sector declaring itself a Turkish Republic and out of bounds to visitors from the South, though day trips can be made.

Mythical birthplace of Aphrodite, goddess of love, Cyprus retains its romantic connections for those with imagination. Marvel at the splendid mosaics of Roman villas at Paphos, a World Heritage Site. Climb the ruins of Crusader castles in the Kyrenia mountains and think of Shakespeare in Othello's Tower in Famagusta. Explore Venetian bastions in Nicosia and Byzantine monasteries in the Troodos Mountains.

Aphrodite's island welcomes you with pine-scented forests, rocky coves, sandy beaches, mountain villages, cherry trees, Byzantine churches, and villages sleeping in the sun...

flying time

To: Larnasa

London: 4 hrs
LA: 16–17 hrs
Miami: 12 hrs
NY: 11 hrs (via London)

climate

Hot, dry summers with mild winters. Rainfall mainly October–March.

when to go

In summer, for swimming, boating, watersports and nightlife. In spring and autumn for sightseeing and touring. In winter for skiing in the Troodos Mountains.

currency

The Cyprus pound. Credit cards are generally accepted.

language

Greek. English is very widely spoken.

getting around

With limited public transport, car rental is the best option.

Mount Olympus, the highest point in the Troodos, rises to 6,450 feet. The wooded slopes and foothills with their quaint villages are ideal for walks and rambles, avoiding the heat of summer. In spring, hikers are rewarded with carpets of wildflowers. In winter, Platres and Kakopetria are good bases for limited but uncrowded skiing.

The coastline alternates between rugged cliffs, hidden coves and golden beaches. Old Paphos dates back to Mycenean times, the centre of the cult of Aphrodite. New Paphos, the port town, was founded in the 4th century BC. Nowadays it is a wonderful mixture of ancient and modern, a popular resort with splendid hotels and attractive restaurants cheek by jowl with archaeological remains.

Farther east, on the way to Limassol, stop at Kourion to see impressive Roman remains including a temple, mosaics, houses and a reconstructed Roman theatre still in use today.

The best finds are now in the museum at Episkopi. Nearby is Kolossi Castle whose square 15th-century keep can be visited.

Limassol itself is a busy port city, but its attractive suburbs have a number of good hotels. Larnaca is now best known for its airport, the island's principal gateway since the closure of Nicosia airport in 1974.

The events of 1974 also transformed the fishing village of Ayia Napa into a bustling seaside resort, with ribbon development along the coast and non-stop nightlife. Here, as elsewhere, enjoy *mezze, dolmas* and kebabs and the excellent local wine, then dance the night away under the stars. Wherever you are in Cyprus, you are never more than a couple of hours from Nicosia, nowadays a divided city but still the island's spiritual heart. Walk the narrow streets, shop for local bargains, explore the Archbishop's Palace, then relax at a pavement café and feel the pulse of this enigmatic yet nevertheless romantic island.

Azia Beach Hotel

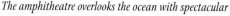

Akamas Avenue
PO Box 2108
Paphos
Cyprus

Paphos 20km

tel +357 6 247 800
fax +357 6 246 883
azlahtl@cy.net

Open all year

Tour operators:
UK: Thomson
     First Choice
US: Argo

The ancient town of Paphos on the western shores of the Mediterranean sea is surrounded by hidden hillside monasteries and historic sights reaching back to the fabled era of Greek legend. Set right on the waterfront, the Azia Beach Hotel exudes the charm and relaxed ambience of a private Greek villa.

The sunlight reflects from dazzling white walls to brighten the modern and elegantly decorated rooms and suites. Most have private terraces overlooking ochre Mediterranean sand and the gleaming expanse of the sea. Many of the larger suites boast a terrace with private garden and are fitted with jacuzzis.

The amphitheatre overlooks the ocean with spectacular Mediterranean sunsets and is the perfect backdrop for intimate candlelit dinners. International and regional cuisine is served in three individually decorated restaurants, each suiting a particular mood. The hotel-owned Morocampos plantation provides fresh produce daily, much of which goes to make the mouth-watering desserts and fruit baskets.

A wide range of watersports is available and visitors may enjoy exploring the historical sights of the area which include tombs of the ancient kings, Aphrodite's baths and stunning mosaics.

The hotel staff are pleased to assist with wedding arrangements. Popular locations for the ceremony include the pretty local churches of Paphos, or the amphitheatre near the outdoor swimming pool.

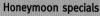

CY£50–146 (183)
CY£150–146 (4)
CY£9–29
included

Honeymoon specials
Champagne, fruit and flowers in room on arrival. Room upgrade if available.

Leisure facilities
Gym, 2 pools, squash, tennis, beauty and health club with extensive range of treatments.

Local attractions
Nearby attractions include Lemba historical village, Tombs of the Kings, the birthplace of Aphrodite, monasteries and mosaics.

38

Four Seasons

PO Box 7222
Limassol
Cyprus

✈ Larnaca 75km

tel +357 5 310 222
fax +357 5 310 887

inquiries@fourseasons.com.cy

Open all year

Member of:
Muskita Hotels Ltd,
International Spa and Fitness Assoc.,
International Hotel Assoc.

Built directly on the seashore, just east of Limassol, this ultra modern, magisterial hotel strikes an excellent balance between present-day convenience and rejuvenating comfort. Located on a sandy beach, only a few minutes drive from the bustling centre of Limassol, guests are within easy reach of all that represents joyous Cypriot life: celebrations, wine festivals and the ever-popular, colourful and exhilarating carnival parades.

Past meets present in the slim-lined, marbled lobby, designed and furnished with beautiful floral arrangements, commanding palm trees and silent, running water cascades. Service is courteous and unobtrusive. A similar theme of classic comfort twinned with the needs of up-to-date convenience continue in the rooms, where attention to detail has been meticulously observed.

Guests can work up a healthy appetite using a selection of the outstanding leisure facilities, take an aqua class, enjoy a game of tennis, or simply lie back in the exclusive Thalasso Spa, where professional consultants will design individual sessions tailored to the needs of each guest.

In the evenings, visitors are spoilt for choice with a wealth of different restaurants, bars and cafes to choose from, perhaps the most romantic being the alluring Palace dining room. With its impressive pillars, beautiful statues and live music, the experience is only enhanced by the delicate cuisine on offer, and the magical panoramic views.

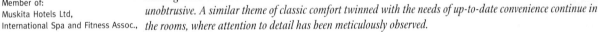

CY£135–150 (306)
CY£210–525 (18)
CY£17
included

Honeymoon specials
Champagne and candlelit dinner on arrival. Room upgrade subject to availability.

Local attractions
Visits to the 9th-century city of Amathus, medieval fortress, Kolossi castle and the ancient city of Curium. Wine festival and carnival parades annually.

Leisure facilities
Swimming, squash, tennis and table tennis. Snooker room and amusement centre. Fully-equipped gym. Aerobic and aqua classes. Variety of watersports. Jacuzzi and sauna. Thalasso Spa for marine-based treatments and massage.

Paphos Amathus

Poseidon Avenue,
PO Box 2381
8098 Paphos
Cyprus

✈ Paphos 14km

tel +357 6 264 300
fax +357 6 264 222

pamathus@logos.cy.net

Open all year

Member of:
The Leading Hotels of the World

Rich in cultural heritage, Paphos lies on the south west coast of the island among significant historical sites and abundant vineyards, encompassed by sparkling, sandy beaches. The hotel sits comfortably on the seashore, a subtle blend of modern facilities, warmth and lofty splendour. Its monastic architecture, tall columns and grandeur combine to make guests feel welcome and special. The bedrooms are decorated in soothing, delicate colours, and have luxurious en suite marbled bathrooms.

A wide, central staircase winds down through the marble-floored lobby to ground level. The beach lies just a short walk away, through the gardens and bright, manicured lawns.

The coffee bar is open throughout the day for a tempting array of culinary delights, a refreshing breakfast or light

buffet lunch. In the warm evenings, couples can enjoy dinner by candlelight in the exclusive La Rotisserie restaurant, accompanied by the lilting music of the resident band, or dine downstairs amid tall columns in The Amorosa, with a table d'hôte menu.

Guests can work off the extra pounds in the health and leisure centre, where professional instructors offer help and advice, or spend the day lazing in the sun by the pool.

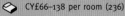 CY£66–138 per room (236)
 CY£102–276 (19)
CY£14–21
included

Honeymoon specials
Room upgrade subject to availability. Candlelit dinner with special menu, vouchers of up to CY£50 per couple for use in the health and recreation centre. Wedding package based on a stay of 7 nights or longer is also available and includes all of the above and wine, flowers, choice of locations, wedding cake and bon voyage champagne.

Sightseeing and leisure
Tsada Golf Club. Troodos Mountains. Abundant vineyards and beaches. Paphos fishing harbour. Local historical sites. Health and leisure centre with gym, sauna, steam bath, solarium, hydromassage and body massage. Squash, swimming pool and tennis. Hair salon.

40

St Raphael

Amathus Avenue,
PO Box 1064,
3594 Limassol
Cyprus

Larnaca 70km

tel +357 5 321 100
fax +357 5 324 394
raphael@spidernet.com.cy

Contact:
Principal Promotions
tel +44 171 485 5500

Open all year
Member of:
Insignia Resorts

On the shores of the beautiful island state of Cyprus, the St Raphael Resort – an oasis of leisure with a golden sandy beach and its own marina – is set within delightful landscaped gardens. Nearby are Medieval castles, remote mountain villages, orange groves and vineyards and ancient relics of such esteemed visitors as St Paul, Alexander the Great and Richard the Lionheart.

The rooms and suites are set around an atrium of cool marble, decorated with trailing plants and graced by the refreshing sound of tinkling waterfalls. The rooms themselves are simply furnished, decorated in warm neutral tones, with full-length windows and balconies looking out onto the warm Grecian seas.

Restaurants and tastes from around the world suit all moods whether it be spicy and exotic Lebanese specialities or colourful Greek salads, mouth-watering ices or delicious pancakes.

Weddings can be held in the cosmopolitan town of Limassol, a stone's throw from St Raphael with receptions arranged to cater for up to 500 guests.

Cyprus is the legendary home of the beautiful and voluptuous Aphrodite, fashioned from the foam of the crystal blue Mediterranean waters. After even a short stay on this fabled isle it is easy to see why the gods chose it as the birthplace for their goddess of love.

 US$140–200 (209)
US$260–360 (7)
US$20–40
included

Honeymoon specials
Flowers, complimentary local champagne. Room upgrade subject to availability.

Leisure facilities
Gymnasium, massage, sauna, jacuzzi, beauty salon, waterskiing, canoeing, windsurfing, sailing, parakiting, day cruises, fishing, tennis.

Local attractions
Archeological and Byzantine art tours. Trips to baths and birthplace of Aphrodite, Temple of Apollo, lace-making village of Lefkara, Latchi fishing harbour. Wine festival in September. Bouzouki tavernas and nightclubs nearby.

41

France

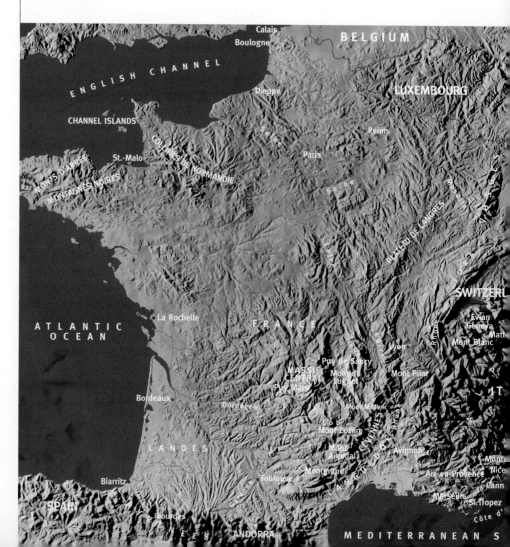

flying time
London: 1 hr
NY/LA: 8–9 hrs

climate/when to go
July and August are the warmest months and the liveliest time, with plenty of special events — especially from 14 July to 15 Aug. Book well in advance and at Easter. June and Sept offer more peace, and nice weather. The south often benefits from warm weather in May and Oct.

currency
The franc. Beware, there is the occasional exclusive restaurant that does not accept them credit cards.

language
French.

health
EU citizens can use the excellent health service, but normally have to pay up front and reclaim.

getting around
There is a close network of airports, an excellent rail service linking major towns and a growing number of *autoroutes* (motorways).

Sparkling champagne, rolling vineyards, the most seductive of cuisines, the grandeur of countless chateaux, historic towns, medieval villages, teeming markets, snow-capped mountains, endless sandy shores, rural bliss...

From the grandeur of Paris to the warm rustic pleasures of southwest France, from the windswept rocks of Brittany to the glamorous resorts of the Côte d'Azur, France is a country to set you dreaming...

The coastline is spectacular for much of its length, with some of the best sandy beaches in Europe on the Atlantic side. Inland, there are châteaux galore, many turned into luxurious hotels where you can sleep in a bedchamber made for a lord and his lady. The Loire Valley is the most famous area for châteaux, which are built in elegant white limestone.

Vineyards beautify many of the provinces. Champagne, Bordeaux and Burgundy count among the most famous wine areas in the world. And, of course, you can taste fabulous French food in every corner of the country.

While the western half of France undulates softly towards the Channel and the Atlantic ocean, the eastern half is marked by magnificent mountains. Below the Vosges and Jura ranges you can go skiing and hiking in the mighty Alps bordering Switzerland and Italy. You can also stay by mountain lakes with snow-capped peaks reflected in their crystal waters. The Alps form the eastern boundary of that earthly paradise, Provence. The most famous slice of the Provençal coast is usually known by the dreamy title Côte d'Azur, the azure blue coast, looking out onto the shimmering Mediterranean.

Hotel Royal
Domaine du Royal Club Evian

South Bank
Lake Geneva
74500 Evian Les Bains
France

✈ Geneva International 45km

tel + 33 450 268 500
fax + 33 450 756 100

reservation.domaine-royal@wanadoo.fr

Closed 6 Dec–6 Feb

Member of:
Leading Hotels of the World

Tour operators:
UK: Elegant Resorts
US: Spa Finders

This splendid Belle Epoque hotel with its colonnades, domes, rotundas and frescoes, overlooks Lake Geneva and is surrounded by 42 acres of magnificent parkland.

The Hotel Royal was built on a grand scale in 1907 in honour of Edward VII. Rooms are spacious, light and airy and furnished with antiques and large brass beds. All have luxurious en suite marble bathrooms, private terraces and wonderful lake or park views. Service is discreet and attentive.

In the resort's nine restaurants, guests can choose from an array of dishes spanning five continents or more traditional fare inspired by local produce.

The spa town of Evian has always been conducive to rest and recuperation. In keeping with this tradition, the hotel's own world-renowned spa, the Better Living Institute, provides a range of revitalising

Honeymoon specials
Champagne, flowers and fruit in the room
on arrival.

 FF700–3,180 (127)

 FF1,500–8,560 (29)

FF110–480

FF110

treatments and special health programmes.

The exceptional geographic location of the Domaine du Royal Club Evian provides an unusually wide range of leisure opportunities. Guests have access to tennis courts, children's club, casino, and year-round sports and music events. Golfers have free access to the Evian Masters' Golf course with panoramic views over the lake into Switzerland.

The Casino Royal Evian provides a great venue for evening entertainment where guests can try their luck in the gambling rooms, enjoy a meal in the restaurants or dance the night away in the Flash night club.

Wedding receptions of up to 250 guests are catered for in the authentic chalet-style Hotel Ermitage, or in the Chalet du Golf overlooking the course, or in the Royal Casino's splendid reception room, the Orée du Lac.

Leisure facilities

Special treatments and programmes in the spa and fitness centres, indoor and outdoor swimming pools, sauna, Turkish bath, jacuzzi, tennis and archery. A range of outdoor pursuits including rafting, paragliding, horseriding, mountain biking and skiing. Private 18-hole golf course.

Local attractions

Evian Music Festival in July. Annual golf tournaments. Exhibitions, painting and sculpture and museums nearby. Trips by old steamer across Lake Geneva. Visits to the historic cities of Annecy and Geneva. Helicopter ride over the romantic site of Chamonix Mont-Blanc with a glass of champagne on the Mer de Glace glacier.

The South of France and the Alps

flying time

Marseille-Provence and Nice are the two major airports along the coast, Lyon and Geneva the two most practical for northern Provence and the Alps. Most flights via Paris.

London: 2 hrs
LA: 12 hrs
Miami 9–10 hrs
NY: 8–9 hrs

when to go

Arts and folklore festivals take place almost year round. Highlights include Cannes Film Festival (early May), Monaco Grand Prix (late May) and Avignon theatre festival (mid July to mid Aug).
In winter, you can get some surprisingly mild and sunny days. The *mistral* thunders down the Rhône at regular intervals throughout the year.

getting around

There is a decent train network between major towns, but you need to hire a car to go exploring.

Glamour is the word in the resorts that line the Côte d'Azur, Provence's main stretch of coastline. St-Tropez, Cannes, Nice and Monte-Carlo, the most famous names, trip easily off the tongue.

The Côte d'Azur is a place to come to see and be seen; vibrant, lively, heady. You can enjoy watersports, wonderful restaurants and casinos here. On the more contemplative side, you could visit some of the coast's fabulous modern art museums or take a trip to the pretty hill-top villages overlooking the Mediterranean. Behind the Côte d'Azur, you enter the rich countryside of Provence. Glorious unspoilt villages lie scattered across the region. Some are full of life, others deeply peaceful, almost all picturesque.

Dramatic hills and mountains form the backdrop to the Provençal countryside. The Alps tower over the eastern side of the region. The range then stretches up towards the Swiss border, close to which you will find magically beautiful lakes such as that of Annecy and Geneva (Léman in French). Luxurious hotels are a speciality in this area, where you can go for a serious pampering in stunning scenery. In winter you can find all the joys of some of Europe's best skiing resorts in the Alps. ●

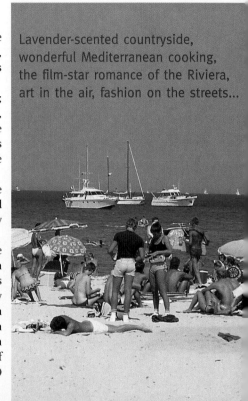

Lavender-scented countryside, wonderful Mediterranean cooking, the film-star romance of the Riviera, art in the air, fashion on the streets...

Hotel Martinez

73 La Croisette
06406 Cannes
France

✈ Nice 25km

tel +33 1 9298 7300
fax +33 4 9394 1694

Open all year

Member of:
Concorde Hotels
The Leading Hotels of the World

Home to the famous film festival, Cannes on the French Riviera is France's Hollywood. Commanding grand views over the city and the bay on the famous Croisette Boulevard is the Hotel Martinez, an Art Deco Palace which has kept all of its 20's and 30's glamour and style with spiral staircases, piano bar and hotel staff in crisp white linen.

The glitz is carried through to the 397 or so spacious, sun-filled rooms and suites. Wooden walnut furniture, Art Deco carriage clocks and fireplaces, stylish lamps and bold print wallpapers and bedspreads make the Martinez a supremely elegant place to stay, continuing the tradition of Cannes as one of the playgrounds of the world.

The hotel's Palme d'Or restaurant has a deservedly high reputation, noted for its 1930's furniture

including black lacquered armchairs covered in pearl-grey and maroon and using period silverware and glassware. The cuisine is international with regional provençal recipes such as bouillabaisse also on the menu.

For those who want to arrive in style, a pier with pink parasols and sun-loungers stretches out into the Mediterranean and a palm-fringed pool and private beach are available for sun-seekers and star-gazers alike.

 FF1,000–3,800 (395)
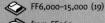 FF6,000–15,000 (19)
 from FF360
 FF115

Honeymoon specials

Deluxe sea view room, continental breakfast, return transfer by helicopter to Côte d'Azur airport, one dinner per person in Palme d'Or excluding drinks. Access to private beach and tennis courts. The package costs from FF2,780 to FF3,380* per room per night depending on the season and includes taxes except local city tax. Minimum stay of 2 nights.

Sightseeing and leisure

Cannes Film Festival in May, Fireworks Festival in July and August. Trips to museums, Provençal markets, Grand Canyon du Verdon, and Grasse (home to France's scent trade). Beauty salon, tennis, pool, watersports.

*not valid during festival periods

Le Moulin de Lourmarin

84160 Lourmarin
France

✈ Marseille 60km

tel +33 4 9068 0669
fax +33 4 9068 3176
lourmarin@silicone.fr

Closed mid Jan–Feb

A delightful 18th-century mill now houses this charming four-star hotel situated in Lourmarin, one of the prettiest French villages in Provence.

There are 22 rooms and suites, all individually designed, some to traditional Provençal style with pretty drapes and wooden furniture; others have a more modern feel with ornate wrought-iron beds and brightly coloured fabrics. One suite has a balcony opening onto a fabulous view of the castle.

In the oldest part of the mill the vaulted dining room is full of surprises, with an ever-changing cuisine prepared using aromatic herbs to take account of the true values and smells of Lubéron.

Claude Loubet and her son Edouard have done their utmost to create a cosy welcoming atmosphere. Guests can pass time sipping wine in the courtyard decorated with an abundance of plants and flowers, swim in the pool, or try their hand at a round of golf nearby. And because the hotel is located between Marseille and Avignon, in the heart of Provence, it is an ideal base for visiting the quaint villages and towns which characterise the region.

Respecting the tradition of the old country farms, the sister hotel La Bastide de Capelongue, ten minutes from Lourmarin, is also a popular base for visiting rural Provence.

The well-tended gardens at both hotels provide a beautiful venue for a wedding reception.

 FF700–1,000 (20)
 FF1,300–2,100 (2)
 FF195–420
 FF85

Honeymoon specials
Champagne in the room on arrival.

Leisure facilities
Golf, tennis, horseriding, swimming, mountain biking and hiking.

Local attractions
Avignon, Marseille and the Camargue are a little over an hour's drive away. Visits to wine cellars, castles, musuems and abbeys nearby. Cultural events such as the annual Worldwide Piano festival of La Roque d'Antheron in August. Discover the aromatic plants and *herbes de Provence* with the hotel's own chef.

Villa Saint-Elme

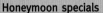

Corniche des Issambres
83380 Les Issambres
France

 Nice 60km

tel +33 4 9449 5252
fax +33 4 9449 6318
101603.1255@compuserve.com

Open all year

Member of:
Small Luxury Hotels of the World

Once a private home, and later a popular haunt for actors and artists including Maurice Chevalier and Edith Piaf, Villa Saint-Elme occupies a prime position overlooking the gulf of Saint-Tropez along the exclusive French Riviera.

All rooms are spacious and individually decorated in Art Deco design, some have pretty Provençal fabrics. Some suites, such as the romantic Froufrou suite with its Baldaquin bed and pale pink interior, have marble bathrooms with jacuzzis. Many have terraces with exceptional views of the sea.

The glass-domed restaurant Saint-Elme overlooking the sea, serves traditional Provençal dishes featuring fresh fruit, vegetables and the day's freshly caught fish. For a lighter meal, grilled fish and salads can be enjoyed any time of the day at the poolside grill.

The hotel is ideally placed for exploring the exclusive resort of St-Tropez – playground of the rich and famous – as well as bustling Provençal markets, the perfumeries of Grasse and some of the region's finest vineyards.

Weddings can be arranged in the beautiful Gothic church of Roquebrune-sur-Argens which dates back to the 16th century and is protected as a historical monument. Hotel staff are happy to arrange receptions for up to 80 guests.

FF750–1,950 (3)
FF1,600–4,600 (13)
FF350–750
included

Honeymoon specials
Champagne, flowers and fruit on arrival. Room upgrade subject to availability.

Leisure facilities
Swimming pool and sauna. Massage and beauty treatments by appointment. Golf, tennis, watersports. fishing nearby. Boats to rent from private quay.

Local attractions
Depending on the season, the hotel can arrange boat trips to nearby islands with lunch on board, helicopter tours along the French Riviera, chauffeur driven tours to St-Tropez and quaint Provençal villages and markets, the Gorges du Verdon and local wine cellars. Monaco, Monte-Carlo and Cannes are all within easy reach.

Biarritz and the Basque Country

The legendary beauty, Empress Eugenie, wife of Napoleon III, made Biarritz one of the most fashionable resorts in Europe. It is still a particularly elegant town; with 19th-century palatial Belle Epoque villas and hotels lining the the shore, along which Atlantic waves crash .

Surfing is a passion among the young of Biarritz today — the town's beaches are considered the best in Europe for the sport. Those who prefer a more leisurely pace can take luxury sea-water treatments at the state-of-the-art thalassotherapy centre, or find a relaxing spot on miles of sandy beaches; one of which is known as the Plage de la Chambre d'Amour (Beach of the Room of Love), because according to local legend this is where Venus, goddess of love, rose from the foaming sea. You might like to try the wonderful seafood restaurants in the port. And don not miss Bidart and Guéthary, two idyllic Basque coastal villages nearby. You can even slip down the coast and over the border into the Spanish Basque country, and compare the glamour of the resort of San Sebastian with that of Biarritz.

This stretch of coastline is cosmopolitan in feel and forms part of that proud region or nation called the Pays Basque. In the Basque hinterland, Bayonne, with its colourful medieval quarters, is one of the very prettiest towns in southwest France. It is also famed for its chocolate shops. Heading further inland towards the rolling Pyrenees, pretty-balconied St-Jean-Pied-de-Port is the main point of departure for exploring the glorious, peaceful Pyrenean scenery. ●

Elegance by the Atlantic,
King Louis XIV's wedding spot...

flying time
To: Biarritz via Paris
London: 2 hrs
LA: 12 hrs
NY: 8–9 hrs

climate/when to go
Big regional festivals take place in high summer, for example the Fêtes de Bayonne (early Aug) and Basque sports finals (Biarritz, early Aug). You can seek out amusing folk festivals further inland. Late summer is especially good for surfing.

language
The Basque language is still alive and well, but everyone also speaks French.

getting around
You will need to hire a car, to go exploring.

Hotel du Palais

1 Avenue de l'Impératrice
64200 Biarritz
France

✈ Biarritz 3km

tel + 33 5 5941 6400
fax + 33 5 5941 6799
palais@cotebasque.tm.fr

Open all year

Member of:
Leading Hotels of the World

Biarritz, set in a dramatically beautiful landscape at the foot of the Pyrenees, has for centuries courted the rich and famous. The Hotel du Palais, formerly the summer residence of Napoleon III and Empress Eugenia, is a splendid example of Second Empire architecture, blending sumptuousness with elegance and restraint. The hotel has been painstakingly restored to combine luxury with period charm.

The bedrooms are especially refined, being individually decorated in light shades, with flowing drapes and period antiques. Most are ocean facing with calming views of the sandy beaches.

Classic French cuisine and regional specialities are served in the hotel's two restaurants: the palatial La Rotonde and the more intimate Villa Eugénie.

Visitors can explore the rolling hills and the small fishing villages, with their brightly painted houses and bustling markets, which characterise the Basque region.

Sports facilities are unusually comprehensive. The town's busy casinos and inns provide a stimulating variety of evening entertainment.

 FF1,200–2,850 (134)

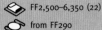 FF2,500–6,350 (22)

from FF290

from FF130

Honeymoon specials
Flowers, fruit basket and perfume on arrival. Double room with sea view, continental breakfast and dinner overlooking the ocean. The package costs from US$420 per couple per day.

Sightseeing and leisure
Romantic walks to Musée del al Mer. Trips to the picturesque villages over the Spanish border and prehistoric caves. Tapas-style gala evenings in a Basque farmhouse. Year-round music festivals. Swimming pool, sauna, fitness club. All watersports, beach diving, tennis, riding. Golf on the 100-year-old Phare golf course.

46

Greece

flying time
To: Athens
London: 3 hrs
LA: 13 hs
Miami: 12 hrs
NY: 10–11 hrs

climate/when to go
The 'season' opens with the tremendous celebration of Greek Easter. Beautiful wildflowers in the spring are followed by long hot summers; you can often swim until mid October.

currency
The Greek drachma. Traveller's cheques and cheque cards are useful, but if you plan to spend time on the more remote islands, it is safest to bring enough drachma with you.

language
Greek, but everyone speaks some English.

getting around
Car hire is not too expensive, but take care on the winding mountain roads. Many islands now have direct flights to both Athens and major European cities.

Tumultuous mountains tumbling into a crystal-blue sea, warm sands and paths through the olive groves, the tinkle of distant goat bells, marble temples in the moonlight...

There is nothing like Greece to make the rest of the world seem blurred, hesitant and grey.

There is an intensity here, and a relish for living. In the transluscent light the Aegean is the bluest of seas, Greek houses are the most dazzling white, and there is no scent so heady as Greek mountain herbs and pines on a summer's day. In Greece you feel more alive, and you are never more than an hour from the sea.

The intensity of the Greek present makes a striking contrast with the haunting beauty of its ancient monuments, and nowhere more so than in Athens, where the Parthenon on the Acropolis overlooks the craziness of the capital.

From Athens, it is easy to reach idyllic Delphi, sacred to Apollo, or see a play at the ancient theatre of Epidauros.

From Athens also you can sail to the islands, or visit the monasteries of Meteora, hanging on pinnacles. You can go walking in the Peloponnese, home of ancient Mycenae and Olympia, where the Olympic Games began, or take a trip to Mystra, a magnificent Byzantine ghost town near ancient Sparta.

The Greek Islands

They come in an astonishing variety, some lush and forested, some rolling and agricultural, others stark rockbound crags rising out of the Aegean; and there are over 3,000 of them, if you count every tiny islet.

Since Odysseus spent ten years wandering them on his way home from Troy, the Greek islands have been a favourite escape from the hurly burly. On some you cannot find a newspaper in any language. Just over a hundred islands are inhabited, and all but a very few have excellent beaches, lapped by the cleanest, warmest, most transparent seas anywhere in Europe.

Islands floating in a wine-dark sea
sprinkled with sugarcube villages,
pine-fringed sandy coves,
jasmine in the evening breeze,
warm nights ablaze with shooting stars...

flying time
To: Athens
London: 3 hrs
LA: 13 hs
Miami: 12 hrs
NY: 10–11 hrs
The national airline Olympic has regular flights to the islands from Athens, at bargain prices if you fly Olympic to Greece. Island-hopping flights rarely last more than an hour.

climate/when to go
April and October, as for Greece. There is a cooling wind in August the meltemi, and this in when the festivals are. But everyone goes then.

festivals
Besides Greek Easter, every village on every island celebrates its patron saint, usually with a feast, music and dancing; the biggest, in honour of the Virgin, happens on 15 August.

getting around
Ferries from Athens' port, Piraeus, serve most islands. Every island with enough roads has car and motorbike hire.

But beyond the common denominators of sun, sea and laid-back atmosphere, each island has its own strong character, and choosing can be hard. Crete, the largest, displays the delightful art of the sophisticated Minoan civilization; Corfu has lovely wildflowers and a Venetian capital; volcanic Santorini has breathtaking sunsets and black beaches; Mykonos parties until dawn; Lesbos, the island of Saphho, is silver with a million olive trees; trendy Hydra is all neoclassical sea captains' mansions; Nissyros is a volcano; Limnos had a culture as old and mysterious as Troy's, and is a best kept secret among its intimates.

Watersports naturally predominate: the swimming, sailing, scuba diving (in restricted areas, as the seas are full of ancient shipwrecks and treasures), and windsurfing are excellent. Spring and autumn are the best time for walking — especially spring, when literally hundreds of species of wildflowers make the islands a botanical paradise.

Shops stay open until the wee hours: best buys are gold and jewellery, at some of the lowest prices in Europe; traditional weavings and ceramics, leather goods, natural sponges, and gift packs of wild herbs and honey. In the summer, people tend to dine quite late on the islands; it is normal to sit down at an outdoor taverna at 10pm or 11pm, and stay until 2am. On a good night, the customers will suddenly burst into song and dance, or move along to a seaside club; the atmosphere is infectious — just try to go to bed early!

Akti Myrina

81400 Myrina
Lemnos
Greece

 Lemnos 26km

tel +30 1 413 7907
fax +30 1 413 7639

Open May–Oct

Akti Myrina Hotel is one of the world's leading hideaway resorts. Surrounded by acres of classical Grecian landscape, it overlooks the breathtaking blue waters of the Aegean which encircle the mythical island of Lemnos.

Traditionally styled stone cottages with quiet and secluded gardens offer privacy in an atmosphere of casual elegance. Meandering pathways lead down to a private sandy beach in a quiet bay of cool, clear water. The hotel's unique architecture blends naturally with the unspoiled beauty of the island, making it an ideal luxury retreat where tranquillity and comfort reign.

Guest are able to choese from the best Greek and international cuisine, as highly trained chefs prepare delicious feasts using fresh local produce. Service is always discreet, courteous and pleasant.

Weddings can be arranged here with the ceremony in the hotel's Santa Barbara church. A reception, including a traditional Greek band and up to 300 guests, may be held at the Beach Gardens or the Taverna overlooking the Venetian fortress, with the Mayor of Lemnos officiating.

 US$247–472 (110)
 US$536–693 (15)
 included
 included

  VISA

Honeymoon specials
Complimentary sparkling wine and fruits.

Leisure facilities
Extensive leisure and sports facilities include fitness centre, floodlit tennis courts, watersports, sailing, beach volleyball, swimming pool, hairdresser on request.

Local attractions
Trip with private caique (typical Greek fishing vessel) to secluded bays, guided tours around the island's historical sites with a local interpreter, to the archaeological museum and the Venetian fortress.

Elounda Mare

72053 Elounda
Crete
Greece

✈ Heraklion 75km

tel +30 841 41102
fax +30 841 41307
elmare@compulink.gr

Closed 1 Nov–31 Mar

Member of:
Relais & Chateaux

Tour operators:
UK: Best of Greece
US: Classic

The mysterious island of Crete, legendary birthplace of ancient Greek myth, was once home to King Minos and his dark labyrinth. The Elounda Mare is a secluded little world that enjoys a privileged position overlooking the winding coastline of Mirabello Bay and the distant mountain range of Sitia.

The bungalows of Elounda Mare are perfect for newly-married couples seeking serenity and seclusion. Each one follows Cretan tradition, blending whitewashed walls with local biege and grey stone and marble. All rooms are beautifully furnished with locally crafted dark wood, Grecian folk art and traditional tapestries in rich colours. Wide windows lead onto elevated private terraces, each fitted with a swimming pool.

Beginning the day with breakfast from a rich buffet, guests can watch the fishing boats haul in the catch of the day. A few hours later this fresh fish is served at the Yacht Club. Crowning the small harbour and sandy beach, the Yacht Club also forms the venue for evenings of traditional Greek food, music and dance. The more intimate Old Mill restaurant offers a refined menu combined with the finest selection of the house's Greek and French wines.

The hotel has a private chapel in the grounds and is happy to take care of any arrangements necessary for a perfect wedding.

US$134–470
US$186–560
US$32–70
US$11

Honeymoon specials
Complimentary champagne, flowers and fruit on arrival. Greek evening with live music and Greek dancing. Fisherman's dinner with piano music.

Sightseeing and leisure
Range of watersports including sailing and scuba diving, sauna, steam bath, hair salon and massage available at the hotel. Local sights include the historic Minoan towns of Knossos and Phaistos, museums, churches and the music festival of Koule in Heraklion.

Italy

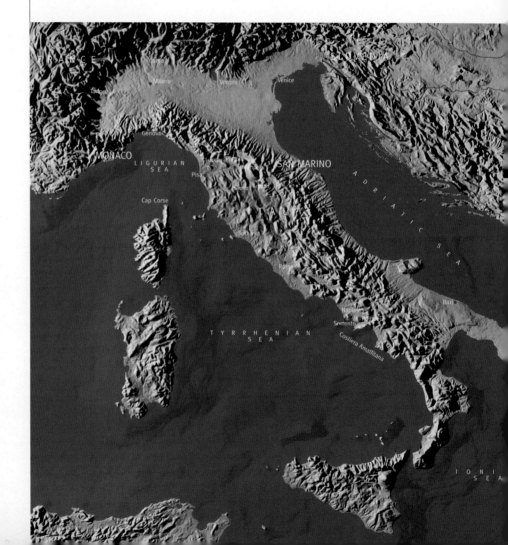

flying time
To: Florence, Milan, Rome.
London: 2–3 hrs
LA: 13–14 hrs
NY: 9–10 hrs

climate
Pleasant but variable;
It rains as much in Rome
as in London in winter.
Summer is hot and dry in
the south, humid and hot
in the northern lowlands;
the Alps and Apennines
stay cool, while the coast is
refreshed by breezes.

when to go
Year round, with exciting
festivals all summer and
major cultural events and
festivals all winter. For
scenery, go in spring or
early autumn.

currency
The Italian lire.

language
Italian. English is very
widely spoken.

getting around
There are numerous small
regional airports, and
efficient train and bus
networks, but hire a car to
explore on your own.

Dining *al fresco* by moonlight,
the splash of a Rococo fountain,
the aroma of a fresh-ground
cappuccino, a glistening marble
piazza, a duet by Puccini...

The Italians have no false modesty.
'The most beautiful country in the world,'
they call their home, and who can argue?
From the snowy Alps to the lacy almond groves
of Sicily, Italy is sensuous and sumptuous,
blessed with a perfect Mediterrenean climate.
Mountains fall sheer into the sea, lakes glimmer
amid vineyards and castles, and each hill wears a
cape of olive groves and a medieval town on top
like a hat.

Nowhere else will you find such a concentration
of art. The country is the size of Britain but
contains half of the great art in the entire world.
Italy was the first country in Europe to recover
after the Dark Ages, and the Italians used this
headstart to build dream cities such as Venice,
Siena, Naples and Rome. They softened the wild
contours of the land with villas and gardens.

Best of all, the Italians learned to cultivate
pleasure and delight to a unique degree; it is no
wonder Shakespeare set so many of his
comedies in Italy. Elegance and grace fill every
detail, from clothes to the precise shape of pasta
for each sauce. For beauty is more than skin
deep in Italy; it is a way of life.

Amalfi Coast

The playground of Roman emperors, sublime and vertiginous, a land of song where cliffs, sea and houses glow in a thousand fauvist colours..

flying time

Naples airport is 4 hours by train or a short air hop from Rome.

climate/when to go

The climate is typically Mediterranean, warm and pleasant, although November to February can be wet. Hot and crowded August is perhaps the least pleasant month, when prices soar.

getting around

Public transport by sea, train and bus is generally excellent and inexpensive, and allows you to take in the stupendous scenery.

shopping

Sorrento for intarsia (inlaid wood), stationery and ceramics in Amalfi, and bargains galore in Naples' outdoor markets.

There are few places that do, literally, take your breath away, and the Amalfi Coast, the most beautiful in the Mediterranean, is one where artificial respiration may well be in order.

The coast is nearly vertical: mountain after mountain plunges sheer into a turquoise sea. Each ledge in the cliffs has a tuft of trees, and where the ledges widen to form shelves, you will find a brightly coloured town — the romantic hideaways of Sorrento, Positano, Amalfi, and Ravello.

Not so long ago the towns were only accessible by boat; now the legendary Amalfi Drive, a corniche road of a thousand bends, offers the most ravishing views this side of paradise — except for the poor driver!

Located just south of the Bay of Naples, the Amalfi coast is surrounded by five-star attractions. Capri, the fantasy island of the Caesars, is only a short sail from Sorrento. A local train from Sorrento, the Circumvesuviana, makes the hop to the slumbering giant, the volcano Vesuvius, and the fascinating ruins of its ancient victims, Pompeii and Herculaneum. Another result of the eruptions is the almost ridiculous fertility of the land; flowers fill every crevice, especially in spontaneous, teeming, exuberant, anarchic Naples. ●

Grand Hotel
Excelsior Vittoria

Piazza Tasso 34
80067 Sorrento
Italy

✈ Naples Airport 60km

tel +39 81 807 1044
fax +39 81 877 1206

exvitt@exvitt.it

Open all year

Member of:
Charming Hotels
ILA

Tour operators:
UK: Abercrombie & Kent Travel

The Excelsior Vittoria is a supremely elegant 19th-century building perched high above the bay of Sorrento on the dramatically beautiful Amalfi coast. The hotel was built in 1834 on the sight of a Roman villa and in the impeccable gardens and orange grove where archeological treasures have been found; some columns can still be seen. Eighteenth-century frescoes, handsome vaults and mouldings and antique furnishings characterise the elegance and refinement of this beautifully maintained hotel, which has been owned by the Fiorentino family for over 160 years.

Most rooms have antique iron beds, spacious marble bathrooms and splendid views over the Bay of Naples.

Guests can dine al fresco against the impressive backdrop of Mount Vesuvius or enjoy traditional Italian and Neopolitan dishes under the majestic painted ceilings of the Vittoria dining room. This grand banqueting room and the adjoining reception hold up to 350 guests and provide a splendid venue for a wedding party. Visitors can sip cocktails on the terrace, enjoy a moment of meditation in the reading room, swim in the hotel pool or take a cruise along the coast.

 ITL353,000–536,000 (95)

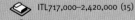 ITL717,000–2,420,000 (15)

 ITL71,000

 ITL15,000

Honeymoon specials
Three nights in a deluxe room with a large terrace, breakfast in room, chauffeur driven transfers to/from airport, dinner for two, Italian Spumante and flowers in the room on arrival. The package costs from ITL1,998,000 per couple.

Sightseeing and leisure
A private lift links the hotel to the lively town of Sorrento. The archeological treasures of Naples. Pompeii and the natural beauty of the surrounding area and islands – Capri, Positano, Ravello, Amalfi, Ischia – are within easy reach.

The Italian Lakes

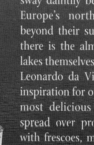

Possessed of an evocative, almost dangerous beauty, the refuge of poets, composers and lovers since Roman times...

flying time

To: Milan,
or Verona forLake Garda.
London: 2 hrs
LA: 13–14 hrs
Miami: 10–11 hrs
NY: 9 hrs

climate/when to go

The Lakes are rarely too hot or cold, but they can be misty in winter. The gardens are magnificent from April; September is the classic month for visiting the lakes — the weather is perfect.

getting around

Boat trips and pleasant walks around the lakes. Rail links to major cities are perfectly adequate.

One of Italy's greatest treasures is a necklace of long, liquid sapphires — Lakes Maggiore, Orta, Como, Lugano, Iseo and Garda.

Although gouged out of the Alps by glaciers, these lakes contain so much water that they each support remarkable microclimates. Palm trees sway daintily below icy peaks; Garda can claim Europe's northernmost lemon groves. But, beyond their surprising Mediterranean climate, there is the almost heartrending beauty of the lakes themselves, the inspiration for the setting of Leonardo da Vinci's 'Virgin of the Rocks'; and inspiration for others to build villas among Italy's most delicious pleasure domes and gardens, spread over promontories or islands, adorned with frescoes, mossy fountains and statues, and intimate bowers, most often built to please a special love.

Each lake has a steamer service, and some of Italy's finest art cities are only an hour or two away: Mantua, Bergamo, Verona (the city of Romeo and Juliet), and high-fashion Milan with its dazzling cathedral and Leonardo's 'Last Supper'. Stunning walking and riding trails, mountaineering, skiing, and windsurfing are only a few of the possible activities, but do not be surprised if you fall under the lakes' magic spell and end up doing nothing at all.

Villa Serbelloni

22021 Bellagio

Como

Italy

 Linate 70km
Malpensa 75km

tel +39 31 950 216

fax +39 31 951 529

hotserb@fromitaly.it

Closed Nov–Mar

Member of:
Hotels de Grande Classe Internationale

Tour operators/agents
US: Premier World Maktg

Surrounded on three sides by deep blue water, the Grand Hotel Villa Serbelloni stands at the extreme point of the promontory which divides the two branches of Lake Como. Green woodland frames the old patrician villa and classically landscaped gardens.

The sumptuous rooms and suites are comfortably decorated in the gracious manner of the Belle Epoque period. Decorated with original frescoes and with elegant antiques and exquisite chandeliers, all have panoramic views over the lake to the Alps beyond.

The hotel kitchens prepare everything freshly, including a delicious range of homemade pasta. International and regional Italian cuisine is served in the Royal Dining Room, where chandeliers, elaborately detailed with gold leaf, are suspended from high ceilings. Gentlemen are requested to wear black tie. For al fresco dining, meals are also served at the terrace restaurant.

Guests can stroll along the stone promenade at the edge of a small private beach, or take a dip in the swimming pool surrounded by flowers and palm trees. Tennis and squash are available in the grounds and the health and beauty centre offers a variety of treatments including massage, sauna and wave therapy. There are several beautiful and historic villas in the area, and a lively village market every third Wednesday.

The hotel is delighted to arrange weddings and can provide flowers, music, a spectacular lakeside location and a traditional Italian wedding menu.

ITL460,000–1,100,000 (83)

ITL900,000–1,810,000

from ITL100,000

included

Honeymoon specials

Welcome drink, fruit and flowers in the room on arrival, dinners, free entry to the fitness and beauty centre, one session of hydro-therapy with massage, tour of the lake by private motor boat, free entrance to Villa Meizi. The package costs between ITL3,094,000–4,474,000 and is based on a stay of three nights.

Sightseeing and leisure

Visits to historic villas nearby. Boat trips on the lake. An hours drive from Milan, Switzerland and the Alps. Health and beauty centre with extensive range of treatments. Swimming pool, gym, tennis, squash, and sauna at hotel. Golf and watersports nearby.

Tuscany

Botticelli's graceful allegories, Medici villas, gorgeous festivals in Renaissance costume, a glass of Chianti in a country trattoria...

flying time

To: Pisa and Florence via London, Rome or Milan.

London: 2–3 hrs
LA: 13–14 hrs
Miami: 11 hrs
NY: 9–10 hrs

climate/when to go

Tuscany's cities are fine for the winter, but if you plan to stay in the country you may find it a bit quiet. November is the rainiest month. April through to the end of October are lovely, although it can get quite hot in August.

getting around

A car really is necessary to enjoy all this glorious countryside has to offer.

Tuscany has, simply, the most perfect and civilized landscapes in the world; so lovely, in fact, that the region wants to have its countryside patented to keep hucksters from exploiting it.

Here each cypress, parasol pine, vineyard and olive tree is just where it should be, as if planted by a master gardener. Each villa, old stone farmhouse or medieval hill town looks as if it were designed and fitted into place by an artist. In Tuscany, art and nature form a unique seamless web. The backgrounds painted five centuries ago by Fra Angelico and Piero della Francesca remain intact.

Tuscany has towns as celebrated and exquisite as its landscapes. Florence, that extraordinary hothouse of the Italian Renaissance, is so full of art that it is best taken in small doses. Florence's medieval rivals, Siena, Pisa, Lucca, Arezzo, and Pistoia are steeped in atmosphere from the very springtime of western civilization.

No matter where you go, the frescoes in the churches and palazzi glow with an irresistible freshness. Even after so many centuries, the sculptures of Michelangelo and Donatello have lost none of their power to move the heart. ●

Special Honeymoon Hotels - Reader Reply Service

Tick all the hotels you are interested in, tear out this page, complete the coupon below and we will pass this to the company concerned - all at no cost to you. (Please note that a free postal service is only available on postage within the UK - overseas readers will need to affix a stamp to the relevant postal amount). Alternatively, fax this page to + 44 (0) 1252 735693

C1 ❏ Celebrity Cruises	29 ❏ Long Bay Beach Resort	59 ❏ Castello Del Sole, Ascona	90 ❏ Royal Palm
C2 ❏ Royal Caribbean International	30 ❏ Ritz-Carlton, St Thomas (The)	60 ❏ Grand Hotel Shönegg	91 ❏ Shandrani
01 ❏ San Ysidro Ranch	31 ❏ Secret Harbour Resort	61 ❏ Palace Hotel	92 ❏ Trou aux Biches
02 ❏ Shutters on the Beach	32 ❏ Spice Island Beach Resort	62 ❏ Cliveden	93 ❏ Le Méridien Barbarons
03 ❏ Breakers (The)	33 ❏ Sandals St Lucia	63 ❏ Gidleigh Park	94 ❏ Fisherman's Cove
04 ❏ Sonesta Beach Resort Key Biscayne	34 ❏ Le Sport	64 ❏ Powder Mills Hotel	95 ❏ Taj Palace Hotel
05 ❏ Ritz-Carlton, Kapalua (The)	35 ❏ Windjammer Landing	65 ❏ Mount Juliet	96 ❏ Taj-View Hotel
06 ❏ Pierre (The)	36 ❏ Hotel Kobenzl	66 ❏ Gleneagles	97 ❏ Rambagh Palace
07 ❏ La Pinsonnière	37 ❏ Hotel Schloss Mönchstein	67 ❏ Eilat Princess Hotel	98 ❏ Lake Palace
08 ❏ Lapa Rios	38 ❏ Azia Beach Hotel	68 ❏ Jerusalem Hotel	99 ❏ Taj Mahal Hotel (The)
09 ❏ Fiesta Americana Cancun	39 ❏ Four Seasons Hotel, Limassol	69 ❏ Royal Beach Hotel	100 ❏ Taj Holiday Village
10 ❏ Fiesta Americana Condesa	40 ❏ Paphos Amathus Hotel	70 ❏ Borana Lodge	101 ❏ Taj Malabar
11 ❏ Las Brisas	41 ❏ St Raphael	71 ❏ Galdessa Camp	102 ❏ Taj Garden Retreat
12 ❏ Ritz-Carlton, Cancun (The)	42 ❏ Domaine du Royal Club Evian	72 ❏ Ol Donyo Wuas	103 ❏ Damai Lovina Villas
13 ❏ Sandals Royal Bahamian & Spa	43 ❏ Hotel Martinez	73 ❏ Beach House on Sandown Bay	104 ❏ Nusa Dua Beach Hotel
14 ❏ Cambridge Beaches	44 ❏ Le Moulin de Lourmarin	74 ❏ Benguerra Lodge	105 ❏ Ritz-Carlton, Bali (The)
15 ❏ Pink Beach Club	45 ❏ Villa St-Elme	75 ❏ Mount Nelson Hotel (The)	106 ❏ Pangkor Laut Resort
16 ❏ Grand Pavilion (The)	46 ❏ Hotel du Palais	76 ❏ Romney Park Luxury Suites	107 ❏ Pelangi Beach Resort
17 ❏ Casa De Campo	47 ❏ Akti Myrina	77 ❏ Amani Beach Club	108 ❏ Penang Mutiara
18 ❏ Couples Resort	48 ❏ Elounda Mare	78 ❏ Ras Kutani	109 ❏ Mines Beach Resort & Spa
19 ❏ Grand Lido Negril	49 ❏ Grand Hotel Excelsior Vittoria	79 ❏ Kinasi Mafia Island	110 ❏ Dusit Laguna
20 ❏ Half Moon Golf, Tennis & Beach Club	50 ❏ Villa Serbelloni	80 ❏ Tongabezi Zambia	111 ❏ Ana Mandara
21 ❏ Sandals Negril	51 ❏ Hotel Terme di Saturnia	81 ❏ Imba Matombo Lodge	112 ❏ Observatory Hotel (The)
22 ❏ Cobblers Cove	52 ❏ Park Hotel Sonnenhof	82 ❏ Katete Safari	113 ❏ NaiTasi Resort
23 ❏ La Cocoteraie	53 ❏ Hotel Quinta do Lago	83 ❏ Sanyati Lodge	114 ❏ Tokoriki Island
24 ❏ Hotel Guanahani	54 ❏ Reid's Palace	84 ❏ Victoria Falls Hotel (The)	T1 ❏ Africa Archipelago
25 ❏ Le Toiny	55 ❏ Villa Vita Parc	85 ❏ Victoria Falls Safari Lodge	T2 ❏ Elegant Resorts
26 ❏ Sandals Antigua	56 ❏ Marbella Club	87 ❏ Soneva Fushi	T3 ❏ Kuoni Travel Ltd
27 ❏ Siboney Beach Club	57 ❏ Hotel Puenta Romano	88 ❏ Taj Lagoon Resort	T4 ❏ Reef & Rainforest Tours
28 ❏ Ottleys Plantation Inn	58 ❏ Na Xamena Hotel Hacienda	89 ❏ Paradis	

Name _____

Address _____

_____

Town/City _____   County/State _____

Postcode/Zip _____   Country _____

Today's Date ____ ____ ____
(day) (month) (year)

Date of wedding ____ ____ ____
(day) (month) (year)

How long engaged to date? _____
months

How old are you? _____

How old is your fiancée? _____

Special Honeymoon Hotels World 1998 Edition
World Destinations Publishing Ltd
Reader Reply Service
FREEPOST
2 Ridgeway Road
Farnham
Surrey GU9 8NW

Hotel Terme di Saturnia

58050 Saturnia (Gr)
Italy

✈ Fiumicino, Rome 150km

tel +39 0564 601 061
fax +39 0564 601 266

info@termedisaturnia.it

Open all year

Member of:
Small Luxury Hotels of the World

Located in the heart of Tuscany, the Terme di Saturnia is an old stone mansion surrounded by ancient park and woodland. Its most striking feature is a large lake right on the doorstep, heated by a natural hot spring which flows into it. Guests can swim in the lake all year round.

The hotel's 90 rooms and suites are quiet and comfortable, decorated in warm, neutral shades with soft lighting. Pattern and ornament are kept to a minimum in the soft furnishings, discreet lighting and full-length curtains. The beds are large and kept low to the floor to add to the uncluttered, minimalist approach.

The food is Mediterranean in flavour but with particular attention to nutrition. Fresh pastas, risotto, virgin olive oil, tomato-rich sauces, grilled fish and game dishes are complemented with herb-rich salads, low fat cheeses, local wines and fruit to produce a menu that is as delicious as it is healthy.

To make the most of the resort's health-giving natural spa, the Institute of Thermal Medicine and Scientific Cosmetology is also on site and Terme di Saturnia offers a wide range of treatments, and spa and fitness programmes. Guests can benefit from skin check-ups, revitalizing and moisturizing treatments, body-toning, massage, stress management, mineral water cures, personal training and fitness and diet classes.

ITL 510,000–610,000 (72)
ITL 890,000 (8)
ITL 75,000
ITL 25,000

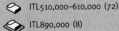

Honeymoon specials
Complimentary flowers and champagne on arrival.

Leisure facilities
Gym, pools, tennis, water gymnastics, golf, horse-riding, birdwatching, walking, guided hikes, mountain bikes, Italian lawn bowling, dancing lessons, lectures and seminars, fishing, archery, photography.

Local attractions
Roman remains, medieval villages, Etruscan tombs.

The Principality of
Liechtenstein

flying time
To: Zurich
London: 1 hr
NY: 8 hrs

climate/when to go
In summer, for romantic
walks through wildflower
meadows and vineyards.
In winter, for snowsports,
downhill and cross-
country skiing, skating
and tobogganing at Steg
(4,300ft/1,300m) and
Malbun (5,300ft/1,600m).

currency
Swiss franc. Credit cards
and traveller's cheques
are widely accepted.

language
German, though English
is widely spoken.

getting around
Taxis are expensive so
the best option is to rent
a car. Zurich is just
90 miles away.

One of the smallest countries in the world, Liechtenstein lies
in the heart of Europe, sandwiched between Austria and
Switzerland, with which it is so closely linked that you cross
the border without knowing it. Its 65 square miles comprise
lowlands, including part of the fertile Rhine Valley, and
alpine valleys in the shadow of jagged peaks.

Visitors to this charming alpine enclave enjoy the novelty of
being in a country seemingly without borders, with no
armed forces, and with almost as many international
companies and corporations registered here as there are
residents. For Liechtenstein, like Switzerland, enjoys
banking secrecy, a favourable tax regime and a healthy
economy. Standards are high, and prices reflect this.

For honeymooners, however, this is a place to relax,
surrounded by clear air and magnificent scenery, and there is
a wide range of hotels, guest houses and chalets. The quaint
capital of Vaduz, where the ruling prince lives in a medieval
castle, has attractive shops, a couple of good museums.

Beyond Vaduz, the countryside gives way to forests and
vineyards, whose products are surprisingly good, especially
Vaduzer, a red wine. The villages, which are scattered among
hills and orchards, are especially charming, and best
explored on foot.

Park Hotel Sonnenhof

Mareestrasse 29
FL-9490 Vaduz
Liechtenstein

✈ Zurich 120km

tel +41 75 232 1192

fax +41 75 232 0053

real@sonnenhof.lol.li

Closed Christmas to mid-Feb

Member of:
Relais et Châteaux

The district of Vaduz, home to the Prince of Liechtenstein, is rich in natural beauty and cultural heritage. The Park Hotel Sonnenhof is located on the edge of extensive woods and vineyards with spectacular views overlooking the upper Rhine Valley and Swiss Alps beyond.

This is a family-owned hotel and the staff are friendly and welcoming.
The rooms are light and airy with balcony or terrace and splendid views of Vaduz castle. Each has a television, radio, safe and minibar.

In the restaurant, guests can indulge in a selection of traditional dishes, and fine wines from the hotel's own wine cellar.

Park Sonnenhof is a haven of peace and tranquillity and an ideal base for avid hikers. Well-marked trails lead visitors through remote countryside and romantic valleys.

Guests can take advantage of the indoor swimming pool, solarium and sauna.

The charming town of Vaduz offers a lively programme of sports and festivals in summer, becoming a thriving centre for skiing enthusiasts in winter.

 SFr300–360 (17)

 SFr360–410 (12)

SFr60–120

included

Honeymoon specials
Flowers and wine on arrival. One free entrance to thermal baths in Bad Ragaz and the national museum nearby. Specially decorated honeymoon table for dinner. This package is valid for a minimum stay of three days.

Sightseeing and leisure
Excursions by horse-drawn carriage to historic sights, local wine areas and thermal springs of Bad Ragaz. Hikes in alpine forests and mountains featured in the filming of 'Heidi'. Swimming, surfing, sailing, golf, riding, squash, tennis, cycling, paragliding and skiing nearby. Health and beauty salons.

Portugal and Madeira

Portugal is a gentle land, with a warm and welcoming people. It is a small country, tucked away at the end of the Iberian penninsula, but it has a long Atlantic coast, a proud history and a thrilling diversity of landscape. The remote northern interior is hauntingly beautiful. Lisbon, the capital, has all the verve of a modern metropolis, with a medieval mantle of churches and palaces.

The Algarve in the south is famed for glorious beaches and, washed by the waters of the Atlantic, the island of Madeira is a miniature paradise.

Portugal is not an expensive place to visit. Life is simple, but standards are high, and you get good value, especially where food is concerned. Fresh seafood and salads, fine olive oil, garlic — then more garlic — are the hallmarks of Portuguese cuisine. Simply prepared, and in abundant quantities, the food is an ideal match for the country's crisp, dry white wines.

A bottle of crisp vinho verde, buckets of flowers in the market place, the soulful sound of fado singing...

Eating out is casual, often *al fresco* — and the whole family joins in.

In Lisbon and in busier spots along the Algarve, discos pound away until the early hours. But in smaller towns nightlife consists dinner and a nightcap in the local café. Fado, that yearning music somewhere between

flying time
To: Lisbon or Funchal for Madeira London: 2 1/4 or 3 3/4 hrs NY: 6 3/4 or 8 1/2 hrs

climate
The mainland is warm and dry (22–30°C) May–Sept. The northern part of the country is cooler and wetter, as is winter. Madeira is mild and sub-tropical with temperatures at a steady 17–30°C. North Madeira can also be damp, but the temperature is mild all year.

when to go
Carnival (Feb/Mar) is a fun time. Madeira celebrates New Year with gusto from early Dec, but hotel prices rise. In Sept, both on Madeira and the mainland, the weather is fine and the crowds are gone.

currency
The escudo. Credit cards and traveller's cheques are accepted, but not in more isolated areas.

language
Portuguese. On Madeira English is widely spoken.

getting around
Taxis are cheap. Buses are generally faster than trains. On Madeira a car is best, though the narrow corniche roads can be hair-raising.

flamenco and the French chanson, starts late in special bars, and continues well into the night. Handicraft shops and markets abound. It is fun to stock up on wickerwork, *azulejos* (brilliantly coloured tiles), chunky ceramics, painstakingly delicate embroidery and handwoven rugs. Madeira lies abpit 450 miles off the coast of Africa and has a climate that has earned it the epithet 'island of perpetual spring'.

It is tiny, with a rugged backbone of mountains running through the middle. Just 30 minutes drive from the coast you can be on a peak overlooking the clouds. The volcanic terrain is lush — camellias her grow up to three storeys high. A network of *levadas* (man-made waterways) makes walking a pleasure, and can transport you into a landscape that could be in the middle of Africa or the Himalayas.

There are no beaches, but a number of hotels have lidos built out over the rocks. On the neighbouring island of Porto Santo there is an 5-mile long sandy beach. The sea is deep and clear close to the shore. Deep-sea fishing can add a dash of excitement, and there is ample opportunity for scuba-diving. Eating out is the main form of evening entertainment. Local fruit and vegetables seem to explode with flavour.

For those who love nature, the dramatic terrain and exuberant flora of this little island provide a romantic and uplifting honeymoon setting. ●

The Algarve

Cut off from the rest of Portugal by a range of hills, the Algarve is known for its mild climate and great beaches.

Tourism is the main industry and the summer season feels like a four-month party. Along the coast you find resorts bursting at the seams with a young crowd heartily intent on having a good time, as well as lonely bays where there is little else but you, the sun and the Atlantic.

The region is incredibly picturesque. A little exploration away from the tourist trail reveals lonely beaches backed by tiny hillside settlements, lush valleys with streams trickling through an abundance of scarlet poppies, eucalyptus- and pine-studded mountains.

The old fishing village of Albufeira is in the tourist heartland, and there is a buzzing nightlife, yet it still has an attractive old town centre. And if you explore the coast, especially if you hire a boat to do so, you can find quiet coves and deserted beaches.

Stunning red sculpted rocks,
long languid beaches, a quiet cove
at sunset, brightly coloured fishing boats,
narrow alleys of whitewashed buildings,
the scent of wild lilies on the roadside...

flying time

To: Faro
London: 2 hrs
Miami: 8–9 hrs
NY: 7 hrs

when to go

April/May for sunny
weather, warm seas,
roadside flowers and
winter rates.

getting around

Buses are faster than
trains. Taxis are cheap.
Hiring a car is the nicest
way to explore inland.

The Algarve had its Golden Age during the Moorish period, and whitewashed buildings trimmed with blue are still in evidence; whilst towns like Loulé, with its mesh of narrow alleys, preserve a strongly North African ambience.

The western part of the Algarve is less developed. Sagres, at the very tip of the peninsula, is a good base for exploring a coastline that alternates between rugged cliffs and sandy beaches. Inland, the countryside becomes even more tourist-free. The Serra do Caldeirão is a range of rolling hills smothered in cork trees and oleander; an ideal place for a peaceful walk, if you do not mind the occasional wild boar.

Most leisure activities are on offer, with the emphasis on gold and watersports. Shopping is fun too. Coppersmiths, basket weavers, lace-makers and ceramists keep crafts markets well supplied. Markets overflow with locally grown fruit, from avocados to damask plums, and delicious local specialities, including memorably indulgent sweets made of figs and almonds. ●

Hotel Quinta do Lago

8135 Almancil

Algarve

Portugal

Faro Int. 20km

tel +351 8939 6666

fax +351 8939 6393

hqdlago@mail.tlepact.pt

Open all year

Member of:
The Leading Hotels of the World
Orient Express Hotels

This luxurious new hotel is situated on the dramatic Algarve coastline beside a tidal estuary in the exclusive Quinto do Lago estate, with its undulating hills, pinewoods and golf courses.

All rooms are spacious and furnished in light, natural wood and pastel shades. Most rooms enjoy views across the gardens to the Atlantic Ocean beyond. All have balconies opening onto terraces.

Guests can enjoy cocktails in the Laguna bar before dining in one of two restaurants offering traditional Portuguese cuisine and exclusive Venetian specialities, or al fresco on the poolside terrace where fish, shellfish and meat are barbecued daily.

A romantic wooden footbridge over the Ria Formosa Estuary links the hotel to the beaches and a wealth of sports activities.

The hotel is ideally placed for exploring the spectacular Algarve countryside or perhaps cruising along the still, clean waters of the River Guadiana, and ending the day with Portuguese folklore dancing.

The 17th-century baroque church of São Lourenço, decorated with astonishingly beautiful tiles (azulejos), provides a romantic setting for a wedding. Buffets and cocktail parties for up to 200 can be arranged in the elegant São Lourenço room or on the extensive hotel lawns.

ESC30,000–72,000 (132)

ESC75,00–250,000 (9)

ESC6,500

included

Honeymoon specials

Champagne and strawberries on arrival. Horseriding or massage. Champagne cocktail followed by candlelit dinner. A guided visit to picturesque Loulé market and the St Lourenço church. A day's car hire. The package costs from ESC153,210 per couple based on a stay of three nights.

Sightseeing and leisure

Romantic walks around the Ria Formosa Estuary and bird sanctuary. Excursions to towns of Silves, Faro and Olhão. Jeep safaris. Visits to local Portuguese potteries. Swimming pools, floodlit tennis courts, health club. Bike hire, clay pigeon shooting, deep-sea fishing and all watersports available close by. Three golf courses on the estate.

Reid's Palace

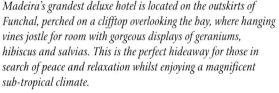

Estrada Monumental 139
9000 Funchal
Madeira

✈ Santa Cruz 22km

tel +351 91 700 7171
fax +351 91 700 7177

Open all year

Member of:
The Leading Hotels of the World
Orient Express Hotel Group

Madeira's grandest deluxe hotel is located on the outskirts of Funchal, perched on a clifftop overlooking the bay, where hanging vines jostle for room with gorgeous displays of geraniums, hibiscus and salvias. This is the perfect hideaway for those in search of peace and relaxation whilst enjoying a magnificent sub-tropical climate.

Built in 1891, this Mediterranean-style hotel, which combines old-world charm and courtesy with luxurious facilities, has always been a favourite of royalty and celebrities. Edward VIII, Sir Winston Churchill and Fidel Castro are amongst those who have passed through its doors. All rooms are spacious, light and airy, and some, such as those in the recently restored Garden Wing, have deluxe marble bathrooms.

There are five restaurants including the turn of the century main dining room, Les Faunes, where guests can savour fine French cuisine while enjoying panoramic views of the harbour. The Trattoria Villa Cliff, set against an amazing open-air backdrop, provides a romantic setting for al fresco dining.

Sports and activities abound, with something for every taste. For those wishing to catch the afternoon sun, there is a private bathing jetty with secluded sun terraces. Other facilities include all watersports, tennis, and a health centre with saunas and massage.

 ESC28,000–67,000
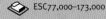 ESC77,000–173,000
 ESC8,100
 included

Honeymoon specials

Portuguese sparkling wine on arrival. Room upgrade subject to availability. Honeymoon packages of 4 and 7 nights cost from ESC130,000 per person and include limousine transfers, flowers and fruit basket, one souvenir Reid's book, honeymoon present, candlelit dinner, champagne breakfast and a visit to Monte church followed by a Tobbogan ride.

Sightseeing and leisure

Daily activity programme which includes walking levadas (irrigation channels), visits to wine lodges and other cultural excursions. Exploring lush green forests on horseback, hiking in volcanic mountains. All watersports, tennis and swimming. Golf nearby.

Vila Vita Parc

PO Box 196
8365 Armaçao de Pêra
Algarve
Portugal

✄ Faro Int. 45km

tel +351 82 315 310
fax +351 82 315 333
vilavitapark@mail.telepac.pt

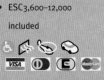

On the rugged and beautiful Algarve coast, set amidst 20 hectares of undulating parkland, is the deluxe hotel and resort complex Vila Vita Parc.

The spacious green terraces of the countryside are dotted with hotels and villas, offering tranquillity and privacy for couples who want to spend time alone. Rooms and suites are furnished in Portuguese and Moorish styles, using gentle natural colours and materials. All have satellite television, minibar and views across the gardens to the Atlantic Ocean.

The resort is also a haven for sports fanatics, with access to two private sandy beaches, a comprehensive range of watersports, volleyball and tennis courts, deep-sea fishing and golf. There are two pools and a supervised adventure playground for children.

Open all year

Member of:
The Leading Hotels of the World

Tour operators:
UK: Cadogan Holidays Ltd

The hotel's Vital Centre provides the perfect retreat for couples wanting to relax and unwind following the hectic events of the wedding day.

 ESC27,300–62,100 (103)

 ESC35,000–107,400 (79)

 ESC3,600–12,000

 included

Honeymoon specials

A 7-night package at ESC50,000* per person includes limousine transfers, wine, flowers and fruit in room on arrival. A candlelit dinner in the room and one in any of the restaurants. One bathrobe engraved with the person's name. Group A car hire with unlimited mileage. Room upgrade subject to availability. *This does not include the price of the room.

All treatments are carried out under medical supervision and based on holistic diagnosis.

There are six restaurants serving a selection of light snacks, international specialities and local cuisine featuring fresh fish and organic produce. Evening entertainment is offered in the club house and discotheque, and the many bars dotted throughout the park.

Wedding receptions for up to 350 guests are catered for in the ballroom.

Vila Vita Parc is an ideal base for exploring the surrounding countryside, caves and grottos, natural springs and picturesque villages characteristic of the Portuguese culture and traditions.

Local attractions

Romantic walks, coastal excursions in the hotel's private yacht, Jeep safaris into the mountains.

Leisure facilities

Tennis, squash, swimming pools, health club with steam-bath, Jacuzzi, sauna, gym and massage. All watersports, including sailing and deep-sea fishing throughout the summer. Mountain biking. Golfing facilities including pitch and put, a driving range and putting green. The Vital Centre, a medically supervised retreat, offers natural treatments.

Spain

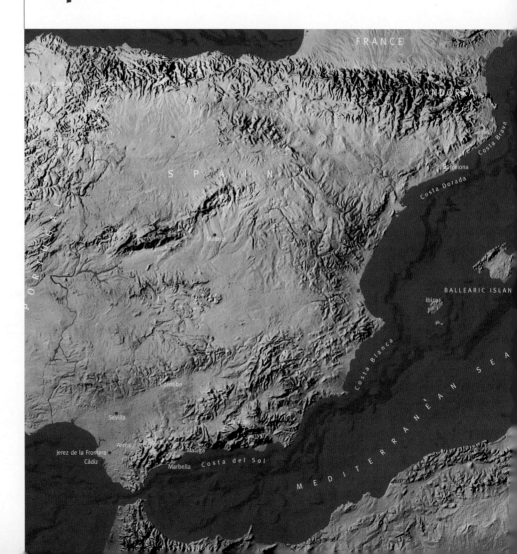

flying time
London: 2 hrs
LA: 12 hrs
Miami: 9 hrs
NY: 6–7 hrs

climate/when to go
Carnival in February is celebrated with gusto, followed in spring by elaborate Easter Week parades and the first bullfights of the season. Summers are dry, hot and crowded but great for fiestas. Autumns are mellow and warm.

currency
The Spanish peseta.

language
Spanish, Basque and Catalan, although it is easy to get by with English on the coasts and tourist destinations.

getting around
There is an efficient, reasonably priced network of public transport, from regional airports to city buses.

Orange groves under China-blue skies,
castles perched on impossible pinnacles,
bar counters crammed with shellfish platters,
endless sandy beaches, fireworks and fiestas...

Romance and Spain have gone hand in hand since the Middle Ages, when Moorish poets introduced the concept of Romantic love and chivalry to Europe.

Spain easily lends herself to dreamy ideals: her land and cities are sweepingly grand and poetic, from the high drama of the Pyrenees and Old Castile down to the sunbaked hills and beaches of Andalucía. Herds of black bulls graze under cork trees, and windmills just like Don Quixote's 'giants' still turn lazily in La Mancha. The ancestral mix of Latin temperment and Moorish imagination shows itself vividly in the fanciful architecture, and in the driving rhythms of flamenco.

For all its old mystique and charm, Spain today might be hipper than any place. After the long Franco dictatorship, the nation fairly exploded with pent-up creativity. Barcelona and Madrid have emerged as the most exciting cities in Western Europe, and their drive and energy, especially when it comes to having the maximum amount of fun, have infected the whole country. Thanks to their hot climate, and the custom of taking a siesta, Spaniards can burst into life again at night — cramming two days into one.

Andalucía

Moorish arches, exquisite
roses and flowing fountains.
Nights in the gardens of Spain...

Sequined matadors and strumming guitars, torrid flamenco and hot-blooded gypsies, orange blossoms and jasmine... Andalucía is everything you expect it would be. Stereotyped perhaps, but these are stereotypes other regions would die for (and they are all true).

Do not worry about the weather. It is always warm and sunny here; Andalucía has the most reliable climate in the Mediterranean. And if it gets too hot, you can always take a ride up to Spain's tallest mountains, the Sierra Nevada, which are situated conveniently nearby. Beyond the mountain peaks are ancient Moorish villages in the narrow valley of the Alpujarras. The southern slopes of the Sierra run right down to the sea, and this is one of the few places in the world where you can ski in the morning and have a dip in the sea in the afternoon. Other possibilities include playing golf on one of Europe's top courses, or tennis by night; going windsurfing or riding — the Andalucians love their horses.

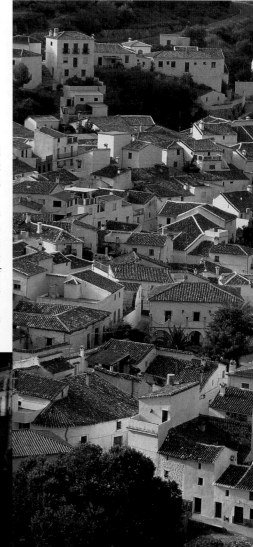

flying time
To: Seville, Malaga
London: 2 1/2 hrs
LA: 11 1/2 hrs
NY: 7 1/2 hrs

climate/when to go
Spring and autumn are usually perfect.

festivals
Spring horse fairs in Seville and Jerez, wine festivals during the harvest season in August and September, not to mention *romerias* (plgrimages).

getting around
There is an efficient local bus service, but trains are slow. A car is always the best option, though parking in cities can be difficult.

For anyone on a honeymoon, it would be hard to beat a stroll through the royal pavilions and gardens of the Alhambra in Granada; in summer you can do it by moonlight. Granada also has excellent shopping the old silk market of the Alcaiceria, and the fairytale Gothic Capilla Real. Continuing through the heart of historic Andalucía, Córdoba offers the enchanting colonnades of its spectcular Great Mosque, and a museum of bullfighting. The most famous of all *plazas de toros* are nearby in Ronda and Seville, the Andalucian metropolis, where you can pick oranges off the trees in the centre of the city. Seville is the home of Carmen and Don Juan, of World's Fairs and the April Fair and endless *tapas* and glasses of sherry. That noble sauce is made in nearby Jerez, where you can visit the famous *bodegas,* and flamingoes at Donaa National Park.

From here, it is only a short hop to Cádiz and its famous carnival, Gibraltar and its Rock, and then the endless beaches of the Costa del Sol. Marbella, summer resort of yachts and film stars, is the glittering heart of Europe's most popular holiday playground, where the nightlife and fine restaurants add to the pleasures of beach and sea. Andalucía's cosmopolitan resorts literally bristle with designer boutiques, but do not neglect the region's fine handicrafts: Córdoba leather goods and filigree jewelry, mantillas from Seville, inlaid wood taracea work in Granada, and fine hand-painted ceramics almost everywhere.

After dinner, choose between the very lively bar scene, which may feature live flamenco (try to find out where the locals go), or put on your dancing shoes. Clubs feature everything from *salsa* to the top ten, and stay open until dawn.●

Marbella Club

Bulevar Principe Alfonso
von Hohenlohe
s/n - 29600
Marbella
Spain

✈ Malaga Int 62km

tel + 34 5 282 2211
fax + 34 5 282 9884
mchotel@wcostasol.es

Open all year

Member of:
The Leading Hotels of the World
Hôtels de Grands Classes
   Internationals

Formerly the residence of Prince Alfonso von Hohenlohe, an Austrian aristocrat, and now an exclusive club resort and hideaway of the rich and famous, the Marbella Club occupies a prime location along the Golden Mile - Spain's fashionable south coast resort.

A luxurious complex of rooms, suites and bungalows built in Andalucían style is surrounded by well-tended, subtropical gardens. There are a wide range of sports facilities to choose from, both on site and in the vicinity, including tennis at the nearby Manolo Santana club, swimming and golf.

The hotel's restaurant serves a range of international dishes featuring seafood and local fish. In summer, hundreds of candles, placed in the trees, light up the terrace to create the perfect scenario for romantic, al fresco dining. A rich buffet lunch is served in the Beach Club beside the sea.

In the evenings, guests can relax to the sounds of live piano music in the bar or venture into Marbella town to sample the nightlife in the many bars and casinos.

The exclusive Beach Club is a popular venue for wedding receptions of up to 250 as guests can enjoy cocktails against a backdrop of incredibly romantic sunsets and breathtaking scenery.

 US$190–367 (84)

 US$273–1,667 (45)

 US$51–80

 US$17

Honeymoon specials
Champagne and flowers on arrival. Room upgrade subject to availability.

Leisure facilities
Sauna and two swimming pools on site. Massage by appointment. Tennis, golf, horseriding, clay pigeon shooting and all watersports nearby.

Local attractions
Visits to Spanish markets and quaint Andalucían villages. Traditional bull fights in season. A short walk to Marbella's old town and the famous yacht harbour with its cafés, restaurants and boutiques. Day trips to Granada and the fabulous, graceful Moorish palace of Alhambra.

Hotel Puenta Romano

PO Box 240
Marbella
Spain

Malaga Int. 55km

tel +34 5 282 0900
fax +34 5 277 5766

hprcpmercial@wcostasol.es

Open all year

Member of:
The Leading Hotels of the World

Marbella is probably the most elegant and exclusive resort on the Costa del Sol. Located in the heart of the Golden Mile, between Marbella and Puerto Banus, the Hotel Puenta Romano nestles along the Mediterranean coast, at the foot of the Sierra Blanca mountains.

The hotel comprises a series of low-rise horizontal buildings constructed in traditional Andalucían style and offering secluded and spacious demi-suite rooms with terraces or balconies overlooking waterfalls, fountains and acres of lush subtropical gardens. The hotel staff achieve the balance between privacy and impeccable service.

The hotel's four restaurants El Puente, La Plaza, Roberto Italian and the Beach Club, each different in style, offer a wealth of gastronomic delights including spectacular buffets and a range of traditional dishes featuring local fish and seafood. Guests can dance the night away at the famous Regine's discotheque, and during the summer months there are themed nights at La Plaza restaurant.

Weddings can be arranged in the grounds or on the ancient Roman Bridge, with receptions for up to 250 catered for in the Plaza restaurant and terrace.

There are many bars and restaurants dotted around town, and in the exclusive marinas of Marbella and Puerto Banus; also a casino and nightclub. Those lucky enough to visit in May, when Marbella's feria is in full swing, will have an experience they are unlikely to forget.

PTS34,800–42,800
included
included

Honeymoon specials
Champagne, fruit and flowers on arrival, breakfast on private balcony and candlelit dinner, room upgrade subject to availability, free entrance to casino. The package costs from PTS34,800–42,800 per double room per night. Special room rates available for accompanying guests. Optional limousine transfers from Malaga airport at cost of PTS26,000.

Sightseeing and leisure
Visits to local markets and boutiques in the old town, rides in a horse-drawn carriage. Roman sites and churches. Festivals and flamenco shows. Romantic strolls along Puento Banus harbour and Marbella promenade. Manola Santana tennis club, fitness centre, sauna and massage. All watersports, polo, horseriding and golf.

57

Ibiza

Outrageous, excessive and hedonistic,
trendy and a little decadent, this island swings...

journey time

Short connecting flights
from Madrid, Barcelona
or Valencia.
The ferry from Valencia
takes 7 hours, from
Barcelona 10 hours.

climate

Ibiza is at its hottest in
every sense of the word
in July and August. The
average maximum
temperature is 29°C.

getting around

Inexpensive boats and
buses provide links to
the beaches, and inter-
island flights make it
easy to visit the other
Balearics, Mallorca or
Menorca.

Off in the Mediterranean, due east of Valencia, Ibiza is an arid island, best known in history as a spot where the ancient Greeks called in for salt. It has a striking, indented coast, golden sandy coves, a beautiful white capital town, and a laidback, tolerant attitude that hippie travellers found convivial in the 1960s.

Year after year they returned, and word got out. Today Ibiza sizzles and glitters, attracting an eclectic crowd of artists, hip designers, gays, and trend-setters, all mixing happily with the relaxed locals and the ageing hippies. The island has become one of the most fashionable destinations in Europe; its boutiques selling the latest look, before Paris or Milan has a clue.

Life is fairly straightforward: up late in the morning, a lazy afternoon on one of the beaches, and then back to the hotel to shower and put on your party clothes. Dressing up is *de rigueur* for a tour of the bars and shops, which stay open until midnight. After dinner everyone hits the clubs and discos to dance the night away to the latest sounds. Typical holiday fare, you might say, but Ibiza does it with more style than anywhere else.

Na Xamena Hotel Hacienda

San Miguel
Ibiza
E 07800
Spain

✈ Ibiza 25km

tel +34 9 7133 4500
fax +34 9 7133 4514

htl.hacienda@vlc.servicom.es

Open Apr–Oct

Member of:
Relais et Châteaux

The north west of the island of Ibiza, with its scattered white fincas and coastal belt of coves, is an area of outstanding natural beauty. Na Xamena Hotel Hacienda sits high up on an impressive clifftop, tucked into pine forests. This privileged setting gives the hotel magical views and a sense of space and isolation which is echoed in the building's simple and elegant design.

All rooms are decorated with delicate wrought iron beds and muslin canopies combining a modern Zen-style with traditional antiques from the pacific islands. Many rooms have a whirlpool bath and afford spectacular views overlooking the sea. Each has minibar, satellite television and safe.

The two restaurants, overseen by top chef Santi Santamaria, serve traditional Mediterranean dishes featuring paella and seafood. At the poolside restaurant, Las Cascadas, Spanish guitarists serenade guests while they dine by candlelight against a backdrop of spectacular sunsets.

Terraces and leafy courtyards provide secluded spots where couples can relax and unwind. For the more energetic, the hotel is within easy reach of sandy beaches and lagoons offering a range of watersports, and the busy nightlife of Ibiza town.

PTS25,000–45,700 (63)
PTS33,100–112,00 (20)
PTS6,850
PTS2,300

Honeymoon specials
Spanish champagne and fruit in the room on arrival. Room upgrade on request.

Local attractions
A 20-minute drive from the centre of Ibiza. Sandy beaches and coves. Concerts, exhibitions and performances in traditional costume.

Leisure activities
Indoor and outdoor swimming pools, mountain biking, tennis courts. Well-being zone with massage, Turkish bath and sauna. All watersports, golf and riding nearby.

Switzerland

Dazzle-white, icing-sugar snow, a fresh cold wind, the scent of pine trees. Only the *whoosh, whoosh, whoosh* of skis breaks the silence...

flying time

To: Geneva or Zurich
London: 1 1/4 hrs
LA: 13 hrs
Miami: 9–10 hrs
NY: 8–9 hrs

climate

Winters are cold, with much snow at high altitude. Summers are warm; the Ticino area has a Mediterranean climate.

when to go

July and August are high season. Prices are highest and pistes busiest at Christmas and New Year, half term and Easter.

currency

The Swiss franc.

language

German in some areas, French in others, Italian in Ticino. Many people speak some English.

health

Health facilities are excellent, but make sure you have good medical and accident insurance.

getting around

The Swiss railway system is efficient and the stunning views on the mountain lines are an added delight.

Dramatic and beautiful, this small country only a sixth the size of Britain boasts mountain peaks that rise 15,000 feet and serene lakes that plunge to unfathomable depths.

Switzerland's loveliest cities hug the lakesides, among them sophisticated and elegant Geneva on the shore of Lac Leman. In winter, the old town's cosy wood-panelled restaurants serve up *kirsch*-laced cheese fondues. In summer, tables are moved into the sunny streets, and windsurfers and sleek yachts take to the water. Trusty steamers carry visitors out of the harbour, past genteel lakeshore villages, to Lausanne and Montreux.

Geneva is a gateway to both the French and the Swiss Alps, and within two or three hours' drive are dozens of mountain resorts offering sports and walking holidays in summer, and some of Europe's best skiing in winter. Switzerland has more than its fair share of glamorous ski resorts, not least chic, traffic-free Zermatt and Gstaad, a favourite of Europe's wealthiest families and film stars. In summer, celebrities who prefer fresh mountain air to the congested beaches of the French Riviera flock to Gstaad's luxury chalets and hotels.

On the Italian border that you find a real gem — the Ticino region. The resorts here could be mistaken for holiday spots on the Mediterranean, by virtue of their sunny weather and long summer season, palm trees and purple bougainvillea, only the blue water here is Lakes Maggiore and Lugano, not the sea. Life goes on simply in the rugged mountains but on the manicured lakefront promenades of Lugano, Locarno and Ascona, the scene appears to be lifted straight from *Hello* magazine.

Castello del Sole Ascona

Via Muraccio 142
CH-6612 Ascona
Switzerland

✈ Lugano-Agno 40km

tel +41 91 791 0202
fax +41 91 792 1118

castellosole@bluewin.ch

Closed 1 Nov–15 Mar

Member of:
Relais & Châteaux
Swiss Deluxe Hotels

The hotel Castello del Sole Ascona, created from the ruins of an old Patrician tavern built in 1532, enjoys an idyllic setting on the shores of Lake Maggiore. In keeping with local tradition, the hotel has been reconstructed using granite, bricks and chestnut wood to retain both charm and style.

Double rooms are located both in the main building and in the newly-built pavilion with garden and inner colonnade, reminiscent of a cloister, which also houses luxurious suites. All rooms have air-conditioning, loggia and wonderful views of the landscaped gardens.

The elegant Tre Stagioni restaurant provides a range of culinary creations prepared with natural products from the estate, including their own Merlot wine.

Service is discreet and attentive.

Guests can choose from a variety of sports activities in the fitness centre, visit the beauty parlour or while away time in the peace and tranquillity of the hotel gardens. There is access to private beaches with small boats, and a private bus service to nearby Ascona.

 SFr480–560 (67)
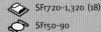 SFr720–1,320 (18)
 SFr50–90
 included

Honeymoon specials
Honeymoon packages of two and three nights cost SFr1,210–2,640 including champagne breakfast with caviar and smoked salmon, candlelit dinner, lunch al fresco, a free beauty treatment for ladies and a free massage for gentlemen.

Sightseeing and leisure
Cycling, hiking and boat trips in the pre-Alpine landscape. Excursions into Italy, or a short stroll around the old town of Ascona. Free use of the hotel's running-track, swimming pool, fitness centre with sauna, thermarium and solarium. Indoor and outdoor tennis, windsurfing, massage and 18-hole golf course at extra charge.

Grand Hotel Schönegg

3920 Zermatt
Switzerland

 Geneva 234km

tel +41 27 967 4488
fax +41 27 967 5808

schonegg@relaischateaux.fr.

Closed May, 10 Oct–1 Dec

Member of:
Relais & Chateaux

Enchantingly sited above the pretty town of Zermatt and surrounded by pine forest, the Grand Hotel Schönegg enjoys spectacular views of the snow-covered peak of the Matterhorn and can be reached via a tunnel bored through the heart of the mountain. Hand carved wooden fireplaces and beams lend a cosy Swiss charm to this family run chalet-style hotel.

The comfortable rooms and suites are classically decorated with dark wood and warm colours, and open out to a spacious balcony. The perfect spot to enjoy the sun, take a siesta, or admire the tapering pyramid of the Matterhorn. The large and luxuriously appointed suites are fitted with private jacuzzis for total indulgence.

The broad and welcoming sun terrace in front of the hotel offers light meals and snacks within sight of the spectacular Matterhorn. Hearty Swiss specialities and delicious international dishes are served in the traditional Gourmet-Stübli Restaurant. Wooden trellises and screens, hand carved lanterns and blazing open fires enhance the romantic and intimate ambience.

In winter, guests can ski from the front door of the hotel or hike along rambling trails during the summer. Cable car stations are within easy reach for those who want to scale the heights of the Alps, and the village of Zermatt is only a thirty second journey in the hotel lift. The hotel also offers whirlpools, sauna and massage parlour where guests can relax within sight of the encircling mountains.

 SFr120–155 (34)
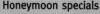 SFr192–252 (2)
SFr65
SFr25

Honeymoon specials
Welcome drink and fruit basket in room on arrival.

Sightseeing and leisure
Hiking trails, skiing, whirlpools, sauna, heated bath, solarium, massage parlour, fitness centre and swimming pool available at the hotel. Local village nearby.

Palace Hotel

3780 Gstaad
Switzerland

 Geneva Int. 160km

tel +41 33 748 5000
fax +41 33 748 5001

palace@gstaad.ch

Closed April and May
1 Oct–18 Dec

Tour operators:
UK: Elegant Resorts

This deluxe hotel, surrounded by pine trees and adorned with castle turrets and towers, is perched atop a hill above the village of Gstaad in the Bernese Alps. Owned and managed by the same family for two generations, the Palace Hotel exudes a friendly and welcoming atmosphere.

The rooms and suites are rustically decorated with soft floral prints, wooden beams and traditionally carved furniture. Most have private balconies with views extending across snow-capped peaks.

Le Restaurant is a perfect setting in which to enjoy a variety of international dishes. For more informal dining, there is La Fromagerie, which boasts delicious traditional dishes such as fondue and raclette, or the canopied terrace set against the backdrop of a superb Alpine panorama.

After dinner, guests can dance the night away to the live band, or try out the GreenGo disco – one of Gstaad's most popular night spots.

Guests may choose to pamper themselves at the hotel's beauty centre, shape up at the gym in the health and fitness centre or take to the surrounding ski slopes. Hot-air ballooning, horseriding and heli-skiing are all available nearby for alternative ways to explore the area.

The hotel is happy to make arrangements for weddings, and will organise everything from flowers and orchestras to a Rolls Royce or horse-drawn carriage to convey the bride and groom.

 Sfr280–1,100 (76)
 Sfr900–2,100 (35)
 Sfr75–90
 included

Honeymoon specials

Flowers, fruit and champagne in room on arrival. Welcome gift. Free access to pools, gym, sauna and the GreenGo nightclub. Special deals available, please enquire. Hire the whole hotel for Sfr1,000 per person (min. 100 people) including 2 nights accommodation, breakfast, wedding reception and dinner.

Sightseeing and leisure

Swimming pools, tennis courts, squash court, gym, beauty centre, fitness centre with sauna, steam bath and massage at hotel. Horseriding, summer and winter skiing, paragliding, hot air ballooning, mountain biking, heli-skiing and golf available nearby. Trips to Church of Saanen and the Lauenen Lake nearby. Several festivals held throughout the year.

United Kingdom

flying time
To: London, Manchester, Glasgow, Edinburgh.
LA: 12–13 hrs
Miami: 8–9 hrs
NY: 7 hrs

climate
Famously wet. Cold but not necessarily icy in winter, warm but not necessarily sunny in summer. You should not rely on the weather.

when to go
May for green landscapes lit by delicate starbursts of wild flowers. Sept/Oct for gentle warmth, mellow light and fewer people.

currency
The pound sterling. In southern Ireland, the Irish pound or punt.

language
English.

getting around
Internal flights to main cities rarely take as much as 1 hour. Public transport is efficient. To appreciate fully the more rural areas, you need a car.

and Ireland

Islands with attitude...

The United Kingdom is an island nation, made up of two main islands and more than 5,000 smaller ones, with a sea which is always near — whether at the tight coves and jaggged cliffs of Cornwall, the wild Atlantic coastline of Connemarra to the west of Ireland, or the gently sloping, pebbly shores of the English Channel.

This is a place of not only of variety but of surprises. The land may be steeped in history, but the people of the British Isles have often led the way internationally — in early days by conquest and colonisation, more recently with street fashion and popular music. Visitors to the cities encounter not only old-fashioned shops, restaurants and markets, and huge museums, but the new and dynamic in art design, music, food and club scenes.

In the countryside, away from the roads and new towns, there are pockets of completely unspoiled scenery lit by a subtle island light. This classically romantic landscape of constant change can look dramatically different depending on when you visit — on a misty morning, perhaps, or in a stormy sunset after a warm summer's day.

England

Cycling and picnics, pretty villages and rolling green hills, soaring cathedrals and ancient market towns, cobbles and castles, the lights of London...

flying time
To: Heathrow, Gatwick, Luton, Stansted.
LA: 12–13 hrs
Miami: 8–9 hrs
NY: 7 hrs

climate/when to go
July and August are busiest and the weather is at its most reliably warm and dry. Out of school holidays, in May and September, sights and cities are more relaxed.

currency
The pound sterling.

getting around
Comfortable and efficient inter-city coaches, a comprehensive if expensive rail network. Hire cars for independent touring in more remote spots such as the Lake District, Yorkshire Moors, and coastal and moorland areas of Devon and Cornwall.

The English countryside is crowded with natural wonders including caves, ancient woods, wild waterfalls, fertile meadows and bleak moorland. It also has many glorious man-made features — stately homes with folllies and manicured parks; Neolithic standing stones, ruined castles and abbeys; old-fashioned Victorian seaside resorts with trimmed Italianate gardens.

Everywhere in England is accessible, and with a hired car you can divide your time easily between jaunts in the country and hectic shopping excursions in London, Manchester or Oxford.

There is a wide range of accommodation for all tastes and budgets, ranging from cheap and idyllic B&Bs, to remote 15th-century farmhouses, to magnificent city- and country-house hotels. ●

Cliveden

Taplow
Berkshire
SL6 0JF
England

 Heathrow 29km

tel +44 1628 668 561
fax +44 1628 661 837

Open all year

Member of:
Preferred Hotels

This beautiful 17th-century country house, surrounded by acres of National Trust gardens and parkland, was once a stately home, often visited by Queen Victoria. Today, it is one of the world's leading hotels.

Majestic sculptured staircases, grand sitting rooms with oak panelling, marble fireplaces, paintings and 300-year-old tapestries all preserve the atmosphere of an English stately home.

The bedrooms, named after famous people connected with Cliveden such as George Bernard Shaw, are each decorated to an individual design in floral fabrics and light pastel shades, with antique furniture and sumptuous canopied beds.

There are two dining rooms: The Terrace, situated off the Great Hall, and Waldo's on the lower ground floor. Both serve fine contemporary cuisine. Three private dining rooms are set aside for special occasions. The magnificent French Dining Room, which seats up to 54 and has stunning views over the formal parterre and Thames Valley beyond, is an excellent venue for a wedding reception.

There are numerous sports and leisure facilities, and guests can enjoy a soothing massage in the Pavilion Spa, which offers a range of beauty and massage treatments.

Cliveden has three vintage boats available for cruising the River Thames, one of which was originally commissioned by Lady Astor.

£230–410 (27)
£410–725 (11)
£35–100
£18

Honeymoon specials
Linen bedmat embroidered with the date of stay for a lasting memento.

Local attractions
Visits to Windsor Castle, Waddesdon Manor and Legoland. Ascot Racecourse and Henley are a short distance away.

Leisure facilities
Two swimming pools, tennis courts, a squash court and gymnasium on site. Horseriding, golf and shooting nearby. Massage and treatment rooms, dry float bed, Canadian hot tubs, steam rooms, sauna and jacuzzi in the Pavilion Spa.

Gidleigh Park

Chagford
Devon
TQ13 8HH
England

✈ Bristol 150km

tel +44 1647 432 367
fax +44 1647 432 574
gidleighpark@gidleigh.co.uk

Open all year

Member of:
Relais et Châteaux

The epitome of a traditional, peaceful country hotel, the refined Gidleigh Park is constructed in acres of gardens and rustling woodland on the banks of the Teign river, deep in the heart of Dartmoor National Park. Acclaimed across Britain as one of the principle areas to view prehistoric settlements, Dartmoor is a place of great historical importance and exquisite natural beauty.

Exuding the ambience of a private home, the hotel was built in 1929 on the foundations of a 16th-century manor house, and is ideally suited to its dramatic and heathland surroundings. Each room is decorated in uplifting and subtle colours, complemented by delicate vases of beautifully arranged flowers. The antique furniture, private bathrooms, and views of the surrounding lawns and trees confirm that this remains a classic country hotel.

The cuisine is expertly prepared by the acclaimed head chef, Michael Caines. With rich sauces, a wide range of delicately steamed fresh vegetables, mouth-watering main meals and luxurious desserts, dining here is a joy.

Hosts, Kay and Paul Henderson welcome their visitors personally. And the wealth of unstudied beauty encircling the estate, including the recently restored water gardens, provide guests with surroundings of luxurious yet homely elegance.

£340–430 (12)
£365–430 (2 cottages)
included
included

Honeymoon specials
Receptions for up to 24 guests can be arranged.

Leisure facilities
All weather tennis courts. Putting course designed by Peter Alliss. Bowling lawn. Two championship standard croquet courts. Hunting, horseracing and riding. Fishing and shooting.

Local attractions
Walking and riding on Dartmoor. National Trust properties a short distance away. Gardens: Rosemoor (RHS), Knightshayes Court, The Garden House, Coleton Fishacre within an hour's drive.

Powder Mills Hotel

Powder Mills Hotel
Powdermill Lane
Battle
East Sussex
England

✈ Gatwick 65km

tel +44 1424 775 511
fax +44 1424 774 540
powdc@aol.com

Open all year

Member of:
Johansens
Best Loved Hotels
Grand Heritage Hotels

The historic 18th-century hotel is set in beautiful woodland and lakes, and adjoins the Battlefields of 1066. This was once the centre for the gunpowder works which operated for over two hundred years and produced the finest gunpowder in Europe.

Now, log fires and richly decorated rooms create a personal welcome in keeping with a traditional English country house hotel.

Most rooms are spacious and all individually furnished, many with antiques. There are sumptuous four-poster bedrooms, one or two allegedly haunted by the Lady in White.

The Orangery Restaurant, with its colonial-style seating, enormous plants and marble floors, offers modern English cooking, and has won many accolades and awards.

Guests can enjoy peaceful walks through scenic woodland trails, which are a naturalists delight, relax by the pool or terrace overlooking the well-tended gardens or try fishing in the specimen lakes. In summer, a rowing boat with champagne picnic may be taken out on the 7-acre specimen lake.

The hotel has a wedding licence too, and its elegant rooms and sweeping gardens provide the perfect setting for a country house wedding.

 £95–120 (29)
 £150 (6)
 £25–40
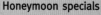 £7.50 (included)

Honeymoon specials
Flowers in the room on arrival.

Leisure activities
Fishing, outdoor swimming pool and beautiful walks through the woods.

Local attractions
Trips to Battle abbey and the town's bustling markets. Romantic Rye – a medieval town with cobbled streets, Bodian Castle and many stately homes are within easy reach.

Ireland

Seaweed baths and diving with dolphins, ancient monuments and grand country houses, music and *craic*, convivial pubs and oyster bars...

flying time
To: Dublin, Cork, Shannon in EIRE; Belfast in the north.
London: 1 1/2 hrs
LA: 12 hrs
Miami: 8hrs
NY: 6–7 hrs

climate
Mild (Jan 4–7°C, July 14–24°C) and very wet, but you can hope for 6 hours of sun a day from May to August.

when to go
May to October, for the best weather and festivals.

currency
The pound sterling in the North, the Irish punt in the Republic.

getting around
Internal flights (excluding Dublin–Belfast), ferries from Great Britain and continental Europe, good trains and buses. Empty roads make driving a real pleasure.

This lovely island has physical and spiritual qualities that are seldom found in the western world. The pace of life is relaxing, and the scenery beautiful and varied, with the sea never far from sight. Dublin, the capital, is cultural, attractive and easy to explore. The people are easy to meet and invariably curteous and friendly. The sunshine, when it comes, intensifies the already beautiful colours of the landscape. The roads are usually empty and traffic jams are still an exception.

It is possible to stay in tranquil country houses where the proportions and the furnishings of the rooms are redolent of a more gracious age. Not only is the food delicious, and made from the freshest seafood, local meat, game and vegetables, but you can also get well-chosen wines and, of course, decent whiskey and beer. The owners and staff of these places will be keen to help with any request you have — whether it is tracing your ancestors, or finding the best fishing, beaches, shopping and sites of historical interest.

If you honeymoon in Ireland, you will be able to enjoy all the conveniences of modern-day Europe and lose yourself in wilderness and beauty. ●

Mount Juliet

Thomastown
County Kilkenny
Ireland

✈ Dublin Airport 120km

tel +353 56 73000
fax +353 56 73019
aohare@mountjuliet.ie

Mount Juliet House open all year

Member of:
Small Luxury Hotels of the World

Mount Juliet is a beautiful walled estate of unspoilt woodland, pasture and formal gardens, hidden away in the south east corner of Ireland. Built by the Earl of Carrick over 200 years ago, the great house still retains an aura of 18th-century grandeur. The elegance of the original decor has been painstakingly preserved and each of the 32 en suite bedrooms has retained its own character and ambience.

Designed around a traditional courtyard, the Hunters Yard is just a 2-minute walk from Mount Juliet's many sporting activities. The en suite courtyard bedrooms provide a rustic contrast to the grandeur of Mount Juliet House and the traditional charm of the Rose Garden Lodges.

Guests can enjoy the finest international and traditional Irish cuisine in the elegantly appointed dining rooms, relaxing afterwards in the convivial atmosphere of the cosy bars with roaring fires.

In the great country house tradition, sport is all around. The Jack Nicklaus championship golf course has often been home to the Irish Open, and the David Leadbetter Golf Academy provides a range of coaching programmes. There is an equestrian centre offering show jumping, dressage and trail riding. Clay target shooting, fishing, archery and a fully-equipped spa and leisure centre are also available.

The seclusion and tranquillity of the estate inspire romance, and the hotel offers a honeymoon package which includes a choice of activities from their extensive range.

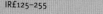 IR£125–255
 IR£210–295
 IR£30*
 IR£12.50*

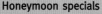

Honeymoon specials

Honeymoon package includes three nights midweek accommodation, Irish breakfasts and dinners, two activities of choice, chocolates on arrival, champagne breakfast in bed and costs between IR£320–540

*Breakfast and dinner is included in the honeymoon package

Sightseeing and leisure

Medieval city and castle of Kilkenny, Waterford Crystal Visitor's Centre, Jeroint Abbey, and Jerpoint glassworks all nearby. Golf, horseriding, fishing, shooting, archery, tennis and croquet available on the estate. Spa and leisure centre with pool, gym, sauna, steam room, and beauty treatments.

Scotland

Breathtaking panoramic views — of mysterious lochs and misty moors, wooded walkways, and heather-clad mountain peaks lapped by clouds...

flying time

To: Edinburgh/Glasgow
London: 1hr
LA: 12–13 hrs
Miami: 8–9 hrs
New York: 7–8 hrs

climate/when to go

Conditions range from quite balmy in the west during the summer to bitterly cold in the north. The Edinburgh Festival takes place over three weeks in August/September.

currency

Scottish pound, equivalent in value to the pound sterling.

language

English/Gaelic in remote North.

getting around

Flights to main cities. Trains traverse the highlands. In the more rural districts public transport is scarce. There are ferries to the islands. Touring is most enjoyable by car.

Home to a vibrant, youthful city culture and some glorious, famously unspoilt countryside, Scotland offers metropolitan pleasures and rural delights in equal measure.

Edinburgh, its sophisticated, cosmopolitan capital, is rightly regarded as one of Europe's most up-and-coming cities and in recent years has become host to Britain's premier New Year's party, when over a million revellers fill the city centre as the clock strikes midnight. Edinburgh has a fun atmosphere and, with a multitude of restaurants, theatres and galleries, not to mention the world-famous arts festival, entertainment is never lacking.

Alternatively, there is Glasgow, Scotland's second city, with its magnificent Victorian architecture including the stunning creations of Charles Rennie Mackintosh. Beyond the towns are a multitude of natural wonders: take a trip to the west coast and bask in balmy Gulf Stream waters whilst watching seal pups frolicking in the shallows. Move inland and experience the glories of the Highlands: snow-capped mountains, mossy glens, rivers and burns gliding gently through granite gorges. To top off the day, wait until nightime when nature puts on its very own electric lightshow, the Aurora Borealis, a dazzling display of red, green and gold.

Gleneagles

Auchterarder
Perthshire PH3 1NF
Scotland

Edinburgh 75km

tel +44 1764 662231
fax +44 1764 662134

ressales@guinness.com

Open all year

Member of:
The Leading Hotels of the World

Once the centre of the Pictish kingdom, the romantic rivers and glens of Perthshire in central Scotland remain quiet and unspoiled. Tucked in the lee of the Ochil Hills, the magnificent Gleneagles hotel is set in 235 hectares looking out towards Glen Devon.

The generous rooms and suites are individually decorated with fine antiques, elegant open fireplaces, beautifully crafted wood and subtle warm plaids to create a warm and convivial atmosphere. The sumptuous Royal Lochnagar Suite boasts a four-poster bed, silk-lined walls and hand woven carpets for the ultimate in luxury. Large windows look out over extensive grounds to the surrounding heather-clad hills.

Walks and trails abound in the secluded woods and hills, and the estate offers a range of world class activities. The golf course, edging the Muir of Ochil, is famous throughout the world. Guests can learn the ancient and aristocratic art of falconry or trek the foothills of the highlands with the equestrian centre.

Salmon and trout abound in the River Tay and the nearby loch and feature in the estate's restaurants. The resort offers a choice of three restaurants. The Strathearn uses only the best produce in Scotland including Highland grouse and delicately-flavoured salmon. The Gallery Brasserie serves a variety of international dishes in a casual atmosphere, while the Bar and Clubhouse Grill with its fabulous views of the golf courses, specialises in earthy modern cuisine with a Scottish slant.

Gleneagles is happy to take care of all arrangements for a perfect wedding, and can provide a Scottish wedding breakfast, resident florist, and romantically secluded locations.

UK£225–365 (215)
UK£515–1,250 (14)
from £45
included

Honeymoon specials
Complimentary champagne and flowers in room. Tailor-made honeymoon packages on request.

Local attractions
Glasgow and Edinburgh about an hour's drive away for shopping, theatres and tourist attractions.

Leisure facilities
Golf courses, shooting school, equestrian centre, off-road driving and falconry at resort. Spa with health and beauty treatments, swimming pools, jacuzzi, squash, gym, tennis, croquet also available. Salmon and sea trout fishing in nearby River Tay.

Middle East

An unforgettable land as ancient as history itself...

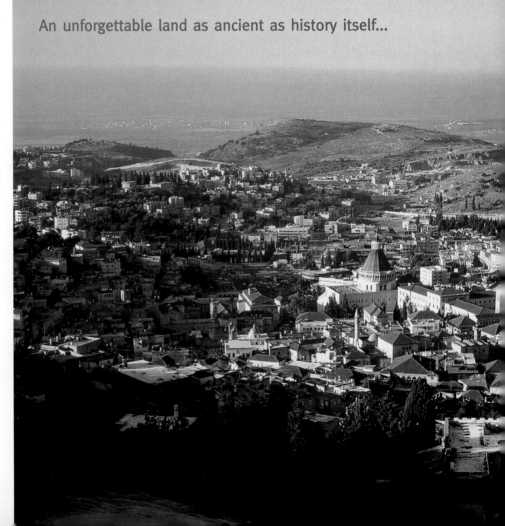

flying time
London: 5–7 hrs
NY: 12–13 hrs

when to go
Summer temperatures can
reach 50°C and it is best to
avoid the crowds around
Ramadan (Dec–Jan).
November to May is usually
fine and dry.

currency
Traveller's cheques, US dollars
and major credit cards are all
readily accepted.

language
Arabic, Hebrew and French.

health
Vaccinations may be required
(Hepatitis B, Typhoid, Polio
and Rabies) and be sure to
take out health insurance

getting around
Planes from country to
country. Within each country,
taxi or hired car.

Travel to most parts of the Middle East and the Western world is left far behind. This is the land of The Thousand and One Nights: a mixed bag of colour and magic, wonderful hospitality, spectacular archeological sites, adventure and surprise.

Romantic Crusader castles perch on mountain ranges in the deserts of Syria while in Yemen's Old City mosque minarets rise high above the ancient houses.

Jordan's one-time capital Petra, built in the 3rd century BC, was forgotten for a thousand years and only rediscovered in the 19th century.

Israel can offer the Dead Sea and, of course, Jerusalem — perhaps the most fascinating city in the world.

As well as the sights, there are beautiful beaches aplenty, snake charmers, lively coffee houses, belly dancers, bazaars bursting with carpets, Bedouin rugs, spices and pearls and a whole range of activities from skiing to desert safaris.

For those with a taste for the strange and exotic, the Middle East can prove to be a richly rewarding honeymoon destination.

Israel

Emerald-green valleys and refreshing waterfalls, bubbling hot mineral springs and soothing black mud. A sand-blasted desert wilderness of sun-warmed rocks, glowing red in the evening light...

flying time
To: Tel Aviv
London: 5 hrs
LA: 16–17 hrs
Miami: 13–14 hrs
NY: 12 hrs

climate
Summers (Apr–Oct) are hot and dry. Winters are mild with some rain, though it can be chilly in Jerusalem, for example. The warmer south can be uncomfortably hot in mid summer.

when to go
Summer is the main season on the Mediterranean coast while autumn, winter and spring are the most popular seasons to visit Eilat and the desert. Spring is a good time for birdwatching.

The State of Israel is a young country, celebrating its 50th anniversary in 1998, but the history of the land is palpable. Names such as Nazareth, appear on the road signs, and landscapes of fertile plains and arid desert seem little changed from descriptions in *The Bible.* These days, although it can feel a little odd at first, you can try your hand at windsurfing on the Sea of Galilee and white-water rafting on the River Jordan.

Israel is an ideal country to tour because its surprisingly small area contains a rich variety of scenery, and ancient and religious sites. ▶

language

Hebrew, Arabic and English. Street and road signs are usually given in all three.

currency

The shekel. Credit cards, and often foreign currencies are accepted.

health

No immunisations are needed; medical services are of a high standard, but be sure your travel insurance covers private treatment. Beware the strong sun on desert trips. Spas at Galilee and the Dead Sea resorts offer health and beauty treatments.

getting around

Organised tours take in the historical sites, but Israel is easy to explore with a hire car, on the good network of roads. Short flights link Tel Aviv, Eilat and other points.

In winter you can ski on the snow-capped slopes of Mt Hermon in the north or take a jeep safari into the southern desert. In summer, you can wonder at Roman monuments in the morning and swim in the Mediterranean after lunch. Indeed, you will never be far from a beach. Along the Mediterranean coast Tel Aviv, Herzliya and Netanya have long stretches of sand, abundant watersports, and a huge choice of eating places and nightlife, while at the Red Sea resort of Eilat you can enjoy year-round sunshine and world-class scuba diving.

Jerusalem must be at the top of any visitor's sightseeing agenda. The stones of this fascinating city breathe history, and it is as sacred to Muslims and Christians as to Jews. While Jews offer prayers at the Western, or Wailing Wall, along the Via Dolorosa, pilgrims follow the alleyways where Jesus is said to have carried the cross to his crucifixion. The narrow, maze-like streets of the Old City are not easy to navigate, so guided walking tours are popular. Most interesting are the ones that involve clambering onto the city walls and over the rooftops for a different perspective on the glistening domes and crowded houses. You can gain a further insight into Israeli life by arranging a visit to a local family through any of the nationwide tourist information offices.

A tour of Israel guarantees some unusual experiences. It seems unbelievable, until you try it, that you really can read a book buoyed up by the warm salty waters of the Dead Sea, or that the black Dead Sea mud you can smear on yourself has therapeutic powers. At Eilat's underwater observatory you can venture into a realm of corals without getting wet, and at Dolphin Reef you can swim, play and dive with the dolphins.

Excursions from Eilat take you deep into the rocky Negev desert, a terrain that you can see from the back of a camel, a four-wheel-drive jeep or a dust-throwing quad bike. And in nature reserves and on guided hikes you may meet the ibex, foxes, snakes and birdlife that thrive in the strangely beautiful desert environment. ●

Eilat Princess Hotel

PO Box 2323
Eilat 88000
Israel

✈ Eilat Airport 10km

tel +972 7 636 5555
fax +972 7 637 6333

Open all year

Poised between the granite rockface of the desert and the immense blue expanse of the Red Sea, the Eilat Princess is set among extensive landscaped gardens on the southernmost tip of Israel.

The rooms are elegantly dressed in cool cotton prints, with king-size beds, and balconies that provide sweeping views across the bay to Jordan and Saudi Arabia. Each floor also offers suites with an exotic theme ranging from Thai to Russian, Indian to Chinese. All are romantic and secluded.

Authentic Creole and Cajun, traditional French, delicate Szechwan, and exotic Japanese are among the several varieties of cuisine prepared by award-winning chefs in a variety of dining venues. The discreet oriental charm of the Mei Garden is complemented by the traditional cosmopolitan atmosphere of the Oak Room, and the Sunrise Terrace Conservatory is set dramatically in the desert rockface.

The countless pools and sundecks of the landscaped gardens are connected by a series of bridges with a Venetian inspiration. Whirlpools, waterfalls, waterchutes, and underwater grottos are among the park's attractions, and a variety of watersports are also available. The semi-private bathing beach offers excellent opportunities for diving and snorkelling, and guests can be pampered at the hotel's spa complex with twelve treatment rooms, beauty parlour and health bar.

The hotel has extensive experience in organising weddings and can provide in-house designers and florists to assist the wedding preparations.

US$234–495 (355)
US$430–1,300 (65)
from US$34
from US$18

Honeymoon specials
Flowers, champagne and cake in the room on arrival. Room upgrade subject to availability. Free entrance to the Sansara Spa and Fitness Centre. This package is based on a stay of three days or more and is complimentary.

Sightseeing and leisure
Trips to underwater observatory, dolphin reef, ostrich farm. Outdoor jacuzzi, waterslides, tennis courts and Spa and Fitness Centre with Finnish sauna, gym, private massage and treatment rooms. Scuba diving, parasailing, windsurfing, snorkelling and waterskiing are available nearby.

Jerusalem Hotel

4 Antara Ben Shaddad St
PO box 19130
Jerusalem
Israel

✈ Ben Gurion 40km

tel +972 2 628 3282
fax +972 2 628 3282
toll free reservations:
US: 1 800 657 9401
Norway: 800 13 115
raed@jrshotel.com

Open all year

Originally built by a feudal lord in the heart of the ancient city of Jerusalem, the Jerusalem Hotel has been carefully and lavishly refurbished in recent months. The authentic Arab architecture of the last century has been retained and accentuated in the arched windows, high ceilings, cool stone flagging and secluded vine garden. The thick stone walls, cut from creamy Jerusalem stone, have been exposed and pointed with a traditional Arabic plaster.

Rooms are timelessly decorated with antiques and have an Eastern inspiration. Private balconies overlook the twisting narrow streets and clamorous markets of Jerusalem's Old City, and the ancient peaceful slopes of The Mount of Olives.

The Eastern influence is continued in the excellent Palestinian cuisine, served in the privacy of the garden. Guests may also try flavourful Bedouin dishes and other local ethnic foods.

From the hotel's convenient location in the heart of Jerusalem, guests can wander among a remarkable number of historical and religious sites, stroll along the city ramparts at sunset, browse bustling markets, or trek into the nearby Judaen Desert.

This is a family-run hotel with a personal, friendly service. Staff are able to arrange weddings and hold receptions for up to 200 people in the historic and romantic courtyard of St Stephen's Basilica.

 NIS347–450 (15)
 from NIS45
 included

Honeymoon specials
Flowers and champagne in the room on arrival. Complimentary night tour into the Windmill Garden, with magnificent views of the Old City walls.

Sightseeing and leisure
Visits to the main markets of Jerusalem's Old City, the Holy Sepulchre, Wailing Wall and Garden Tomb. Hiking trails nearby. Musical and cultural events throughout the year. Beauty salons and health spas available in the area.

Royal Beach Hotel

Eilat

Israel

Eilat Central 2km

Contact:
Central Reservation Office,
North Beach, Eilat 88000

tel +972 7 636 8888
fax +972 7 636 8811
royal-beach@isrotel.co.il

Open all year

Part of the Isrotel Hotel Chain

Eilat, home to the Royal Beach Hotel, is situated at Israel's southernmost tip. Here, nature's bounty converges as shimmering desert and red-hued mountain ranges meet the azure-blue, coral-filled waters of the Red Sea. The resort boasts three exotic swimming pools with cascading waterfalls and wide expanses of green lawns dotted with sunbeds and shaded by majestic date palms which overlook the hotel's beach.

All 366 luxuriously appointed rooms and suites boast south facing balconies which command sweeping views across the bay. Works of art and rich furnishings, full-length sliding glass doors, wooden furniture and stylish lighting lend a regal feel, while bright floral arrangements add a welcoming touch.

American, Italian, Chinese and Jewish cuisine, all prepared with the freshest ingredients, are served with elegance and style in a variety of speciality and ethnic restaurants.

More than anything else Eilat is characterised by the Red Sea and offers every possible experience in, on, under and around the water. The Coral Beach nature reserve is one of the richest displays of corals and other marine life in the world – to be observed by anyone either by diving, snorkelling, glass-bottom-boat excursions or at the magnificent underwater observatory. Visitors to the natural environment of the Dolphin Reef on the shores of the Red Sea can view and even swim with these amazing mammals.

£709 (315)
£1,269 (18)
US$50–150
US$13

Honeymoon specials
Complimentary dinner for two, special VIP treatment, surprise gifts in the room, 2 T-Shirts of the hotel, room upgrade subject to availability, photo album.

Leisure facilities
Health club, gymnasium, sauna, jacuzzi, Synagogue, all watersports. Deep-sea fishing.

Local attractions
Safaris, dolphin watching, desert exploration by camel, mountain bike, air-conditioned car or all-terrain vehicle. Trips to Timna Valley National Park featuring King Solomon's pillars, Red Canyon, biblical wildlife reserve and bird-watching park.

Africa

Africa! Next to Asia, the largest continent in the world and a heady mixture of peoples, languages, climates and landscapes.

If camping out under a star-filled sky while a herd of elephants slowly make their way across the grassy plains is appealing then Africa is the place to be. Likewise, if living it up with the jet-set

A continent of dramatic landscapes —
ancient rift valley, sweeping savannah plains, snow-capped mountains,
wide stretches of arid desert, tropical beaches and Indian Ocean islands...

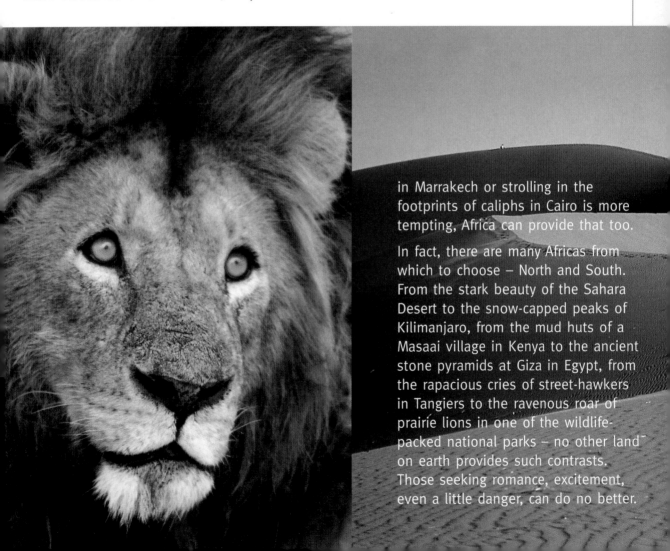

in Marrakech or strolling in the footprints of caliphs in Cairo is more tempting, Africa can provide that too.

In fact, there are many Africas from which to choose – North and South. From the stark beauty of the Sahara Desert to the snow-capped peaks of Kilimanjaro, from the mud huts of a Masaai village in Kenya to the ancient stone pyramids at Giza in Egypt, from the rapacious cries of street-hawkers in Tangiers to the ravenous roar of prairie lions in one of the wildlife-packed national parks – no other land on earth provides such contrasts. Those seeking romance, excitement, even a little danger, can do no better.

Southern Africa

flying time
London: 12–13 hrs
LA: 23 hrs
NY: 19–20 hrs

climate
Very hot year round. Southern Africa operates the opposite system to the Western Hemisphere, being rainy Dec–March and hot Sept–Nov.

when to go
Try to avoid rainy seasons, but note that in dry season some places such as Tanzania are unpleasantly hot.

currency
US dollar traveller's cheques or cash are widely accepted.

language
English, French and a variety of indigenous languages such as Swahili and Zulu.

health
Imunisation against Yellow Fever is mandatory; against Hepatitis B, Typhoid, Polio and sometimes Meningitis, advisable. Malaria pills are usually prescribed. Do not drink the water.

getting around
Usually by plane. Off–road vehicles are used on safari but road transfers are usually ardous if not unfeasible.Trips to Southern African can be combined with the beaches of South Africa or the islands of Mozambique or Mauritius.

One of the world's last frontiers...

There are endless ways to create a memorable honeymoon in this vast and historic land. Each country offers diverse experiences. The East African Swahili countries of Kenya and Tanzania make easy 'beach and bush' locations, combining safari drives through such famous African national parks as The Masaai Mara, Serengeti and Ngorongoro Crater, with lazy days on their Indian Ocean coastlines and exotic islands.

Zambia, often described as 'real Africa', offers exciting safaris in the wild and remote parks of Kafue and the South Luangwa, and relaxation on the golden sands of Lake Malawi.

Zimbabwe is defined by the path of the Zambezi river, which cascades over the mighty Victoria Falls. Visitors often take a raft or canoe over her tempestuous rapids, and explore the many tiny riverine islands set in the magnificence of the powerful landscape.

In Botswana, the islands and crystal-clear water channels of the Okavango Delta, 'Jewel of the Kalahari, are best explored by dug-out canoe, or even from the back of an African elephant.

The desolate landscapes of Namibia are intensely dramatic; many who visit the richly coloured desert dunes of Soussesvlei and the elemental Skeleton Coast find breathtaking beauty. The waterholes of Etosha attract large numbers of southern African wildlife.

South Africa is a land of extremes. From the cosmopolitan cities of Johannesburg and Cape Town to the safari experience of Kruger national park, the beautiful Garden Route and its many fabulous beaches, it has something to offer every visitor.

Kenya

Kenya is one of the oldest and most traditional safari destinations, and seems to capture the romance of Africa. The country has a colourful diversity of wildlife, scenery and people; its coastline is lapped by the Indian Ocean, and has long carried the influence of Arabian traders who first found their way to these shores nearly ten thousand years ago.

Much of Kenya is perceived to have been over-developed by mass tourism, but there remain many wonderfully unspoilt locations, and elegant colonial homesteads where hosts can recount tales of an Africa that existed long ago. The airport at Nairobi is well served by international flights, and local airlines make travel within the country extremely easy.

The ancient rift valley stretching out before you, proud Masaai herding cattle, graceful *dhows* plying the coastline, freedom and the call of the wild...

flying time

To: Nairobi
London: 9 hrs
LA: 22–23 hrs
Miami: 19–20 hrs
New York: 17 hrs

when to go

Apr–May sees the long rains, Jun–Oct is hot and dry, November sees the short rains, and Dec–Mar is very hot and humid.

currency

The Kenyan shilling, but US dollars are widely accepted. Credit cards are accepted at many hotels.

language

The official language is Swahili, though English is widely spoken.

getting around

Air Kenya and many private airlines connect the national parks and towns. There is a daily railway service from Nairobi to Mombassa.

The Masaai Mara is characterised by huge expanses of rolling savannah grassland and flat-topped acacias, and its open plains make for good game viewing. As the name suggests, it is the homeland of the nomadic Masaai tribe who continue to herd their cattle across this land and Northern Tanzania, still living in accordance with their age-old traditions and distinguished by their proud nature, and a distinctive red cloth that they wear. In August the Mara provides fresh pasture for the millions of wildebeest that also follow the seasonal change across the border. The spectacle of the wildebeest migration across the Sand River can be viewed in spectacular fashion from the elevation of a hot-air balloon, a trip which can be arranged from most of the surrounding lodges.

Nearby, the Amboseli National Park is set against the staggering backdrop of Mount Kilimanjaro, which is actually a surprising 30 miles distant, in Tanzania. Both parks are rich in wildlife, and permission for vehicles to leave the road means visitors can get close to enough to observe the fascinating rituals of life in the African bush ▷

No trip to Kenya would be complete without a visit to the Rift Valley Lakes, where thousands of greater and lesser pink flamingos flock together to colour the saltwaters of Magadi, Nakuru, Elmenteita and Turkana, and the fresh waters of Naivasha and Baringo. These tranquil surroundings provide perfect settings for walks in nearby national parks and private reserves.

The confluence of the Arab, Portuguese, Indian and African cultures add a hint of spice to any time taken on Kenya's coast, or on its offshore reefs and islands so rich with aquatic life. This exotic coastline provides the ideal finale to any Kenyan honeymoon.

Borana Lodge

Borana

Kenya

✈ Borana airstrip 3km

Contact:

PO Box 24397, Nairobi

tel +254 2 568 801/04/567 251

fax +254 2 564 945

ROYAL.AFRICASAF@commsol.sprint.com

Closed 15 Apr–15 May

In a valley which meanders out of Laikipia Plateau onto the plains of Northern Kenya is the deluxe hideaway retreat – Borana Lodge. The lodge appears to be cut off from the outside world and yet is within easy reach of Kenya's famous national parks and reserves.

Six cottages made of stone, cedar and thatch are gathered around a main house in the shadow of Mount Kenya blending into the natural surroundings. Each cottage is different in design and layout and has its own bathroom and verandah. All have fireplace and some have large four-poster beds. The interiors echo the spirit of Africa with furniture made of rough hewn cedar, leather and hand-woven and hand-painted fabrics and fine East African art.

The main house has a morning room where guests can relax and take in the easterly views over the river gorge and beyond before enjoying a meal estate-style around the large rosewood table. Good homemade traditional and exotic fare is served, with the emphasis on fresh produce obtained every day from the ranch.

Trips to Borana can be combined with luxury tented safaris led by professional guides into the heart of Kenya, for a truly memorable experience.

 US$360

 included

 included

Honeymoon specials

Wine, sundowners, activities on the ranch, guided walks and game drives all included. The package costs US$360* per person per night in a double room. *Champagne and spirits are not included.

Leisure facilities

Swimming, horseriding. Massage available on request.

Local attractions

Game walks and drives with professional guides. Day trips to Samburu National Reserve, famous for its wildlife, and Aberdare National Park, a forest with incredible scenery and wildlife. Flights to Lake Turkana to visit archaeolgical sites. Cultural visits to local Samburu community highlighting aspects of their life, from spear making to traditional dance.

Galdessa Camp

Nairobi

Kenya

✈ local airstrip 10km

Contact:
c/o Corecodi S.A.
5 rue de la Fontaine, 1204 Geneva
Switzerland

tel +41 22 311 0002
fax +41 22 311 0021

geneva@galdessa.com

Open all year

Tour operators:
UK: Abercrombie & Kent
    Cazenove & Lloyd
US: Sue's Safaris
    Frontiers International

Set in the middle of Kenya's largest national park, Tsavo East, the elephant park, Galdessa is one of the country's newest and most private hideaways.

The camp, which caters to a maximum of sixteen guests, is located on the southern bank of the Galana river, the sole source of permanent water in the area and home to some of Tsavo's best wildlife. Elephant, rhino, buffalo and antelope come to drink, while predators lurk in the shade.

The Honeymoon Suite enjoys a private location well away from the rest of the camp, faces the river, and has its own adjoining seating area with a water wallow and elevated viewing platform. Inside, through the use of natural woods, stone and canvas, an authentic contact is maintained with the world outside – manifest in the stone sink and tables, timber floors, ostrich-egg lamps and enormous beds made out of wood from the park. Truly an eco-tourism camp, electricity here is solar generated and all wastes, including water, are recycled or treated.

The cuisine is known to be the best in East Africa and 22 experienced staff will attend to guests' needs 24 hours a day. Meals can be enjoyed in the comfort of a spacious lodge in the middle of the untamed wilderness, or, for more intimate moments, privately in the suite.

Guests can both relax in the peace of Galdessa, and discover the many mysteries of this wild and untamed part of Africa on foot or in one of the open land cruisers, for a truly memorable time.

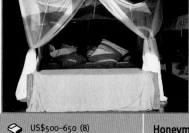

📖 US$500–650 (8)

📖 US$600–750 (2)

🍽 included

☕ included

👤

    for bookings only

Honeymoon specials
Honeymooners can enjoy meals in the privacy of their suite with dedicated waiter service. Romantic dinners are served al fresco in the moonlight. All drinks*, meals and activities are included. Room upgrade is subject to availability.

*except French champagne

Sightseeing and leisure
Safaris in Kenya's largest national park, Tsavo East. Game drives during the day and at night, walking safaris with professional guide, meals in the bush, sundowners, fishing along the river.

Ol Donyo Wuas

Chyulu Hills

Kenya

✈ own airstrip 50 min. from Nairobi

tel +254 2 882 521

fax +254 2 882 728

Contact:
Richard Bonham Safaris
c/o Roxton Bailey Robinson
25 High St, Hungerford, RG17 0NF

tel +44 1488 683 222

fax +44 1488 682 977

Closed in May

Tour operators:
Roxton Bailey Robinson Worldwide
Richard Bonham Safaris

Stunningly situated among the rugged Chyulu Hills and overlooking the snow-capped peaks of Mount Kilimanjaro, the private lodge Ol Donyo Wuas has exclusive access to one of the few remaining wilderness areas of East Africa.

Each of the six thatched cottages has a cosy open fireplace and verandah with panoramic views across the vast unspoilt plains toward distant mountain peaks. The beautifully crafted furniture is locally made and establishes an intimate and comfortable atmosphere.

A typical day at the lodge might well begin when dawn is still reflected in the snow of Mount Kilimanjaro's summit. Early morning and late evening are the best times for game viewing. Trekking into the bush on foot, horseback, or in a specially converted open-top landrover, guests can watch oryx, gerenuk, zebra, eland, giraffe and wildebeest roam the plains, always on the lookout for cheetah and lion. The early evening is the perfect time for observing predators in action, and as the heat of the sun dies down, guests are taken to a suitable spot for a 'sundowner' cocktail. Back at the lodge, an invigorating hot shower and then a romantic candlelit three course dinner under the stars round off a perfect day.

Other optional activities include an early morning charter around the top of Mount Kilimanjaro, or some excellent bird shooting. The lodge can also arrange for guests to stay at the sister lodge – Sand Rivers in Tanzania's largest game reserve to enjoy a different kind of safari experience.

Weddings can be organised in a variety of wildly romantic locations around the lodge.

 US$315–360

 included

included

Honeymoon specials
Wine in room on arrival. All drinks are included.
A stay at Ol Donyo Wuas can be combined with days at other romantic safari lodges or time spent relaxing along the shores of the Indian Ocean. A full itinerary, including international flights, can be arranged.

Sightseeing and leisure
Tailor-made riding and walking safaris with support crew and mobile tented camp are available at an extra cost of US$50–100 per person per day. Bird shooting can be arranged during the season July to October. Trips to local Maasai village and Amboseli National Park.

VISA for bookings only

South Africa

Mist rolling from Table Mountain,
cascading waterfalls on the Garden Route,
graceful colonial homesteads,
cheetah racing across the savanah...

In this cosmopolitan and sophisticated country, reminders of a fascinating history abound, and its sheer size and diversity means that there is something here for every visitor, including a wide range of accommodation catering for all budgets.

In addition to safaris to its national parks, South Africa offers activities that tend not to be found on the rest of the continent such as hiking, walking, riding, cycling, wine tasting and scenic

flying time
To: Johannesburg or
Cape Town
London: 11 hrs
LA: 21 hrs
NY: 15 hrs

climate/when to go
Cape Town is best visited
Sept–Apr. The rest of the
country experiences rain
in the summer Oct–Mar.

currency
South African Rand.

Language
A wide variety including
English, Afrikaans, Zulu,
Xhosa and South Sotho.

getting around
South African Airways'
efficient network of
internal flights connects
most of the major towns,
the national parks and
other attractions.

train journeys. For wildlife enthusiasts, the Kruger National Park and its surrounding private reserves offer extremely good game viewing and luxuriously appointed lodges. Open-sided vehicles and well trained guides, who are adept at spotting the 'big five', ensure that your safari is as memorable as possible.

The famously lovely Garden Route from Port Elizabeth to Cape Town follows the coastline. The secluded bays and beaches, waterfalls and forests make this one of the most dramatic drives in the country, and its destination is one of the most romantically situated cities in the world.

Table Mountain provides a magnificent backdrop to many fine beaches, and acres of vineyards and gardens, and the Waterfront is an ideal spot to relax and sample the fine cuisine that is on offer.

There is so much more to experience in South Africa — perhaps the verdant hills and valleys of the Waterberg, the stark landscapes of the Kalahari Desert, or the Indian Ocean coastline around Durban. For those who wish to end their trip in a tropical paradise, Benguerra Island off the coast of Mozambique is a short flight from Johannesburg, and can provide a marvellous finale to your African honeymoon.

The Beach House
on Sandown Bay

PO Box 199
Kleinmond 7195
Western Cape
South Africa

✂ Capetown Int. 110km

tel +27 28 271 3130
fax +27 28 271 4022

bhrelais@satis.co.za

Open all year

Member of:
Relais Hotels

Nestling between the protective shoulders of rugged mountains and directly overlooking the pristine golden beaches of the famous Cape coastline, The Beach House rejoices in its enviable natural setting.

All bedrooms are individually decorated in light shades, with wood furniture and pretty floral fabrics. Many are either seaward-facing with breathtaking views of the sweeping shoreline, or look out over an endless stretch of craggy mountains.

A particular highlight of the stay is the food, which features ingredients harvested from the sea and served either by the pool, in the elegant Tides restaurant or, weather permitting, on the front terrace overlooking the sensational panorama of Sandown Bay.

Guests can take advantage of the many sporting activities on offer including cycling, tennis, golf and swimming, or can simply take a relaxing walk in the tranquil English gardens surrounding the hotel.

This is an area of stunning natural beauty, home to numerous birds and penguins. From June to Novermber, guests can spot whales from their bedroom window. The Overburg Whale Coast is one of the best land-based viewing areas in the world.

ZAR250–365 pp (20)
ZAR385–405 pp (3)
ZAR75–95
ZAR40 (included)

Honeymoon specials
Welcome sherry and fruit platter, wine and flowers in room on arrival. Room upgrade subject to availability. Candlelit dinner can be served on the private verandah by arrangement.

Sightseeing and leisure
Cycling, golf, tennis, swimming, bowling, horseriding, walking and hiking. Trips to the nature reserves at De Hoop and Bontebok, and the Harold Porter Botanic Gardens. Visits to the Stony point penguin colony and birdwatching spots. Arts and crafts in the town at Hermanus, a short drive away.

Benguerra Lodge

PO Box 87416

Houghton 2041

South Africa

Vilanvulo 25km across sea
airstrip on the island

tel +27 11 483 2734

fax +27 11 728 3767

benguela@icon.co.za

Open all year

Member of:
Classic Camps of Africa

Situated off the coast of Mozambique and accessed by air, the luxury Benguerra Lodge offers unsurpassed exclusivity in a tranquil and remote setting. The island is encircled by silver beaches, turquoise seas and coral reefs supporting a vast array of jewel-like fish.

The luxury thatched lodge is flanked by secluded chalets merged into a natural milkwood forest bordering Benguerra Bay. Each chalet, built on stilts with reed walls and thatched roofs, has a double room with en suite bathroom and a private balcony with magnificent views overlooking the ocean.

A mosaic of forest, savannah and wetland ecosystems sustain a diverse abundance of flora and fauna in this idyllic island getaway, which is now a designated nature reserve.

Fresh seafood and exotic Portuguese dishes are served at the lodge where service is attentive and discreet. A comprehensively stocked bar offers a wide range of wines and imported liqueurs.

This is a haven of peace and tranquillity and an ideal base to try out a wealth of activities from snorkelling, scuba diving to sailing on a dhow. Guests can drive to a remote part of the island and picnic and sunbathe in seclusion, explore the birdlife along the freshwater lakes or simply comb deserted beaches in solitude and serenity.

US$224

included

included

Honeymoon specials
Champagne in room on arrival. All meals and accommodation, teas and coffees, daily laundry, snorkel trip with lunch, landrover trip, island tour and sunset cruise in a dhow. 3-,4-,5- and 7-night packages cost from US$1,312.

Sightseeing and leisure
Visits to mainland markets, crocodile farm and local church services. Sailing to see flamingos. Talks with local witchdoctor. Romantic walks along secluded beaches. Birdwatching. Sunset cruise on dhow or yacht. Deep-sea and fly fishing and snorkelling. Fully equipped diving facility. Sailing on catamaran.

The Mount Nelson Hotel

76 Orange Street
Cape Town 8001
South Africa

✈ Cape Town Int. 3km

tel + 27 21 231000
fax + 27 21 247472

orientex@iafrica.com.za

Open all year

Member of:
Orient Express Hotels

Tour Operators:
UK: A&K,
    Southern African Travel,
    Elegant Resorts,
    Carrier Travel,
    The African Connection
US: A&K, African Travel Inc

Nestling at the foot of mountains amidst landscaped gardens, the colonial-style Mount Nelson is one of South Africa's oldest and most famous hotels.

Four separate wings, set in the splendid Edwardian gardens, provide luxurious accommodation that is ideal for couples seeking serenity and seclusion. All rooms are prettily decorated with delicate wooden furnishings, floral fabrics and drapes over the beds. Each has satellite television, video and minibar, and some have mountain views. In the main building, guests can enjoy a wealth of sports and health facilities. There are two restaurants one serving traditional Cape Malay fare, inspired by French, Dutch and Eastern cuisine.

The hotel is ideally placed for exploring the cobbled squares and lanes of old Cape Town and the Cape's legendary vineyards and beaches.

Elegant rooms are available for wedding receptions, and the hotel staff will be happy to arrange anything from a champagne picnic on top of Table Mountain to a banquet in the Whale Well.

 from ZAR1,670
 from ZAR2,410
 from ZAR150
 from ZAR95

Honeymoon specials

Fruit basket, welcome card, wine, rose and the hotel book in room on arrival. Room upgrade subject to availability. Room service and breakfast included. A tour operator package at a cost of ZAR755 for a stay of 3 nights is also available and includes all of the above (excluding accommodation) and Rolls transfers, dinner with wine and picnic hamper.

Sightseeing and leisure

Galleries, museums, markets within 15 minutes' walk. Excursions to vineyards, beaches and nature reserves. Champagne on Signal Hill at sunset. Swimming pools, floodlit tennis and gymnasium. Therapeutic treatments, massage, aromatherapy and reflexology in the Bodycare Centre. A full range of water sports at nearby beaches. Golf courses nearby.

Romney Park Luxury Suites

PO Box 171
Green Point 8051
Cape Town
South Africa

Cape Town Int. 20km

tel +27 21 439 4555
fax +27 21 439 4747
rprelais@satis.co.za

Open all year

Member of:
Relais Hotels

Flawlessly designed in grand Cape Colonial style, Romney Park Luxury Suites are set in a convenient central location, with magnificent views across Green Point Common and the clear blue waters of Table Bay.

The integral grace and charm of Romney Park Luxury Suites combines sensitively with stylish, contemporary decor, and all the enjoyment and comfort of modern living. All bedrooms are sea-facing and have a large private terrace.

Guests can enjoy the cosmopolitan variety of cuisine on offer in Cape Town's most elegant restaurants, or simply order in and enjoy an evening of intimate dining in the privacy of their apartment.

There are any number of world-renowned beauty spots nearby, such as the awe-inspiring Table Mountain, The Victoria and Alfred Waterfront, or the famous golden beaches of the Cape which lie only a short distance from Romney Park Luxury Suites. Alternatively, a pleasant afternoon can be spent relaxing by the swimming pool, idyllically situated on a landscaped deck, or enjoying the tranquil surroundings of the immaculate and charming esplanade.

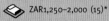 ZAR1,250–2,000 (15)*

N/A

ZAR45 pp

Honeymoon specials
Wine, fruit and flowers in room on arrival.

Leisure facilities
Health and raquet club and golf nearby.
Beach close by.

*per apartment

Local attractions
Visits to Table Mountain, Cape Town, Kirstenbosch, Cape Point and The Castle, South African Museum, Houses of Parliament. Victoria and Alfred Waterfront with shops, pubs and restaurants.

Tanzania

Enjoy unparalleled game viewing on a walking, riding or boating safari, snorkel and dive over pristine coral reefs, or simply lie back and relax...

From the snows of Mount Kilimanjaro, across the endless plains of the Serengeti, and to the crystal clear waters of its Indian Ocean islands, Tanzania is one of the most beautiful countries to visit in Africa. It is ideally suited to a honeymoon that combines the timeless elegance of a safari with some of the most unspoilt beaches in Africa.

A safari into the northern or southern national parks is the highlight of any trip. Far from demanding that you suffer the hardships of the early pioneers, these parks offer luxurious accommodation and fine cuisine. And the natural wonders of world-renowned parks such as the Serengeti and Ngorongoro crater lie waiting to be discovered, are now easily accessible from the airport at the foot of Mount Kilimanjaro.

Few things can compare with the joys of watching the spectacles of nature unfurl before you — the migration of the wildebeest, a solitary leopard languidly sleeping in the branches of an Acacia, cheetah racing across the sunbleached savannah. You can start the day with a dawn balloon ride over

flying time
To: Tabora
London: 11 hrs
Miami: 20 hrs
New York: 17 hrs

when to go
April and May are the
months of the long rains,
Jun–Oct is hot and dry,
November brings the
short rains, and Dec–Mar
is very hot and humid.

currency
The Tanzanian shilling,
though US dollars are
widely accepted. Credit
cards are accepted at
many hotels.

language
The official language is
Swahili, though English is
widely spoken.

getting around
Specialist transfer
operators and internal
airlines connect major
towns, national parks
and airports.

the plains, and end it by watching the African sun set whilst taking cocktails on your verandah. Whether you choose to stay in a beautifully appointed hotel or to sleep under canvas, the sounds of the African night will envelop you.

The southern parks of Selous and Ruaha offer an insight into the Africa of old. Vast and remote, these parks remain the preserve of some of the most discerning safari operators, who offer game walks for guests seeking a chaperone into the heart of the bush. Take boat rides along the waterways of the Selous, where colourful birdlife flourishes alongside an abundance of hippo and crocodile, and, if you are brave enough, take up your rod and fish for 'Tigers'.

The magnificent palm-fringed beaches of Tanzania are complemented by freshwater lagoons and verdant forests that reach to the white coral sands and azure waters of the Indian Ocean. On the mainland there are idyllic resorts, and offshore islands such as Zanzibar, Mafia and Mnemba offer some of the best diving, snorkeling and big-game fishing in the Indian Ocean. These islands, just a short flight from Dar es Salaam, offer the ultimate barefoot luxury and are rich in history and exotic culture.

Tanzania remains unspoilt by tourism. The people of this land are proud of their heritage, and are some of the most friendly and welcoming you could hope to meet.

Amani Beach Club

Dar es Salaam
Tanzania

 Dar es Salaam
20 min. flight to local airstrip

tel +255 51 600 020/601 721
fax +255 51 602 131

Contact:
Africa Archipelago, England
tel +44 181 780 5838
fax +44 181 7809482
worldarc@compuserve.com

Closed Apr–May

On a glorious expanse of soft coral sand and just a short flight from Dar es Salaam, Amani Beach Club is the ideal setting for a secluded honeymoon in paradise.

There are ten luxury air-conditioned suites, each with a garden terrace facing the warm waters of the Indian Ocean. The Swahili-inspired architecture is decorated with local and Pan African art pieces that reflect the true exotic flavour of the setting, and the atmosphere is cool and comfortable, whatever the heat of the midday sun.

The beach bar and restaurant serves a range of international and exotic dishes including freshly caught fish from the region. Staff are delighted to arrange al fresco dining under the stars, or picnics in secluded areas for honeymooners who want a romantic evening alone.

Afternoons can be spent strolling along the endless white sandy beaches and beautiful gardens, or simply relaxing by the swimming pool or in a hammock on private verandahs. For the more active, scuba diving and deep-sea fishing can be arranged. The coral reef, which lies offshore, makes the bay a haven for safe swimming, windsurfing and fantastic snorkelling.

Personalised itineraries that combine a safari to the Selous, or trips to Zanzibar or Mafia can easily be arranged.

 US$290

 included

 included

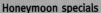

Honeymoon specials
Champagne and flowers on arrival. Private meals on your verandah and a personal valet. The package costs US$290 per person.

Leisure facilities
Windsurfing, snorkelling, diving, tennis and swimming.

Local attractions
Safaris to Selous Game Reserve, Ruaha and the parks of northern Tanzania. Birdwatching and walks to secluded beaches.

Ras Kutani

Dar es Salaam
Tanzania

 Private airstrip 2km

contact:
Selous Safari Co Ltd
PO Box 1192
Dar es Salaam

tel +255 51 34 802

fax +255 51 112 794

selous@twiga.com

Closed mid-April to end May

Tour Operator:
UK: TTI Ltd

Hidden in tropical forest and flanked on one side by a freshwater lagoon, Ras Kutani lies beside the Indian Ocean on a crescent of deserted beach, white sands and gentle surf, cooled by trade winds.

Traditional bamboo and thatch cottages, with interiors furnished to an international standard, harmonise perfectly with this serene and idyllic setting. Located on a hill overlooking the ocean, alongside the lagoon or directly facing the beach, each cottage offers complete privacy. All have king-size beds, and spacious verandahs with hammocks for those lazy afternoons.

A selection of fine wines from around the world complements exotic menus which often feature the area's abundant seafood.

The full range of watersports is available. Those keen on deep-sea fishing can fish in world renowned areas such as Pemba Channel and Latham Island.

Hotel staff are happy to organise wedding receptions for up to 40 in the hotel or the surrounding area. A stay at Ras Kutani can be combined with a visit to the Selous Game Reserve – the largest in Africa where guests can enjoy the truly authentic experience of sleeping under canvas. Mbuyuni Luxury Tented Camp offers first-class accommodation 'in the bush'.

 US$360 (18)

 US$720 (1)

 included

included

Honeymoon specials
Sparkling wine with the first dinner. Room upgrade subject to availability. Daily bouquet of flowers in the room. Airport transfers and laundry are included.

Leisure facilities
Full range of watersports including laser sailing, surfing, windsurfing, fishing and snorkelling.

Local attractions
Safaris to Selous Game Reserve. Game drives, boat and walking safaris led by professional guides. The capital of Tanzania, Dar es Salaam, a journey of just ten minutes by light aircraft.

Kinasi, Mafia Island

Mafia Island
Tanzania

✈ Dar es Salaam 130km

Contact:
PO Box 18033
Dar es Salaam
Tanzania

tel +255 51 843 501
fax +255 51 843 495
kinasi@intafrica.com

Africa Archipelago, England
tel +44 181 780 5838
fax +44 181 780 9482
worldarc@compuserve.com

Closed Apr–May

Mafia Island, with its studded islets, sandbanks and beaches lapped by clear waters, lies a short distance off the great Rufji Delta and was once a regular stop for Arab and Persian dhows plying the coastal waters from Mozambique.

Kinasi, a small, luxury lodge, is in an idyllic spot to the south of the island in the beautiful Chole Bay. Accommodation is in 12 luxury palm-topped bungalows spread throughout acres of coconut plantation. All rooms are decorated with traditional, brightly coloured African fabrics, with furniture designed by Kinasi's own carpenters, and hand-blown glassware and works of art to create a stylish but personal feel. Each has a large verandah and en suite bathroom. There is electricity 24 hours a day and a reliable water supply.

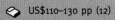 US$110–130 pp (12)

 included
 included

Honeymoon specials
Champagne and flowers in the room on arrival. Private dinners and personal valet. Entertainment by the local choir and drummers. Laundry included.

Staff in traditional dress serve delicious local dishes featuring fresh seafood, tropical fruit and vegetables. Staff are friendly without being intrusive. Activities centre on the sea. The diving here is amongst the most spectacular in the world. Isolated islets and beaches, coves and channels provide many places to swim or picnic in private. More intrepid guests can fish in traditional style with local fishermen on jahazis or ngalawas or go on safari to the northern end of Mafia. The terrace overlooking the Bay is a romantic setting for a wedding ceremony and receptions for up to 30 guests can be arranged in the grounds or on the island atolls. Years of hard work and attention to detail have gone into transforming what used to be a private house into a perfect hideaway with a homely feel.

Local attractions

Thai massage, croquet, badminton, tennis and swimming pool on site. Game fishing, scuba diving, snorkelling and and sailing (lasers and windsurfers).

Leisure facilities

Visits to local villages, Persian ruins and other archaelogical sites, coastal forest and traditional boat-building yards. Guided tours to commercial coconut plantations. Birdwatching on the tidal flats and mangroves. Romantic picnics in coves and channels around the island. Forest walks.

Zambia

To many, Zambia is the 'real' Africa. Its vast, protected wilderness areas are home to a wide range of flora and fauna and its relative inaccessibility means it is still untouched by the mass market.

There are a number of small, owner-run camps and lodges spread throughout the national parks. Many of these lodges can be linked by game drives or walking safaris and frequent charter flights connect the national parks. Zambia has some of the best wildlife guides in Africa and it was here that the walking safari was first pioneered.

There are many ways to experience the magic of this beautiful country including day and night game drives, walking safaris and portered walks, canoe safaris and white-water rafting.

Leopard stalking against the moonlight, canvass billowing in the wind, the thrill of foot safaris through the undergrowth, the sweep of the mighty Zambezi...

flying time
To: Lusaka
London: 10 hrs
Miami: 20 hrs
NY: 18 hrs

climate/when to go
May to November are
the dry months.

currency
The Zambian Kwacha.
US dollars and sterling
cash and traveller's
cheques are accepted.

language
English is widely spoken.

getting around
Internal airlines connect
most of the major towns
and national parks.
Most lodge operators will
arrange airport transfers.

The spectacular and dramatic scenery of the South Luangwa and Kafue National Parks provides a supertb backdrop for game viewing. Both parks have high concentrations of the African predators, and night safaris to see nocturnal hunters such as leopard and lion are easily arranged. The birdlife in these parks is glorious and varied, especially on the flood plains of Luangwa.

No visit to Zambia would be complete without viewing the spectacle of the Victoria Falls. Here you can relax with a sundowner looking out across the Zambezi before it cascades over the Falls. The adventurous may brave its white-water rapids on a raf,. More gentle options include canoeing along the Upper Zambezi, exploring the many riverine islands, and lunching on an island right on the edge of the Falls.

A honeymoon in Zambia can easily include neighbouring Malawi, Botswana or Zimbabwe or an Indian Ocean island such as Mauritius. ●

Tongabezi Zambia

Private Bag 31
Livingstone
Zambia

✈ Livingstone 20km
tel +260 3 323 235
fax +260 3 323 224
tonga@zamnet.zm

Itinerary valid Apr–November

Member of:
Classic Safari Camps of Africa
Classic Retreats

This unique 13-day package into the heart of Zambia, one of the most unspoilt countries in Africa, captures the mystery and spirit of old Africa.

The first three nights are spent at Tongabezi Lodge which enjoys an idyllic position on a sweeping bend of the Zambezi River. Accommodation is in one of the Tongabezi Houses, with magnificent views of the river, vast open-air bedrooms, four-poster beds and sunken bathtubs. Old fashioned wind-up telephones connect rooms to the kitchen, where a great cooking team prepare culinary delights such as filo baskets with spinach and groundnuts and Zambian dishes such as Tongabezi Mahuluhulu fruit cheesecake.

During their stay at Tongabezi, guests are taken on a sunrise boat trip and champagne lunch on Livingstone island, perched on the edge of Victoria Falls, followed by a canoe trip to an island for sundowners and a romantic candlelit dinner, each course paddled out by canoe. Daredevils can experience the thrill of white-water rafting over the rapids of the Fall's gorges or try out the world's highest bungee jump from the railway bridge.

From there, guests are flown to Kafue National Park, the third largest in Africa and home to an

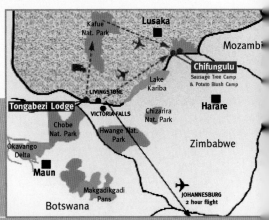

US$338
Tents:US$268–288
included
included

Itinerary
3 nights Tongabezi Lodge (Victoria Falls, Zambia)
5 nights Tongabezi Expedition (Kafue National Park)
5 nights Chifungulu (Lower Zambezi National Park)
comprising: 3 nights Sausage Tree Camp
and
2 nights Potato Bush Camp

VISA MasterCard

abundance of wildlife, for a five-day safari. Nights are spent under canvas in exclusive tented camps, one of which is located under the shade of Waterberry trees on a wide bend of the Kafue River. Days are passed discovering the beauty of the remote wilderness with a professional guide.

From Kafue the six-seater Cherokee transports guests way off the beaten track to the unspoilt Lower Zambezi National Park for a three-night stay at Sausage Tree Camp. Guests end their stay at Potato Bush Camp for an authentic back-to-nature experience, arriving by canoe or motorised banana boat. Both camps are pitched high on the banks of the Zambezi, overlooking scenic channels dotted with water lilies where hippos bathe. Accommodation is in luxury tents. All are privately located with river views, large en suite bathrooms and hammocks in which to while away lazy afternoons.

Days can be spent exploring the river channels by canoe, game viewing in the park, tiger fishing and walking. In the evening, dinner and drinks are served around the camp fire. For a truly romantic evening, honeymooners can dine by candlelight against the backdrop of the Zambezi escarpment.

For an unforgettable wedding, a local pastor can carry out blessings on the paradise island of Sindabezi to the accompaniment of the Tongabezi African choir.

Honeymoon specials
Complimentary champagne in room on arrival at Tongabezi Lodge.

Leisure facilities
Guided walks, game drives, trips by canoe or Zambian banana boat and fly-fishing. Aromatherapy massage, swimming pool under a rock cliff, grass tennis courts and croquet available at Tongabezi Lodge. The lodge is an ideal base for whitewater rafting, bungee jumping, visits to museums and markets in nearby Livingstone and walks around Victoria Falls.

Zimbabwe

Zimbabwe is thought to have been the site of King Solomon's mines, being rich in mineral wealth and good farmland, with beautiful and varied landscape scenery. The country is also home to the spectacular Victoria Falls, one of the natural wonders of the world. Its many national parks are considered some of the best in the continent, with the greatest variety of means to take an adventurous safari — day or night drives, walking safaris, boat game drives, canoeing, kayaking, white-water rafting or floating on a houseboat. An ideal introduction to the many wonders of Africa.

Though it is land-locked, Zimbabwe is easily combined with the tropical paradise of Mauritius or a Mozambique island. All the major attractions of the country itself are linked by the national airline.

The Zambezi River that marks the boundary with Zambia is a must on any visit to Zimbabwe; especially at the Victoria Falls. Here, many thousands of tons of water cascade down the escarpment sending spray up to

The thundering Victoria Falls,
herds of majestic elephant drinking at a waterhole,
African sunsets, fish eagles swooping for their prey...

flying time
To: Harare
London: 13 hrs
Miami: 21 hrs
New York: 18 hrs

when to go
Dec–Mar is wet. The
hottest dry time of year
is Sep–Nov.

currency
The Zimbabwe dollar,
though US dollars are
widely accepted. Credit
cards are accepted at
many hotels.

language
English.

getting around
Air Zimbabwe connects
major towns and national
parks. There is a train
service between Harare
and Bulawayo.

500 metres in the air, giving the falls the name 'the smoke that thunders'. The adventurous may raft through the rapids or bungee-jump from the top. There are also some excellent canoe trips on the Upper Zambezi involving fly-camping on its riverine forest islands.

Hwange National Park, the largest reserve in Zimbabwe, is famous for its huge population of over 25,000 elephant. Also home to all the major African predators and plains game, including black rhino and wild dog, Hwange is a superb park in which to be captivated by the magic of life in the bush.

Lake Kariba is one of the world's largest man-made lakes; guests can watch the wildlife that comes to the water's, edge from luxurious lodges on the shoreline, from islands on the lake, or even from a houseboat. Lake Kariba and the bordering Matusadona national park have prolific birdlife and compelling scenery. The Matopos National Park, just south of Bulawayo, is the last resting place of Cecil Rhodes. Huge balancing boulders, piled like strange natural totems, are the most intriguing feature of this area, as they seem to defy gravity. This is the site chosen by the San bushmen for their intriguing rock paintings, still miraculously preserved in well-camouflaged caves.

Lesser known Zimbabwean parks are worth a visit, such as the Bubiana Conservancy where conservationists have brought together Zimbabwe,s greatest concentration of the endangered species of black rhino, and Chizarira National Park which specialises in superb wilderness walking safaris.

Imba Matombo Lodge

3 Albert Glen Close
Glen Lorne
Harare
Zimbabwe

Harare 20km

tel +263 4 499 013/4
fax +263 4 499 071
imba@harare.iafrica.com

Open all year

Member of:
Relais et Châteaux

The Lodge occupies a majestic position on a hill in Harare's tranquil suburb of Glen Lorne and commands views stretching 30km into the distance.

Accommodation is in luxurious, thatched lodges which are spread throughout well-tended grounds, creating an informal and intimate atmosphere, perfect for couples wishing to spend time alone. Honeymoon suites feature bright, African designs and polished teak furniture, in keeping with the natural surroundings. Each has en suite bathrooms, two queen-size beds and a private verandah.

Guests can enjoy a game of tennis, an hour in the gym or simply sunbathe beside the sparkling 25-metre pool, which affords panoramic views across Domboshawa. In the early evening, guests are invited onto the verandah for sundowners.

The Conservatory Restaurant serves gourmet foods, created from Imba's own recipes, and an extensive selection of fine wines from South Africa and Zimbabwe. The thatched gazebo next to the pool is an ideal setting for romantic al fresco dining. Weddings for up to 100 guests can be arranged within the grounds; the gazebo is a particularly pretty and popular spot.

 US$110–160 (10)

 US$25–50

 included

Honeymoon specials
Champagne and flowers in the room on arrival. Room upgrade subject to availability.

Leisure facilities
Swimming pool, tennis court, gym, jacuzzi and sauna. Golf courses, tennis coaching and horseriding nearby.

Local attractions
Ceramics, stone and wood carvings, teak furniture and world renowned silverware nearby. Trips to Mbare art and crafts market, Domboshawa rock mountain and botanical gardens. Centre of Harare only 15 minutes away.

Katete Safari

PO Box 41
Kariba
Zimbabwe
✂ 15 min. transfer
private landstrip

tel +263 61 2353
fax +263 61 2354

Open all year

Tour Operators:
UK: Southern Africa Travel
UK: Elegant Resorts

This luxurious thatched lodge in the heart of the African Bush, downstream of the legendary Victoria Falls, has been built to blend into the banks of the spectacular Lake Kariba — a huge man-made inland sea, home to buffalo, elephants, lion and waterbuck.

The rooms are spacious with large en suite bathrooms and Victorian furnishings in the style of 'Out of Africa'. All have a private balcony, from where guests can watch elephants move graciously along the lakeshore or witness the famous African sunsets cast red and orange hues across the water.

Safaris, on foot, by boat or vehicle are an ideal way to explore the vast bush landscape and national parks teeming with game and birdlife.

All are led by professional guides and leave twice daily at dawn and sunset.

Guests dine al fresco by candlelight, in great style, with silver service, five-course meals and an excellent range of wines.

 US$323 (16)

 US$969 (1)

 included

included

Honeymoon specials
Fruit and wine on arrival. All meals, drinks and safaris are covered by the all-inclusive rates, which start at US$323 per person per night.

Sightseeing and leisure
Visits to craft markets nearby. Safaris. Swimming pool, fishing and birdwatching.

Sanyati Lodge

124 Josiah Chinamano St.
PO Box 1718 Harare
Zimbabwe

 Kariba 20km

tel +263 4 706 408
fax +263 4 732 542
ldf@mail.pci.co.zw

Open all year

Tour operators:
UK: On safari

Situated alongside the spectacular Sanyati Gorge, Sanyati Lodge nestles against the steep rugged hills of the Matusadona mountain range overlooking the vast gleaming waters of Lake Kariba. Natural stone walls, rough plaster, indigenous timber and thatch make this skillfully designed lodge merge quietly into the landscape in harmony with the surrounding environment.

Eleven luxury rooms are scattered throughout the extensive gardens. An elegant blend of natural fabrics in light neutral colours, layers of cream muslin, wrought iron and local basket weave has created a cool, gracious interior. Guests can experience magnificent views of the lake while bathing in the glass-fronted bathroom or watch the stars above while taking an open-air shower.

For a romantic dining experience, the Lodge offers a five-course candlelit dinner, silver service-style, with tasty local dishes such as Kariba Bream and Inyanga Trout on the menu. Staff are friendly and discreet.

The nearby Matusadona Game Park is home to a spectacular variety of wildlife, including the rare black rhino. Guests can view the game from Landrovers, take a cruise, or follow the tracks of big game on foot. Other outdoor pursuits include fishing and canoeing down the spectacular Sanyati Gorge.

Weddings can be arranged at the local Kanba chapel or within the romantic wilderness of the lodge grounds.

US$250 (9)
US$250 (2)
included
included

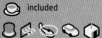

Honeymoon specials
Flowers, fruit and champagne in room on arrival. Upgrade to the honeymoon suite subject to availability.

Sightseeing and leisure
Game viewing cruises, fishing, walking in the nearby Matusa Dona game park and game drives.

The Victoria Falls Hotel

PO Box 10
Victoria Falls
Zimbabwe

Victoria Falls Int. 22km

tel +253 13 4761
fax +253 13 4586

Open all year

Tour Operators:
UK: Southern Africa Travel
UK: Elegant Resorts

An opulent building in the grandest of colonial styles, the Victoria Falls Hotel occupies a prime site in front of one of the most spectacular natural wonders of the world.

The hotel was built in 1904 and has been recently restored to bring back the full glory of the original Edwardian features, creating an atmosphere of elegance and grandeur. Some bedrooms have awe-inspiring views of the world's largest sheet of falling water.

The award-winning Livingstone Restaurant offers silver service, à la carte and table d'hôte menus. The Pavilion Brasserie serves light snacks and buffets, whilst Jungle Junction is an informal restaurant for barbecues. Afternoon tea is served on the verandah affording views of the gorge of The Falls and Bridge linking Zimbabwe to Zambia.

Activities include helicopter rides, games drives and Sunset Champagne cruises along the Zambezi. A private path leads from the hotel directly to the Falls.

Hotel staff are delighted to arrange wedding ceremonies in the hotel's own chapel, in front of the Falls Bridge or in the beautiful extensive grounds of the hotel. Wedding receptions are fully catered for.

Team the romantic Victoria Falls Hotel with the exclusive Katete Safari Lodge for a unique safari experience in the heart of Zimbabwe.

US$189 (171)
US$567–756 (9)
from US$20
included

Honeymoon specials
Flowers and sparkling wine on arrival. Room upgrade subject to availability.

Leisure facilities
Swimming pool, tennis courts and touring desks for booking activities at the hotel. White-water rafting on the rapids of the Zambezi, bungee jumping.

Local attractions
Visits to the spectacular Victoria Falls, crocodile farm and nature sanctuary and two national parks. Sundowners on the Zambezi, sipping champagne. The Flight of Angels, helicopter tour providing a fabulous vista of the river. Visits to craft markets, local villages, African Spectacular – a traditional African dance show.

Victoria Falls Safari Lodge

PO Box 29
Victoria Falls
Zimbabwe

Victoria Falls 24km

tel +263 13 3211/16
fax +263 13 3205
rachelma@vfsl.gaia.co.zw

Open all year

Tour operator/booking:
UK: Three Cities Hotels
    Utell International

Set high on a natural plateau, the Victoria Falls Safari Lodge rises up above the Zambezi National Park and enjoys uninterrupted views and spectacular African sunsets. Hot days, cool nights, vibrancy and colour go to make this a distinctive African paradise.

Matabele-inspired thatch, rustic finishes, lavishly coloured ethnic fabrics and extensive use of local hardwoods and clay tiles give the 72 rooms a warm and relaxed ambience. All are simply furnished marrying together traditional African art and design with modern convenience and comfort. Each has a balcony looking down onto a local waterhole, which attracts a huge variety of wildlife including elephants, buffalo, antelopes, and even the occasional lion. For pure indulgence, there is a honeymoon suite with spa bath.

The à la carte menu in the Makuwa-kuwu restaurant, overlooking the bush, is succulent and beautifully prepared with the accent on local ingredients and cuisine.

Only five minutes away are the famous Victoria Falls, known to the Zimbabweans as Mosi-oa-tunya or 'the smoke that thunders'.

This is an ideal location for a wedding reception of any size, from 2 to 150. Popular venues include the library at the top of the lodge which commands magnificent views of the area, and a boat on the Zambezi with hippos and crocodiles as spectators.

 US$154–169 (66)*
 US$205–225 (6)*
 US$35–50
 US$7.50

Honeymoon specials
Zimbabwean Sparkling wine, fruit and flowers on arrival. Suite upgrade subject to availability.

Leisure facilities
Swimming on site. Golf, tennis, squash, white-water rafting, horseriding nearby. Sauna, jacuzzi, hair and beauty salon.

Local Attractions
Professional guide-led safari in unspoilt African bushland, flights over Victoria Falls, excursions to nearby villages, displays of tribal dancing. International rafting festival in October.

*Prices are per person per night for B/B accommodation

Africa Archipelago

Through many years of experience we know that choosing the right honeymoon requires meticulous planning and detailed and up-to-date knowledge. We specialise in tailor-making honeymoons to East and Southern Africa, as well as to some of the more exotic islands in the Indian Ocean.

We have taken care to select some of the most untouched and romantic destinations in Africa. Most of the accommodation we recommend is in small, exclusive camps, lodges and beach and island hideaways, all of which offer the very best in personalised service.

The African dream is one of the most evocative. Just imagine waking to the sound of the Indian Ocean lapping the coral sands of your private island, gazing down on the migrating wildebeest as your hot air balloon soars over the Serengeti, or sipping cocktails on your verandah as the African sun sets over the Zambezi...

This vast continent has a huge range of landscapes, wildlife and activities, as well as a beautiful coastline and islands, and it is very important to us that we arrange exactly the right honeymoon for our clients.

Please contact us in London, where we can arrange a personal presentation, or over the internet where we have many pages devoted to honeymoon ideas, and let us arrange the African honeymoon of your dreams.

Contact:

Africa Archipelago
6 Redgrave Road, Putney
London SW15 1PX
England

Tel: +44 181 780 5838
Fax: +44 181 780 9482
worldarc@compuserve.com

T1

Indian Ocean

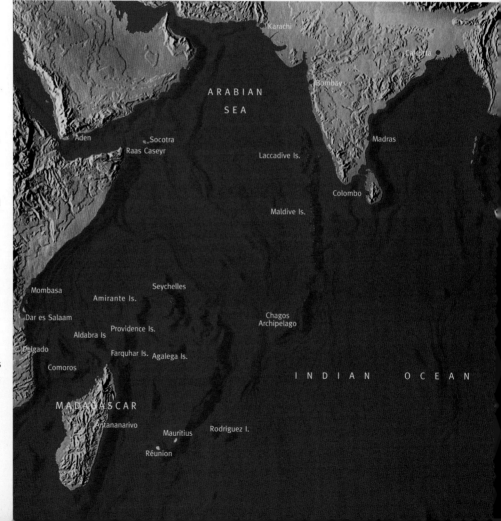

flying time
A few international flights via Sri Lanka or Madagascar.
London: 10–11 hrs
Miami: 20–21 hrs
NY: 17–18 hrs

climate
Weather patterns vary from tropical and hot all year (Maldives), to subtropical with distinct dry, rainy and cooler seasons (Mauritius).

when to go
Any time, but watersports and diving are affected by occasional cyclones.

currency
Local denominations apply. Credit cards are accepted in up-market tourist locations.

language
English is widely spoken.

health
Innoculations and malaria pills required for some islands.

getting around
Mauritius and Southern Africa make an excellent combination. Island-hopping within the Seychelles or Maldives, by plane or boat is extremely enjoyable.

Birdsong, the caress of a warm tropical breeze, and beneath the surface of the purest turquoise sea, a rainbow-tinted underworld...

A thousand miles from anywhere, scattered like petals on the waters between the coasts of India and Africa, dozens of Indian Ocean islands fringed by dazzling white beaches make perfect honeymoon retreats.

Their very remoteness is part of their charm. The Seychelles, the Maldives, the Comores and the larger island-nations of Mauritius and Madagascar share the magic of being well and truly away from it all. On any of these isles you find yourself adapting to a slower pace and tuning into nature.

On Madagascar, sometimes described as 'an evolutionary laboratory' because of its thousands of unique plants and animal species, you are entranced by wide-eyed lemurs.

In the Seychelles you wonder at giant tortoises, and in the markets of the Comores or Perfume Isles, you breathe in the heady scents of ylang ylang, jasmine and patchouli.

Yet more natural wonders lie beneath the ocean.

For scuba divers this is a magical part of the world and non-divers can explore the underwater marvels with a snorkel, mask and flippers.

On Mauritius you can walk among the corals on the sea bed wearing a special helmet, and from Mahé in the Seychelles you can stay dry, but still get glorious close-ups of the reef from a sub-sea viewer.

Maldives

There is a place on this earth where you go to do nothing but chill out — the Maldives. These 1,190 dots of land in the Indian Ocean are the closest you can get to being castaways.

If it is peace, quiet and your own private palm tree that you want, look no further. Hotels here do not have their own garden, they have their own island, with dazzling white-coral sand beaches and temptingly tepid azure sea. About eighty of the tiny, scattered islands have been developed for tourism so far, with just one resort hotel apiece. These are car-free zones you can walk around in a matter of minutes. Some are of the 'no news, no shoes' variety, with few facilities and no hot water, which is what some folks like. Others have air conditioning, a swimming pool, tennis courts and a choice of restaurants — essential ingredients in other peoples' idea of honeymoon heaven. All are very informal, but you will need evening dress.

The time-honoured way of getting about this country — 99 per cent of it being sea — is by *dhoni*, a wooden-hulled water-taxi, though nowadays there are speed boats and helicopters for long distances.

The islands are grouped in 26 atolls, each atoll being surrounded by coral reef teeming with fish; no wonder more than half the visitors to the Maldives go scuba diving. This is one of the world's very best dive sites and a superb place to take up the sport.

Corals glow like jewels
in the realm of sea turtles,
sharks and majestic manta rays...

flying time
London: 13–14 hrs
Miami: 22–23 hrs
NY: 19–20 hrs via London

climate/when to go
Tropical. Always hot at
25–30°C. High season is
November to April when
the weather is dry and
hot. May to October, it is
wetter with high humidity
and the possibility of
heavy monsoon showers.

currency
The Rufiyaa. Prices at
resort hotels are usually
in US dollars.

language
Dhivehi. Many people
speak some English.

getting around
By *dhoni*, speed boat, sea
plane or helicopter.

Certified divers should be sure to take their log book and certificates, and to take out insurance. All the resort islands have scuba diving schools offering a range of internationally recognised PADI (Professional Association of Diving Instructors) courses, and usually two boat dives daily. All the equipment you need can be hired. For convenience, choose an island with its own 'house reef' within easy reach for scuba diving and snorkelling. Snorkelling may be a less ambitious option than diving, but in these 27°C waters, where you swim surrounded by shoals of multi-coloured tropical fish, it is a wonderful experience.

For non-divers, the sightseeing above water level is usually a *dhoni* trip to a neighbouring island, and a visit to a Maldivian village where the locals might set up a few souvenir stalls. Some resorts offer deep-sea fishing trips and, if you long for the sight of traffic, you can take a *dhoni* to the country's capital, Malé

After dark, the Maldives is not clubbers' territory and entertainment is very low key. Try your hand at moonlit line fishing and maybe land a grouper or two if you are lucky. The country is strictly Muslim and Maldivians do not drink alcohol, though it is available on the resort islands.

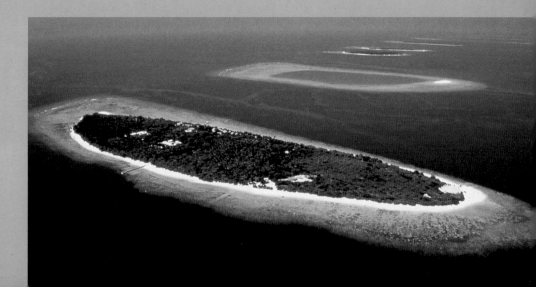

Soneva Fushi

Kunfunadhoo Island
The Maldives

✈ Malé Int. 115km

tel +960 230 304/5
fax +960 230 374
soneva@dhivehinet.net.mv

Contact:
Soneva Pavilion Hotels & Resorts UK
tel: +44 181 743 0208

Open all year

Member of:
Small Luxury Hotels of the World

Blessed on all sides by a private shallow lagoon encircled by a coral reef, the tiny island of Kunfunadhoo is a Robinson Crusoe-style hideaway in the middle of the Indian Ocean. At the edge of the lapping, clear waters, just a few steps up on the beach, are the villas of the Soneva Fushi resort.

All the rooms are naturally styled with thick wooden frames and cane blinds in soft, light colours to reflect the vibrance and warm ambience of the island. Some have ornate four-poster beds. Modern furnishings are tastefully concealed inside natural objects – such as a coconut desk, or rattan – maintaining modern living standards in the midst of nature.

During the day, guests can lunch under a canopy of trees by the beach, or enjoy a simple, romantic, desert island picnic on one of the many surrounding islands that make up The Maldives. In the evening, the restaurant serves a range of delightful dishes including Western, Asian and New World cuisine. For romantic dining, guests can choose to dine al fresco on a private beach by lantern light.

Experienced beauty and body therapists are on hand to ease the mind and soul into glorious relaxation with a soothing massage.

Weddings receptions can be arranged for up to 124 guest in the restaurant or on the beach. Staff are happy to take care of every detail, from flower arranging to providing traditional music.

 US$205–775 (55)
 US$555–1,075 (7)
US$20–50
US$10

Honeymoon specials
Champagne on arrival. Desert island picnic, free beauty treatment at the health spa, breakfasts, complimentary house wine throughout the stay and a candlelit dinner, and transfers. This package is available from 20 April to 25 July 1998 and costs US$1,735–5,585 for 7 nights.

Sightseeing and leisure
Local fishing village, excursions to the islands of Mahlos and Eydhafushi. Maldivian band Bodubeeru every Friday. Spectacular coral reef and underwater life. A wide variety of watersports including snorkelling, windsurfing, diving and game fishing.

Taj Lagoon Resort

PO Box 53
South Malé Hotel
Maldives

 Malé Int. 8km

tel +960 444451
fax +960 445925

tajlr@dhivehi.net.mv

Contact:
Taj Toll Free Reservations:
US/Canada: +1 800 458 8825
UK: 0800 282 699

Open all year

Part of The Taj Group of Hotels

Tour operators/booking
UK/US: Utell International

Set in the midst of the island-dappled waters of the vast Indian Ocean and on the southwestern tip of India, lies the Maldives comprising 1,000 or so low-lying coral islands. A short boat ride from the capital of Malé is the Taj Lagoon Resort – a cluster of beach bungalows and lagoon rooms situated close to the sparkling white sands and turquoise ocean.

The lagoon rooms are built on stilts with palm-thatched roofs. All have private balconies and sun decks. They stand at the water's edge and when the tide is in guests can sit out on the porch imagining they are in a boat at sea. The bungalows are built further back amid the lush island palms. Both beach bungalows and lagoon rooms are spacious and well-appointed.

The resort boasts a dining room and lounge bar serving sumptuous international cuisine and local favourites such as fish curry and rice and fish soup. Beach dinners can also be organised for those who enjoy the fresh sea-breezes.

Being on an island, excursions in glass-bottomed boats and fishing trips are well worth trying. The Padi Diving School, attached to the resort, offers diving classes for beginners and advanced to get a closer look at the abundance of coral and sea life.

 US$140–220*
included
included

Honeymoon specials
Complimentary basket of fruit, al fresco dinner for two.

Leisure facilities
Diving school, snorkelling, watersports, indoor games. Herbal massage by appointment.

Local attractions
Coral reefs, boating and fishing trips. Gift shop.

*Please note: prices are subject to change.

Mauritius

This is one of the largest Indian Ocean islands. Its 720 square miles pack in an amazing variety of landscapes, from the soaring mountain peaks of extinct volcanoes to gushing waterfalls and field after field of wind-rippled sugar cane.

Around the coastline there is an almost unbroken circle of coral reef. The gentle north coast gives way to wildly rugged southern scenery, and an east coast of sugary white beaches and shallow lagoons with warm, waist-high waters.

The one million people who live here are a harmonious mix of races and cultures. African, Indian, Chinese and European settlers have given the island its different faces, traditions and religions. In even the smallest village you will find a mosque, a Hindu temple and perhaps a Christian church. Everyone joins in the spectacle and jollity of festivals that seem to happen almost weekly.

A skyline punctuated by sturdy church steeples, slender minarets and the blazing primary colours of ornately decorated Hindu temples...

The food is a pot pourri too, featuring spicy samosas and 'gateaux piments', Chinese sweet-and-sour, and the delicate home-grown flavours of smoked marlin and the palm heart that is nicknamed 'millionaire's salad'.

flying time
London: 11–12 hrs
NY: 17–18 hrs via London

climate/when to go
Any time, but do not
expect tropical weather
from May to Oct.
Hindu festivals, Cavadee
(Jan/Feb) and Divali (Oct)
are spectacular.

currency
The Mauritian Rupee. Credit
cards are widely accepted.

language
The official language is
English. French, Creole,
Hindi and Chinese are
also spoken.

getting around
Local bus, taxi or hire car.

Millionaires and celebrities feel at home on Mauritius, which has some of the region's most sophisticated hotels. The island's infrastructure is well developed and things work pretty efficiently. In the capital, Port Louis, tower-blocks are starting to dwarf the old colonial buildings, though it only takes a walk through the Victorian wrought iron gates of the central market to find yourself in a scene that hardly seems to have changed in a century.

Odorous halls are thronged with housewives eyeing up freshly caught sailfish and the goat that goes into a tasty curry. Grains and pulses overflow from huge sacks in the warren of stalls, where you haggle with vendors over the price of gaily printed beach clothes, carvings, vanilla pods and spices to take home as souvenirs.

If you enjoy sports, Mauritius is the island for you, with scuba diving, yachting, deep-sea fishing for marlin and tuna, and all sorts of watersports with the latest equipment. There is also the opportunity to play golf on a choice of 18-hole courses, and the spectacle of horse-racing at the Champ de Mars.

When you want a change from the beach, take a day trip on a catamaran, or join a bus tour round the island. Or jump in your own hired car — an open jeep is fun — and seek out the dodo (stuffed) in the Mauritius Institute museum; the 85 types of palm trees in the marvellous Botanical Gardens at Pamplemousses; and history-brought-to-life at Domaine des Pailles, the island's nearest equivalent to a theme park, where you can see how sugar cane is made into rum — the islanders' favourite tipple.

Paradis

Paradis
Le Morne
Mauritius

 Mauritius Int. 70km

Contact:
Beachcomber
tel +44 1 483 533 008
fax +44 1 483 532 820

b@bctuk.demon.co.uk

Open all year

Lying on a private peninsula at the south-westerly tip of Mauritius, the Paradis resort nestles between le Morne and the Indian Ocean in beautifully landscaped gardens. Spread out on a seemingly endless strip of golden beach where one can always find a quiet secluded spot to be alone, the Paradis is an idyllic setting for romance.

All the rooms extend along the expanse of beautiful white beach encompassing the peninsula. The 280 rooms and 13 luxury villas are elegant and spacious and are traditionally designed to retain the typical Mauritian architecture combined with the comforts of modern day life.

The resort's four restaurants serve a delicious range of national and international dishes in stylish and intimate settings.

Surrounded by some of the island's most spectacular natural wonders, guests can hike around waterfalls or visit the volcanic lake at Grand Bassin. For golf fanatics there is the challenging 18-hole championship course, which blends perfectly into the relief of the peninsula. Free and unlimited land and watersports, tennis, squash and aerobics are also available. Guests may decide to laze around the swimming pool, rejuvenate in the massage parlour or shape up in the gym.

 RS3,614–8,359
 RS7,227–20,000
 included
 included

Honeymoon specials
Flowers, fruit and wine in the room on arrival. Candlelit dinner with wine, souvenir gift from the management. The package costs from £1,629 based on two weeks for the price of one. Another package available throughout the year includes a 33% discount for wives arriving with their newly wed husbands.

Sightseeing and leisure
Rochester and Tamarind Falls, Black River Gorge, Grand Bassin Lake and the Casela bird park nearby. Sauna and massage. Extensive land and watersports including deep-sea fishing and scuba diving. Swimming, golf and full use of the gym.

Royal Palm

**Royal Palm
Grand Baie
Mauritius**

 Mauritius Int. 75km

Contact:
Beachcomber
tel +44 1 483 533 008
fax +44 1 483 532 820
b@bctuk.demon.co.uk

Open all year

Perfectly positioned on a golden stretch of one of the most exclusive beaches in Mauritius, the Royal Palm blends European comfort with tropical elegance.

The rooms are brightly furnished with silk carpets and Indian artefacts handpicked by the manager. All are sea facing. Ground floor rooms open onto private verandahs, with only a small neat lawn separating them from the beach. For pure indulgence, the three-bedroomed Royal Suite has a personal valet service, en suite bathrooms with jet bath, jaccuzi and steps leading directly to the beach.

French-trained chefs create a range of culinary delights featuring seafood and local dishes such as rougaille made from the hearts of palm trees.

There are a wide range of sports on offer including waterskiing, sailing and windsurfing. Guests can work out in the fitness centre, relax in a Turkish bath or have an invigorating massage to replenish energy levels.

Visitors can explore the historic streets of the island's capital, Port Louis, or stroll through the renowned Pamplemousses botanical gardens.

 Rs5,402–9,198 (52)

 Rs11,826–34,493 (27)

 approx RS1,200*

 included

Honeymoon specials
Flowers, fruit and wine in the room on arrival. Souvenir gift.

Leisure facilities
Hotel fitness centre with gymnasium, Turkish bath, sauna and massage. Waterskiing, sailing, wind-surfing, tennis and squash available.

Local attractions
Trips to the local fishing village of Grand Baie and the island's capital city, Port Louis with its shops, restaurants, markets and festivals. Visits to Domaine les Pailles, a restored former colonial sugar estate, or Pamplemousses botanical gardens.

* an à la carte menu is also available

Shandrani

Shandrani
Plaine Magnien
Mauritius

Mauritius Int 6km

Contact:

Beachcomber
tel +44 1 483 533 008
fax +44 1 483 532 820
b@bctuk.demon.co.uk

Open all year

Overlooking Blue Bay in the south east of Mauritius, the Shandrani, (meaning 'Goddess of the Moon' in Hindi), is surrounded by badamiers, flame trees, palm trees, bougainvilleas and many other exotic plants. The resort features finely worked thatch roofs, stone colonnades set with ceramics and delicately sculptured woodwork.

The rooms are spacious and bright, and furnished primarily with wood and rattan. Guests can gaze out across the lagoon from the privacy of the secluded terraces, or relax in the luxurious bathrooms which also provide views of the sea less than 20 metres away.

Excellent restaurants, each one cultivating a different ambience, offer a range of dining options from Chinese and Indian to Creole and local seafood specialities.

The resort is happy to arrange excursions to many historic sights and natural wonders that can be found on the island. Most notable is the volcanic lake at Grand Bassin. Guests may prefer to spend their days sailing, playing tennis, utilising the pitch and putt golf course, or trying out one of the vast range of watersports on offer.

Wedding and honeymoon couples are invited to attend a blessing of love by a Hindu priest, and the staff are happy to provide assistance with wedding arrangements.

 RS3,176–5,767

 RS6,497–11,534

 included

 included

Honeymoon specials

Flowers, fruit and wine in the room on arrival. Candlelit dinner with wine, souvenir gift. Blessing of love by a Hindu priest. This package costs from £1,538 based on two weeks for the price of one. Another package available all year includes a 50% discount for wives arriving with their newly-wed husbands. Discounts available for wedding guests.

Sightseeing and leisure

Trips to Curepipe, Grand Bassin, Rochester and Tamarind Falls and the naval museum in the historic town of Mahebourg. The resort has a resident band, folkdancing, theme evenings and astronomy evenings. Extensive land and watersports including scuba diving, sailing, tennis and golf nearby. Sauna and massage available.

Trou aux Biches

Triolet
Mauritius
Mauritius

Mauritus Int. 70km

Contact:
Beachcomber
tel +44 1 483 533 008
fax +44 1 483 532 820
b@bctuk.demon.co.uk

Open all year

Ideally positioned on the north west coast of Mauritius, the romantic chalet-style accommodation of Trou aux Biches sits on the pristine shores of a calm and protected lagoon.

The shingled and thatched chalets typical of the island are discreetly set in extensive tropical gardens. Traditional prints and furnishings are combined with contemporary comforts in the wooden chalets, and each has a private terrace.

The two restaurants are beautifully positioned close to the lagoon with wonderful views of the reef, and are especially romantic in candle light. Themed evenings with traditional dancing and food allow visitors to taste a little of the local culture.

Land and watersports on offer include waterskiing, sailing, windsurfing and tennis. Excursions can be arranged to the local village or nearby botanical gardens. A beauty centre and massage parlour allows guests to unwind in luxury. For golf enthusiasts, there is the splendid 9-hole golf course with a thatched roof club house.

The beautiful beach house, La Bella Vista, is a delightful location for a wedding ceremony and staff at Trou aux Biches are happy to make the necessary arrangements. Each newly-married couple is offered the chance to plant a palm tree in celebration of their marriage.

 RS3,614–6,643

 RS7,227–11,534

 included

included

Honeymoon specials
Flowers, fruit and wine in the room on arrival. Candlelit dinner with wine, souvenir gift. This package costs from £1,629 for two weeks for the price of one. Another package is available all year including a 50% discount for wives arriving with their newly-wed husbands. Discounts available for wedding guests.

Sightseeing and leisure
Trips to the local fishing village of Grand Baie and the island's capital city, Port Louis. Shops, restaurants, markets and festivals nearby. Visits to Domaine les Pailles, a restored former colonial sugar estate, or Pamplemousses botanical gardens. Extensive land and watersports including scuba diving are available at no extra charge. Beauty centre with massage.

Seychelles

You cannot return from the Seychelles without having acquired a new skill — Sega dancing. The sexy, hip-wiggling dance is the traditional accompaniment to folk tunes that tell two hundred years of history on these beautiful, far-flung islands.

The Seychelles archipelago is made up of 115 islands, spread over such a vast area that getting between them often involves flights rather than boat trips. Only a handful are inhabited and 90 per cent of the population live on Mahé, where inter-national flights land and most visitors stay.

A white ribbon of sand, empty but for a myriad of shells in delicate shades of pink and beige, washed up by a gentle tide...

It is here that you find the country's tiny capital, Victoria, with its echoes of former British rule. The island's main beach, and by far the busiest on the Seychelles, is a long curve of pale sand known as Beau Vallon Bay. This is excellent for watersports and people-watching, but if you want a beach all to yourself, hire a car for a day and explore the coastline.

flying time
London: 10–12 hrs
Miami: 21–22 hrs
NY: 18–19 hrs
via London or India

climate/when to go
Tropical. Hot and humid
Nov to Feb although
slightly cooler and drier
Mar–Oct. The temperature
stays at a constant
20–30°C all year.
Seas can become rougher
from May to Oct.

currency
The Seychelles Rupee.
Credit cards are accepted
by hotels but not all
restaurants and shops.

language
Creole (a French-based
patois). English and
French are widely spoken.

getting around
By ferry, plane or
helicopter between the
islands. By bus, taxi
or hire car on Mahé
and Praslin.

A worthwhile day trip takes you on a glass-bottom boat or a submarine to see the coral reef of the Marine National Park, then to Moyenne Island, where you can meet the giant tortoises and bask in the blissfully warm waters of a shallow lagoon.

Mahe and the other main island, Praslin, are both granitic and have huge granite boulders littering their powdery white sands. Both are lush and hilly, with jungly tropical scenery and splashes of pink, purple and scarlet flora highlighted against the emerald green. A walk in Praslin's mysterious Valley de Mai brings you under the shadow of rare and exotic plants, like the *coco de mer* palm, found only in this part of the world.

From Mahé you can take day trips to other islands, but as they differ in scenery and style, the very best way to experience the Seychelles is to island-hop. Frequent flights make it easy to combine islands. On La Digue, where there are no cars, you do your sightseeing from an ox-drawn cart or a bicycle, and become part of a way of life that seems stuck in a time-warp.

Cousin, Aride and Bird islands are breeding grounds for millions of seabirds but you do not need to be a keen birdwatcher to marvel at the colourful parrots, weaver birds, magpie robins and fairy terns.

Watersports, diving, snorkelling and game fishing are on offer at most of the island resorts and on Mahe and Praslin you find some nightlife. Be prepared to attempt the latest variation on the sega, even at the local disco.

Do venture beyond the sometimes bland 'international' food on the hotel menus and try some typical Seychellois cooking. Local produce — tuna, octopus and crab, chicken, breadfruit and yams — is jazzed up to delicious effect, with coconut milk and generous dashes of spice. ●

Le Méridien Barbarons

PO Box 626
Mahé
Seychelles

   Seychelles Int. 15km

tel +248 378 253
fax +248 378 484

Open all year

Tour operators:
UK: Kuoni UK

Situated just below the equator, the Seychelles are a blaze of tastes, scents and colours. Coconut palms, flowering shrubs and a huge variety of rare and exotic birds are to be found here, as is Le Méridien Barbarons, located on the west coast of Mahé: a tropical island set in the lap of a shimmering lagoon.

All rooms are split-level, each with their own private balcony or terrace leading onto fabulous views of a white, sandy beach lined with palms, veloutiers and takamakas. A bright interior decor is enhanced by polished wooden floors and colourful rugs.

The cooking at Barbarons features local produce and comprises such Creole favourites as steamed parrotfish, fish curries and crab cooked in coconut milk. These are to be found in Le Mangrovia, the main restaurant, which also puts on theme evenings. Two other restaurants, as well as two bars, ensure that guests are never short of choice.

Guests can try out snorkelling and discover a multitude of colourful fish without venturing too far from the hotel.

For those intrepid explorers Victoria, the capital of Mahé, is nearby and offers an interesting variety of creole restaurants, art galleries and fruit markets, bursting with local colour. Other neighbouring islands such as La Digue and Praslin, can be reached by chartering a boat.

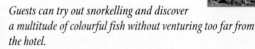

 US$220–280
 US$320–375
 US$50
US$12

Honeymoon specials
Champagne, flowers and gifts for bride and groom in room on arrival.

Leisure facilities
Swimming, scuba diving, snorkelling, tennis, golf, volleyball, billiards, boules, ping-pong, deep-sea fishing, sailing, watersports. Bicycle hire.

Local attractions
Visits to nature reserves, bird sanctuaries, coral reefs. Trips by chartered boat to neighbouring islands particularly La Digue and Praslin. World music day in May, Jazz and international food festival in July. Discovering the capital – Mahé with its restaurants, art galleries and markets.

Fisherman's Cove

PO Box 35
Mahé
Seychelles

✕ Seychelles Int. 15km

tel +248 247 247
fax +248 247 742

Open all year

Tour operators:
UK: Kuoni UK

The Seychelles archipelago is a jewel set in the transparent lagoons of the Indian Ocean. On the island of Mahé, home to rare and exotic birds and lush flora and fauna, Le Méridien Fisherman's Cove is a little paradise in its own right. Situated at the tip of the beautiful beach of Beauvallon, the local architecture of simple stone and slate blends well with the tropical gardens which surround it.

The rooms and cottages all have their own terrace affording ocean views. The cottages have small private gardens where couples can relax in serenity and seclusion. The decor is bright and comfortable with wood panelled walls, colourful rugs and bedspreads, cane furniture and pottery lamps. All the rooms have direct access to the beach.

The hotel has two restaurants. On the menu are Creole specialities of the region with the emphasis on fish, crab, lobster and other seafood delicacies. Grilled, curried, served with ginger – all are delicious. The more adventurous might even try turtle soup or grilled bat.

In the evening the Blue Marlin Bar, with its ocean views, is a popular retreat serving cocktails and pre-dinner drinks to the tones of light classical music and jazz.

There is plenty to do here, whether it be swimming in the pool, taking fins, mask and snorkel for a casual underwater exploration or just enjoying a game of ping-pong. Many other activities, such as deep-sea fishing, are also available in the area.

US$500–665 (48)
US$780 (2)
US$40
US$25

Honeymoon specials
Champagne, fruit and gifts for bride and groom in room on arrival.

Leisure facilities
Swimming, scuba diving, snorkelling, tennis, golf, volleyball, billiards, boules, ping-pong, deep-sea fishing, sailing, watersports. Bicycle hire.

Local attractions
Visits to nature reserves, bird sanctuaries, coral reefs. Trips by chartered boat to neighbouring islands particularly La Digue and Praslin. World music day in May, jazz and international food festival in July. Discovering the capital – Mahé – with its restaurants, art galleries and markets.

South East Asia

Bangkok, Bali, Borneo, Java, Kuala Lumpar, Mandalay, Manila, Rangoon, Sumatra – the very names conjure up a land of mystery and promise where ancient temples, jungles, mountain ranges and bustling cities all compete for attention.

The region offers the perfect way of escape, and sipping long, cool drinks on the palm-fringed shores of the Indian Ocean or the South China Seas while gentle breezes caress the warm waters is about as luxurious a way to spend a honeymoon as anyone could hope for.

Those wanting more excitement will not be disappointed either, whether trekking the hills of Thailand or exploring the underwater world off Maylaysia's Sipadan Island.

Add to these ingredients delicious food, a fascinating culture and some of the world's most beautiful scenery and South East Asia has the perfect recipe.

India

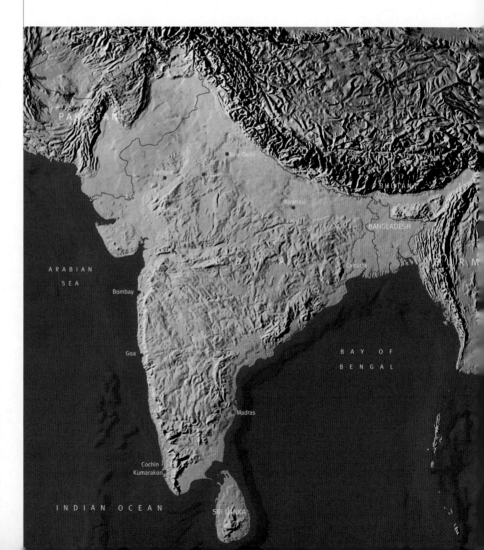

flying time

To: Delhi/Bombay/Calcutta/Madras.
London: 10–12 hrs
NY: 17–19 hrs

climate

Four seasons: spring, autumn and two monsoons. Climate varies according to location and altitude. The mountain resorts of the north stay cool at 10–20°C. Further south and inland things hot up; in May Delhi sizzles at up to 40°C.

when to go

Whatever the month, there is always somewhere on this vast continent to enjoy a relaxing holiday. The tourist season is, roughly, Oct–Mar.

currency

The rupee. Traveller's cheques are exchanged by most banks. Credit cards are useful for tourist areas.

language

There are over 1,000 languages and dialects. Hindi is perhaps the most popular altough there are plenty of English speakers.

health

Have inoculations against typhoid, tetanus, polio, hepatitis and meningitis. Take a supply of malaria pills.

getting around

Unless you are flying, travel in India is slow, even on the famous rail system. Buses, taxis, cycle and sutorickshaws are good for short hops. For even quite extended sightseeing trips, taxis are cheap.

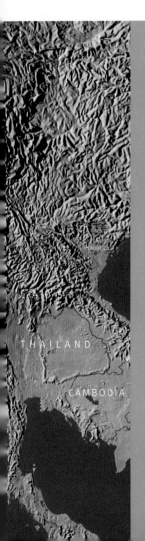

Wandering through ruined temple cities, bargaining in bazaars, inhaling the scents of spices jasmine and incense, staying in a maharajah's palace, sleeping on a beach under the stars...

Whatever you want from a honeymoon, it is here — royal palaces, desert fortresses, beach resorts, hill stations, temples, mountains, lakes and lots more besides.

This is one of the oldest civilisations known, in its heyday one of the richest, dating back about five thousand years. Here you can enjoy some of the most wonderful man-made structures in the world, and some of the best music, dance and theatre in Asia.

Away from the expensive capitals, you can live like royalty for a relatively small sum, and there are all sorts of tempting shopping bargains to be had — silks and brocades, paintings and furnishings, carvings and carpets, gems and jewellery. If your tastes run to sports and recreation, many cities have facilities for swimming and golf, tennis and squash, fishing and riding, while in outlying areas you can explore wildlife parks on elephant-back or cross the desert on camel safari.

Finally, international cuisine is now available, although it is normally cheaper, tastier and much, much more interesting to eat Indian food.

North India

The north is the most visited area of the country, by virtue of its cooler climate, imposing Mughal architecture and wide range of attractions — the fairytale desert forts of Rajasthan; the hill stations of Himachal Pradesh; the pilgrimage sites of Bihar and Uttar Pradesh, Bodhgaya, and Varanasi on the sacred river Ganges; and, most famously, the unforgettable Taj Mahal.

Old Delhi is still a medieval place of forts, mosques and bazaars; colonial New Delhi is an elegant metropolis of broad avenues, stately homes and landscaped gardens. Here you find some of the best hotels, restaurants and facilities in the county.

Close to Delhi are three places that together provide many of the images with which India is associated — Agra, Khajuraho and Varanasi. If Agra's Taj Mahal, the most extravagant monument to love ever built, can be said to define the romance of India, then the erotic temples of Khajuraho must describe its sensuality, and the holy city of Varanasi its divine mystery.

Mighty forts and exquisite temples, busy bazaars and teeming traffic, the Taj Mahal, the sacred River Ganges...

flying time
To: New Delhi
London: 9 hrs
NY: 16 hrs

climate/when to go
Between Oct–Mar the weather is at its most pleasant in Delhi, Rajasthan and Uttar Pradesh. Late Mar/early Apr is hotter, but there are significantly fewer tourists. Delhi can be quite chilly around the turn of the year. The resorts of the north are best visited between Apr–Oct or Dec–Feb.

getting around
Short, daily flights link all the main sights and cities. Surface transport is efficient but can be arduous. It is always advisable to agree a fee before travelling in a taxi or rickshaw.

Further west, the desert territory of Rajasthan, 'Land of Princes', is as famous for its gardens and lakes, festivals and handicrafts as for its fortress theatres of war. It encompasses the Pink City of Jaipur, the towering fort of Jodphur, medieval Jaisalmer and elegant Udaipur, a famous lake city of charming gardens and palaces.

In the extreme north are cool hill stations and towns with resonant names — Manali and Shimla, Dalhousie and Dharmsala, present home of the Dalai Lama. Each trapped in its own time warp, these picturesque resorts are places for relaxation and contemplation, scenic promenades and fond recollections of the Raj. ●

Taj Palace Hotel

Sardar Patel Marg
Diplomatic Enclave
New Delhi 110 021
India

 Indira Gandhi Int. 21km

tel +91 11 611 0202
fax +92 11 611 0808

Contact:
Taj Toll Free Reservations:
US/Canada: +1 800 458 8825
UK: 0800 282 699

Open all year

Part of The Taj Group of Hotels

Member of:
Leading Hotels of the World

Tour operators/booking
UK/US: Utell International

New Delhi, designed by the British architect Sir Edward Lutyens to replace Calcutta as the capital of India, is home to the Taj Palace Hotel. Offering convenience and a gentle ambience within a large landscaped garden, it is minutes from the airport and city centre. Though modern, New Delhi embraces the foundations of seven earlier cities dating back to the eighth century, and temples, ruins, gateways and citadels are all within easy reach of the hotel.

From the white marbled staircase sweeping down from the main lobby visitors can make their way to elegantly appointed rooms and suites. Once there, comfortable armchairs and sofas, wooden furniture and king-size beds and relaxing neutral decor offer an indulgent sense of gracious living. The luxury terrace suites are spacious and individually appointed with a separate lounge and terrace garden – ideal for al fresco dining.

The hotel boasts no fewer than six restaurants and bars offering a range of international cuisine from The Tea House of the August Moon designed on a Chinese temple theme with its authentic Sichuan and Dim-sum specialities to Handi, specialising in the cooking of Northern India with live Indian classical music and dance every evening.

Cocktail receptions for up to 2,500 guests can be organised as can multi-cuisine catering.

 US$315–425 (381)*
 US$475–975 (40)*
 approx. Rs425
 approx. Rs275

Honeymoon specials
Basket of fruits, Indian sweets, flower arrangement, Limousine transfers on request.

Leisure facilities
Pool, fitness centre, beauty parlour. Golf and tennis on request.

Local attractions
Boutiques, fine shops, Jama Mashid, Red Fort, Parliament House, Rashtrapati Bhavan (President's residence), Humayum's Tomb.

Please note: prices are subject to change.

Taj-View Hotel

Taj Ganj
Fatehabad Road
Agra 282 001
India

✈ Agra 10km

tel +91 562 331 841/59
fax +91 562 331 860

tvhgm.agr@tajgroup.sprinrpg.ems.vsnl.net.in

Contact:
Taj Toll Free Reservations:
US/Canada: +1 800 458 8825
UK: 0800 282 699

Part of The Taj Group of Hotels

Open all year

The Taj-View Hotel received its name for the simple reason that it enjoys uninterrupted views of the greatest monument to love ever built – the Taj Mahal. Built in the 17th century by the heart-broken Shah Jehan in memory of his beloved wife Mumtaz Mahal, it took 20,000 workers from India and central Asia 22 years to complete.

Gracious marble interiors welcome the traveller and well-proportioned suites and rooms with occasional lamps and scattered cushions offer ample room for privacy and relaxation. Large beds, comfy sofas and chairs, and vases of flowers add to the feeling of comfort and indulgence. Outside, lazy days can be spent by the palm-fringed pool or in the lush, landscaped gardens.

Speciality cuisine is on the menu in Nazara, the hotel's restaurant. Gourmets can savour such delights as dal makhani (pulses with a dash of butter), paneer pasanda (a rich dish made from cottage cheese) and skewered lamb kebabs, all of which reflect flavours true to Northern India.

The Taj Mahal is not the only site of special interest in the area and visitors may want to take in the massive Agra Fort or the city of Fatehpur Sikri built by Akbar, the 16th-century Mogul Emperor.

 US$65–150 (95)   *
 US$220 (5)*
 approx. Rs350
 approx. Rs210

Honeymoon specials
Complimentary basket of fruit, Indian sweets, special flower arrangement in room, romantic dinner on request.

Leisure facilities
Pool, fitness centre and badminton. Massage by appointment.

Local attractions
Marble curios, fine carpets, jewellery and leather works on sale locally. Visits to the Taj Mahal.

*Please note: prices are subject to change.

98

Rambagh Palace

Bhawani Singh Road
Jaipur 302 005
Rajasthan
India

✈ Jaipur 11km

tel +91 141 381 919
fax +91 141 381 098
rambagh@jpl.vsnl.net.in

Contact:
Taj Toll Free Reservations:
US/Canada: +1 800 458 8825
UK: 0800 282 699

Open all year

Part of The Taj Group of Hotels

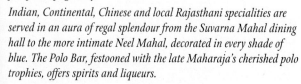

The legendary palace of Rambagh, once home to none other than the Maharaja of Jaipur, stands majestically in gardens renowned for their elegance and exotic foliage. Peacocks preen themselves on the lawns, exotic migratory birds nestle in the Bougainvillea and Lantana trees and dazzling flower beds and expansive lawns make this one of the horticultural wonders of the world.

The interior of the palace is breathtaking. Guests can stay in the former personal chambers of the Royal family such as the Prince's suite with marble floors, golden sculptures and an indoor fountain. Antiques, wood panelling and high ceilings give the Potikhana, once the Maharaja's study and now a lavish bed-sitting room, an elegant warmth. Each of the 19 large luxury rooms are indivually decorated. Intricate painted ceilings, chandeliers, sumptuous beds and original furniture hark back to an age of pomp and pageantry.

Indian, Continental, Chinese and local Rajasthani specialities are served in an aura of regal splendour from the Suvarna Mahal dining hall to the more intimate Neel Mahal, decorated in every shade of blue. The Polo Bar, festooned with the late Maharaja's cherished polo trophies, offers spirits and liqueurs.

In the evenings the Palace's original amphitheatre comes to life with song and dance, performed by folk artistes under a canopy of trees.

 US$145–370 (108)*
 US$350–675*
 approx. Rs650
 approx. Rs275

Honeymoon specials
Complimentary basket of fruit, Indian sweets, special flower arrangement in room. Buggy and elephant ride on request.

Leisure facilities
Pool, fitness centre, beauty parlour, tennis, squash, badminton. Golf and horseriding on request.

Local attractions
Area known for fine emeralds, antiques, jewellery, tie-and-die fabrics, Jantar Mantar, Hawa Mahal, Amber Fort, City Palace, museum. Astrologer by appointment.

*Please note: prices are subject to change.

Lake Palace

PO Box 5
Pichola Lake
Udaipur 313 001
Rajasthan
India

✈ Maharana Pratap 26km

tel +91 294 527 961/73
fax +91 294 527 974

Contact:
Taj Toll Free Reservations:
US/Canada: +1 800 458 8825
UK: 0800 282 699

Open all year

Part of The Taj Group of Hotels

Built two and a half centuries ago by Maharana Jagat Singh II, the Maharana of Udaipur, the Lake Palace is situated on a rocky island which rises from the broad waters of Lake Pichola. The slender columns of pure white marble, fountains, filigreed screens, domed chattris, rippling ponds and intricate mosaic were once the sole preserve of princes. Today it is a luxury hotel whose guests have included the likes of HRH Queen Elizabeth II, actress Vivian Leigh and Jackie Onassis.

The suites echo with historic memories. Walls are frescoed with ancient water colours, inlaid with miniature paintings. Light dances on the walls, reflected from the waters of the lake through stained glass of every hue. High ceilings, chandeliers, marbled and wooden flooring, Indian rugs and balconies looking out onto the lily pond below make this a hotel as beautiful as it is unique.

In the hotel's two restaurants and bar, secret recipes, passed down through the years by word of mouth, are still on the menu for the best of Rajasthan's creamy yoghurt sauces, delicately spiced fish dishes and fiery stews. Meals may also be taken on one of the barges which make their way in serene splendour around the lake.

In the evening, guests can wander around the lily pond or watch the lights reflected in the lake's glassy waters as the night settles to the liquid strains of a soulful sitar playing a raag older than the Lake Palace itself.

 US$150–235 (68)*
 US$300–550 (13)*
 approx. Rs700
approx. Rs225

Honeymoon specials
Complimentary basket of fruit, Indian sweets, special flower arrangement in room, late night champagne cruise on request.

Leisure facilities
Pool, multi-gym. Horseriding on request.

Local attractions
Trips to local markets with clothes, silks, antiques, paintings, City Palace and museum, Fateh Sagar Lake, Kumbhalgarh Fort, puppet museum.

*Please note: prices are subject to change.

South India

Southern India has become increasingly popular with travellers — especially the beaches of Gokarn and Kovalam, and historic Cochin. And since the loss of Kashmir as a holiday destination, the scenic attractions of the backwaters of Quilon and Alleppey have to some extent replaced those of the mountainous north. Bombay, a traveller's gateway, is a dynamic, go-ahead city. Above the clutter rise tycoons, skyscrapers, film studios — the nearest thing to the West in the East. Despite chronic overcrowding and teeming traffic, it is a fabulous place to be with some fine hotels and restaurants, and a gracious sweep of seafront.

Winding, wooded inland waterways
and warm, sandy beaches,
dazzling sunlight on the great brass
headdresses of temple elephants,
lush fields of rice and cashew,
the glint of silk and scent of sandalwood...

flying time

To: Bombay/Madras
London: 9–10 hrs
NY: 16–17 hrs

climate/when to go
Bombay and Goa are best
from Nov–Feb, thereafter
hot and humid until the
monsoons break in early
June. Further south is
coolest Nov–Apr and
receives the rains as early
as late May. Avoid
Bombay during March,
when the city is packed
with travellers. Off season,
discounts of up to 50%
are offered by hotels.

getting around
By plane, train, bus, taxi
and rickshaw. Motorbikes
are popular in Goa and
other country areas. In
quieter towns bicycling is
fun. Driving/car hire is
more hassle than it is
worth. Scenic boat
journeys include the
catamaran trip from
Bombay to Goa, and
small-boat trips through
the backwaters of Kerala.

Madras, the region's second gateway city, is a pleasant introduction to India, being unusually green and spacious, with friendly locals.

On the south west coast, in the old Portuguese colony of Goa, with its unique subtropical blend of Asia and the Mediterranean, fishermen leave their long hardwood boats to worship at the white-fronted Baroque churches, and grand colonial houses share space in the villages with huts made of palm thatch. Everywhere you travel inland, you are surrounded by lush green fields of rice, coconut and cashew. For visitors, the emphasis is on fun and relaxation, with good food and wine, and partying all night.

Inland, the mountain forests offer some of the best wildlife viewing in Asia, and there is excellent trekking around Ooty and Coorg.

Further south, Tamil Nadu is a land of a thousand temples. And on the backwaters of Kerala, villages appear amid the coconut palms and the water is cloaked with blue-flowering water hyacinths. If time stopped here, you would be content.

The Taj Mahal Hotel

Apollo Bunder
Mumbai (Bombay) 400 001
India

✈ Sahar Int. 32km

tel +91 22 202 3366
fax +91 22 287 2711

Contact:
Taj Toll Free Reservations:
US/Canada: +1 800 458 8825
UK: 0800 282 699

Open all year

Part of The Taj Group of Hotels

Member of:
The Leading Hotels of the World

Along with the Gateway of India, the Victoria Terminus, the Rajabai Clock Tower and the High Court the Taj Mahal Hotel is one of the great Victorian and Edwardian landmarks of Bombay's architectural history. From the ornate iron-work of the old stairwell to the regal finery of the Crystal Banqueting Room, the hotel is as much an architectural marvel as it is home to luxurious accommodation.

Even the corridors of the Old Wing resemble art galleries as they lead to rooms and suites. All are different in decor and furnishing. Original artifacts and antiques, intricately carved wooden chairs, traditional Indian bedspreads and original works of art mean that every room is an individual statement of India's living heritage.

Dining at the Taj is itself a cultural experience whether it be in the Tanjore Restaurant, noted for is South Indian cuisine or the authentic Sichuan dishes served in The Golden Dragon. Aperitifs or after-dinner brandies may be had in The Harbour Bar where dinner is also served.

Outside, the bustle of Bombay, home to 12 million people, offers many sights and attractions which are within walking distance or a short taxi ride from the hotel's historic doors.

US$290–435 (592)*
US$500–1,700 (48)*
approx. Rs950
approx. Rs300

Honeymoon specials
Complimentary basket of fruits, Indian sweets and special flower arrangement in rooms.

Leisure facilities
Pool, fitness centre, beauty parlour. Golf, badminton, squash and tennis on request.

*Please note: prices are subject to change.

Local attractions
Trips to Chor Bazaar, Hanging Gardens, Prince of Wales Museum, Haji Ali Mosque, Elephant Caves, Tata Theatre, Nehru Planetarium, Jehangir Art Gallery, Taraporevala Aquarium, Film City, Afghan Church and Mahatma Gandhi's residence (Mani Bhavan). Boat cruises.

Taj Holiday Village

Sinquerim
Bardez
Goa 403 519
India

✈ Dabolim Airport 50km

tel +91 832 276 201/10
fax +91 832 276 045

Contact:
Taj Toll Free Reservations:
US/Canada: +1 800 458 8825
UK: 0800 282 699

Open all year

Part of the Taj Group of Hotels

Tour operators/booking
UK/US: Utell International

Less than an hour from the airport, Goa's Taj Holiday Village has a rustic appeal. Terracotta-roofed cottages cluster together under palm trees amidst beautiful landscaped gardens to make a charming hamlet fringing the sands of Calangute Beach.

Surrounded by flowering jasmine and passion flower, the cottages are of Moorish designs with vaulted wooden ceilings and ornate glass windows. Wicker furniture, rush matting, exuberant house plants and lantern-style lighting add to the charm.

The Beach House Restaurant serves Indian and traditional Goan cuisine. With the Arabian Sea lapping at the coastline, seafood is a speciality. Pomfret Recheado – whole pomfret stuffed with red hot spices and then pan-fried – is a particular favourite. Shellfish, tamarind-flavoured sambars, dosa, bhel puri and brightly-coloured Indians sweets add to the exotic creations which this privileged portion of Western India has to offer.

A cool fresh water pool and sunken pool bar provide a refreshing alternative to the Arabian Sea while in the evenings guests can view a magnificent sunset in the Portuguese-inspired Caravela bar accompanied by the lilting melodies of the Goan mandolin.

 US$60–130 (144)*
 approx. Rs950
approx. Rs300

Honeymoon specials
Basket of fruit, Indian sweets, flower arrangement.

Leisure facilities
Pool, sports complex, all watersports, tennis, squash, badminton, golf and fitness centre with sauna, steam, jacuzzi, gymnasium.
*Please note: prices are subject to change.

Local attractions
Visits to churches and temples, historic monuments of Portuguese architecture, Church of St Francis of Assisi, Bascilica Bom Jesu in Old Goa. Beach tour, river and sunset cruises. Trips to Mapusa market, flea markets on beach and pottery centre. Bird watching. Goa Carnival in February. Astrologer on request.

Taj Malabar

Willingdon Island
Cochin
682 009 Kerala
India

✈ Cochin 3km

tel +91 484 666 811
fax +91 484 668 297

Contact:
Taj Toll Free Reservations:
US/Canada: +1 800 458 8825
UK: 0800 282 699

Open all year

Part of The Taj Group of Hotels

This hotel located on Willingdon island in Cochin affords panoramic views of the harbour and backwaters. The Old Wing, built in 1935 and extensively refurbished over the years, still retains a delightful air of old world elegance and style.

The charming interiors hark back to the Victorian era with brass lamps, solid wooden furniture and thick, richly coloured carpets. Many of the hundred rooms and suites offer soothing harbour views where spectacular sunsets illuminate the porpoise at play. Others look out onto the gentle setting of the scented garden.

Kerala's famous seafood specialities, coconut-rich stews and curries can be enjoyed at the Waterfront Café with the accompaniment of a lively band. Cochin's historic maritime links with China are reflected in the authentic Sichuan cuisine served at the Jade Pavilion.

Alternatively, guests can climb aboard the hotel's boat, the Pathira Manal, and cruise the night away with cocktails and dinner while taking in the area's natural beauty. It is even possible to spend the night afloat.

Kerala is an eclectic mix of cultures and there is much to see nearby such as India's oldest European-built church and the Jewish Synagogue built in 1568. For something a little more lively, performances of Kathakali – a spectacular Indian dance-drama – offer colour and excitement.

 US$110–170 (91)*

 US$250–300 (9)*

 approx. Rs300

approx. Rs175

Honeymoon specials
Complimentary fruit basket, Indian sweets and special flower arrangement in room.

Leisure facilities
Pool, bookshop, boating, Ayurvedic massage.

Local attractions
Famous spice market, shops selling jewellery, antiques and fabrics. Trips to St. Francis Church, burial site of Vasco da Gama, 1st century Jewish town, Jewish Synagogue, Dolghatty and Mattancherry Palace, sound and light show at Kerala Museum.
*Please note: prices are subject to change.

Taj Garden Retreat

1/404 Kumarakom
Kottayam 686 563
Kerala
India

✈ Cochin 85km

tel +91 481 524 377
fax +91 481 524 371

Contact:
Taj Toll Free Reservations:
US/Canada: +1 800 458 8825
UK: 0800 282 699

Open all year
Part of the Taj Group of Hotels

Set on the banks of the tranquil waters of Vembanad Lake in Kerala, southwestern India, is the Taj Garden Retreat. The land is rich and fertile, lush with wonderful crops of rice, coconuts, cassava and cashew nuts, while the surrounding bird sanctuary is home to rare migratory birds like Siberian Storks and egrets.

Reflected in Vembanad's mirror-still waters are the 22 rooms which make up this rustic idyll. Quiet, intimate moments, day-dreaming and restful solitude are in plentiful supply here whether guests stay in the century-old baker's bungalow, on one of the two traditional Kerala houseboats moored in the lagoon or in one of the newly built cottages with their own patios.

Guests can sit by the lake and watch the glorious sunset as the fishing boats put out their nets or take out a row boat and fishing line to dawdle the day away catching their own supper on the lagoon. If the fish aren't biting there's no need to worry as gourmets can expect a veritable feast in the resort's restaurant which serves Kerala dishes such as Karimeen Pollichatu (Pearl Pot fish wrapped in banana leaf), Appams (Lace hopper) and Chemmeen Curry (spicy prawn curry).

A romantic stroll along the waters edge will bring an end to a wonderful day.

 US$60–150 (22)*

 approx. Rs300

approx. Rs,150

Honeymoon specials
Complimentary fruit basket, Indian sweets, special flower arrangement in the room.

Leisure facilities
Speed boats, row boats, kayaks, banana boats, fishing, windsurfing, massage, steam therapy, yoga and meditation.

Local attractions
Back water cruises, Vembanad Bird Sanctuary, Vembanad Lake, Coconut Lagoon.

*Please note: prices are subject to change.

Indonesia

To: Jakarta
London: 17 hrs
LA: 20 hrs
NY: 26 hrs

climate
Temperatures are 25–32°C, but coastal breezes and inland heights help to create a generally agreeable tropical climate. The wet season, (Nov–Mar), despite the presence downpours and high humidity, is still a rewarding time to travel.

currency
The rupiah. Traveller's cheques and credit cards are accepted in the the main tourist areas.

language
Bahasa Indonesia, which is similar to Malay. English is spoken only in areas visited by tourists. There are also nearly 300 local languages.

health
Recommended vaccinations include polio, typhoid, tetanus, tuberculosis and hepatitis. Malaria protection is advised. Avoid untreated drinking water.

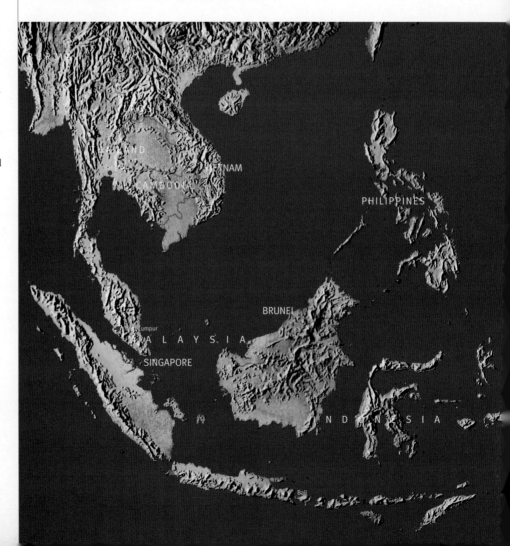

and Spice Islands

Blasted volcanoes smouldering above lush forests and palm-fringed coasts, outrigger yachts scudding over the coral reefs, silver-domed mosques and ancient Hindu temples, gentle villages set among the rice terraces, dancers of exquisite poise, undulating gamelan music, markets redolent with tropical fruits and spices...

A bejewelled necklace of over 13,000 tropical islands lies scattered across the coral seas of South East Asia — a kaleidoscope of colour and cultures united under the flag of Indonesia. Their rich variety offers every kind of honeymoon possible, from lotus-eating luxury in some of the world's most pampered resorts to jungle adventures and voyages on the high seas on traditional trading schooners and outriggers.

There are great Buddhist and Hindu temples at Borobudur and Prambanan, testifying to Java's past as the seat of mighty empires that dominated the region in medieval times. Ancient temple-dance traditions are preserved in the old sultan's palaces around Yogyakarta, although Indonesia has been predominantly Islamic since the 16th century. Hundreds of villages still glimmer in the lamplight of a shadow-puppet show, playing out the eternal battles of the Hindu epics.

Remote forest peoples live in the thatched villages of Kalimantan and Irian Jaya, while the Toraja of Sulawesi are famed for the arching roofs of their elaborate houses. Deep in the forests of Sumatra there are families of orangutans, and the world's largest flower, the pungent Rafflesia.

Luxury cruisers travel along the chains of smaller islands, to the multi-coloured lakes of Flores and to Komodo, home of world's largest lizard, the Komodo 'dragon'. These are the original spice islands. Everywhere is bathed in the evocative scent of kretek, cigarettes laced with crushed cloves. Cloves, nutmeg, ginger, pepper, vanilla and coconut find their way into the food, a healthy blend of fire and spice, made with ingredients fresh from the market or the sea.

Bali

This mountainous island of startling beauty is the jewel in Indonesia's crown. Emerald-green rice terraces hug the contours of the hills, reflecting the clouds scudding over the frittering palm fronds. Everywhere there are tiny shrines, adorned with mossy statues and offerings — incense sticks laid on tiny rice packets, and gifts of magnolia, hibiscus and richly scented frangipani flowers.

Bali is a prayer to the gods, where heaven and earth are held in balance by daily obeisance. The Balinese know their luck: this is one of the world's most charmed places.

In about 1520 the royal Javanese court fled to Bali, establishing a set of Hindu princedoms, while Islam suffused through the surrounding seas.

Their elegant, complex and deeply artistic culture survives in dance traditions of mesmeric enchantment, and in knockabout masked pantomime of dragons and monkeys and blood-curdling witches, all played out to complex rippling melodies of gamelan music. These are sacred temple

flying time
London: 18 hrs
LA: 18 hrs
NY: 24 hrs

climate/when to go
May–Sep, in the dry
season, is ideal. But any
time of the year is good,
although you might need
to shelter under a
banana-leaf umbrella
during a wet-season
downpour in Dec–Feb.
The high season for
spectacular religious
ceremonies is Oct–Nov,
but there are thousands
of smaller ceremonies
throughout the year.

getting around
By taxi, bus, *bemo*
(covered pick-up truck),
or *dokar* (horse-drawn
trap). It is also easy to
hire your own car, jeep,
motorbike or bicycle.

traditions, performed to tourists only so that they may be better performed to the gods during moonlit festival nights in countless the thousands of village temples.

Tourism has come to Bali, but it has been skilfully marshalled. The biggest hotels are clustered on the palm-fringed peninsula of Nusa Dua in the south, away from the more raucous backpacker streets of Kuta, or its quieter twin Sanur. Ubud, set among wooded valleys inland, is the old artistic capital, where low-cost lodging can be found — thatched cottages, with simple bamboo furniture and a private bathroom or *mandi*, where you can slake off the day's dust with a coconut-shell scoops of water beneath open skies. Set apart from the town are a handful of hideaway hotels of utter charm and deep luxury, overlooking spectacular river ravines. Bali is the perfect place for honeymooners, deeply poetic and spiritual, yet comfortable and accessible. The Balinese regard marriage as a sacred union of the physical and the spiritual, blessed by the gods. 'Where is Wayan?' they ask all young couples, 'Where is the first born?' Families are at the centre of their lives, and you will have a special place among them.

Damai Lovina Villas

Jalan Damai
Lovina
Bali

 Ngurah Rai 80km

tel +62 362 41008
fax +62 362 41009
guests@damai.com

Open all year

Nestled in the gentle hills overlooking the bay of Lovina, among rice paddies, spice plantations and stunning jungle-clad ravines, are the Damai Lovina Villas. Quiet, secluded and very romantic, they make a perfect hideaway. Located only a couple of hours' drive from the airport and the crowds of the south, they are a secret gem offering two of the greatest luxuries of all – beauty and tranquillity.

The eight bungalows are built in traditional Balinese style and have a cool, open-plan opulence. Stylish four-poster beds, antiques, meticulously crafted teak furniture, textiles recreating ancient Indonesian patterns and beautiful open-air bathrooms with spas create a warm atmosphere of tropical style and elegance.

A mouth-watering blend of French and tropical cuisine – as colourful as it is varied – is presented simply and beautifully by the resident French chef, who creates a new set menu each night.

A full Balinese wedding ceremony with a reception for up to 40 guests can be arranged on request.

Being off the beaten track, the Damai takes a bit of effort to find but, once discovered, it is almost impossible to leave.

 US$140–212 (8)
 US$40
 US$10

Honeymoon specials
Champagne, a basket of tropical fruit, and a beautiful arrangement of flowers each day.

Leisure facilities
Diving, swimming and golf in the volcanic crater at Bali Handara Golf Course. Beautician by appointment. Traditional Indonesian massage,

Local attractions
Watching dolphins playing at sunrise. Walks in the unspoilt countryside, watching the sun set behind Java's volcanoes. The waterfalls of Git-Git, the hot springs of Banjar and spice plantations.

Nusa Dua Beach Hotel

PO Box 1028 Denpasar
Bali, Indonesia

Bali

✈ Ngurah Rai 15km

tel +62 361 771 210

fax +62 361 772 617

ndbhnet@indosat.net.id

Open all year

Member of:
The Audley Group
The Leading Hotels of the World

Set on Bali's southern shores, the Nusa Dua Beach Hotel is immersed in the pageantry of one of the world's most vibrant cultures. An aquamarine ocean, azure skies stretching into the distance, silver sands, a golden sun and the deep greens of the beach-side palms are the palette with which the Balinese gods painted this fabled isle.

The guestrooms are regal and celebrate the richness of Balinese culture in a sumptuous tapestry of classical decor and unmatched comfort. Personalised rooms offer a rich panoply of the island's arts and crafts, including Balinese ikat and batik textiles and ornately painted wall panels.

Guests can dine in high style in any number of fabulous venues ranging from gourmet Asian cuisine enjoyed al fresco to a colourful Italian bistro or a sizzling beachside barbecue.

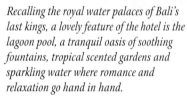

Recalling the royal water palaces of Bali's last kings, a lovely feature of the hotel is the lagoon pool, a tranquil oasis of soothing fountains, tropical scented gardens and sparkling water where romance and relaxation go hand in hand.

 US$200–350

 US$450–2000

 from US$35

 US$15

Honeymoon specials

Flowers, fruit and chocolates on arrival.

Leisure facilities

Massage treatments, exotic body scrubs blending native herbs, flowers and spices, spa (sauna, lap pool, steam rooms and jacuzzi), hair and beauty salon and a fully-equipped gymnasium.

Local attractions

Traditional open-air theatre for classic cultural performances at hotel. Club Tabuh, the hotel disco, presents a variety of evening programmes throughout the week. Ulu Watu (temple to the sea spirits) is nearby.

The Ritz-Carlton, Bali

Jalan Kerang Mas Sejahtera
Jimbaran
Bali 80364
Indonesia

✈ Ngurah Ria 10km

tel +62 361 702 222
fax +62 361 701 555
ritzbali@dps.mega.net.id

Perched high on a bluff, with panoramic views of the Indian Ocean and vibrant tropical sunsets, this deluxe hotel provides its guests with a taste of paradise.

Exotic flowers, including cascades of sweet-scented bougainvillea, and trees such as the almost-mythical banyan are set amidst tiered lawns featuring lily ponds, sculpted fountains and waterfalls. Stone steps, cut into a cliff, lead to a lush ravine that forms the entrance to secluded beaches that stretch for miles.

Thirty six thatched-roof villas are part of the hotel's distinctive Balinese design. Each features a carved door opening onto tropical gardens, private plunge pools and bale bengongs (open-air lounges) with an interior of Balinese furnishings and art, and a two-person bathtub. Intricately woven coconut-leaf baskets filled with flowers and incense are placed in the room daily as an offering to the gods for a harmonious sejourn.

Open all year

Member of:
The Leading Hotels of the World

 US$220–340 (323)
 US$550–2,500 (30)
 US$35–65
 US$17–23

Honeymoon specials
Ocean Suite for US$988, based on a stay of three nights, includes dinner in room, massage, Turkish Bath, Balinese sarongs, flowers, strawberries and limousine transfers.

The hotel combines the romance of this enchanting island with attentive service and excellent cuisine. There are six restaurants ranging in atmosphere from informal to intimate, serving dishes ranging from Balinese Hot Pot to Japanese Sushi. Most dramatically, skewers of meat, chicken and seafood are flamed by the tables in a sand-floored restaurant carved out of the cliff. After dinner, cigars, brandy and robust Indonesian coffee or spiced teas are served on the Damar Terrace, romantically illuminated by dozens of candles.

Marriage blessings in Balinese costume can be arranged in the hotel's temple. Receptions for up to 540 guests are catered for in the Canang Sari, a traditional Balinese wedding gazebo constructed of coconut-palm wood and limestone flooring. Young Balinese girls welcome the bride and groom, dressed in traditional costume, while a musician plays the gender – a local instrument.

Local attractions
Trips to Denpasar's Bali museum, Sangeh's sacred monkey forest, Mount Batur volcano, art centre, sacred springs and temples and giant sea turtles on the island of Serangan.

Leisure facilities
Tennis, golf, swimming. Boating, rafting, diving, deep-sea fishing, hiking, surfing, windsurfing and snorkelling. Fully-equipped spa with saunas, Turkish bath and private massage rooms.

Malaysia

The world's tallest structure, the Petronas Twin Towers complex, soars above Malaysia's capital Kuala Lumpur — a new and powerful symbol of the country's headlong race into the 21st century. Malaysia has embraced manufacturing industry and the latest technology, but it is still a destination where you can discover untamed nature at its most tropical. Also, compared with a year or two ago, Malaysia is a real travel bargain, as the local currency has weakened considerably against the dollar and the pound.

Driving through peninsular Malaysia, the land link between Singapore and Thailand, you soon escape the cities and find yourself amid plantations of rubber and palm oil trees. A day's drive from Kuala Lumpur brings you to the Taman Negara National Park where you can go jungle trekking, on the look out for giant monitor lizards and brilliant butterflies. On the jungle-clad island of Borneo, which contains the Malaysian states of Sarawak and Sabah, you can climb South East Asia's highest mountain, Mount Kinabalu, see orangutans, take a river trip through tropical rainforest and stay in

Curried chicken,
salted fish,
cucumber,
a boiled egg
and fried peanuts.
That's nasi lemak.
That's breakfast...

flying time
To: Kuala Lumpur
London: 12 1/2 hrs
LA: 18–19 hrs (via Tokyo/Taipei)
NY: 20 hrs (not direct)

climate/when to go
Tropically hot and humid all
year. Try to avoid wet seasons,
which affect beaches and
watersports. The west coast of
the peninsula gets most rain
Apr–May and Oct–Nov; the east
and parts of Borneo, Nov–Feb.
There are many Chinese, Indian
and Christian festivals eg
Chinese New Year (Jan/ Feb) and
Deepavali (Oct–Nov).

currency
The Malaysian ringgit, or 'dollar'

language
Bahasa Malaysia. Chinese, Tamil
and English are widely spoken.

health
Air pollution from forest fires in
Indonesia in 1997 has been a
serious health hazard, especially
to travellers with respiratory and
heart problems. Doctors
recommend immunisation
against typhoid, tetanus, polio,
hepatitis and, for some areas,
anti-malaria tablets.

getting around
A good rail service and the
luxurious option of the *Eastern
and Oriental Express*. Flights
and long-distance buses link
main cities; ferries go to the
islands. Touring by car is the
best way to explore.

traditional bamboo longhouses with families of
the Dayak tribe, sharing communal meals and
finding out about their still quite primitive
way of life.

Malaysia has fine, empty beaches for those who
like solitude, and newly developing beach
resorts like Kuantan and Cherating on the east
coast of the peninsula, where watching
leatherback turtles lay their eggs in the sand is
one of the night-time attractions.

Off the peninsula's more built-up and industrial
west coast are the islands of Langkawi and
Penang, where you find busier resorts, though by
the standards of, say, Thailand's Pattaya, even
these are sleepy.

As a contrast to the sun-baked beaches and
steamy jungles, there are the cooler highlands,
places like Fraser's Hill, Genting Highlands and
the Cameron Highlands, all within easy reach of
Kuala Lumpur. For British civil servants in
Malaya in the 19th century, the hill station in the
Cameron Highlands, with its fruit orchards and
tea plantations, was like a little chunk of home. It
still has something of the old colonial
atmosphere and today's recreation includes
tennis, golf and walking in the hills.

To get a feel for the country's earlier colonial
history, go to Melaka and see the legacy of
16th-century Portuguese churches and rusty
pink-brick mansions put up by Dutch traders in
the 1600s. Like the rest of Malaysia, Melaka has
a mixed population of Malays, Indians and
Chinese. It is in the old Chinese quarter that you
feel most sharply the clock being turned back as
you walk between the old-style shop houses and
dragon-roofed temples. Medicine shops sell
dried snakes and strange potions, tinsmiths beat
metal into shape on the street, and darkened
doorways reveal coffin-makers at work. ●

Pangkor Laut Resort

Pangkor Laut Island
32200 Lumut
Perak
Malaysia

Kuala Lumpur 250km

tel +60 5 699 1100
fax +60 5 699 1200
plr@po.jaring.my

Contact:
Pangkor Laut Resort Mkt Office
UK: tel +44 1628 771 171
US: tel +1 212 465 0619

Open all year

Member of:
Small Luxury Hotels of the World

The private island paradise of Pangkor Laut is situated off the west coast of Peninsular Malaysia and offers a rare opportunity to experience the natural wonders of a 2-million-year-old tropical rainforest coupled with the luxury of a 5-star deluxe resort. Surrounded by a coastal fringe of palm trees, rocky headlands and sweeping bays, the island is a place where stillness is interrupted only by the song of the jungle and the gentle sound of the sea.

Individually designed villas are set either on a hillside with breathtaking views of the sea, amidst lush tropical gardens or, strikingly, on stilts over the emerald waters. Each spacious room offers a king-size bed and luxurious en suite bathroom with huge open-air tubs. Many have views over the forest or out to sea. Private balconies provide a place to relax whilst listening to music.

Guests can enjoy the tranquil ambience of the resort's six restaurants and a range of gastronomic delights, from traditional Hockchew Chinese cooking and speciality seafood, to wonderful Asian cuisine served in a spectacular over-water setting at the Samudra Restaurant.

Visitors can explore the many wonders of the fascinating rainforest, try out a wealth of activities including the relaxing alternatives of sunbathing at Emerald Bay – one of Asia's most beautiful beaches.

 M$575–805 (179)

 M$1,250 (2)

 M$20–100

 M$40

Honeymoon specials
A romantic 'reaffirmation of vows' ceremony, including the planting of a tree in the couple's name which will be nurtured, replanted and tracked by a resident naturalist who will send annual updates on its progress.

Sightseeing and leisure
Trips by boat to nearby islands. Jungle treks and sunset cruises. Swimming, tennis, squash, watersports, sauna, massage, jacuzzi, fitness centre.

Pelangi Beach Resort

Langkawi Pantai Cenang
07000 Pulau Langkawi
Kedah
Malaysia

✈ Langkawi Airport 13km

tel +60 4 955 1001

fax +60 4 955 1122

pbrl@tm.net.my

Open all year

Member of:
The Leading Hotels of the World

Stretching across dazzling white beaches on one of the largest islands off the north west coast of Malaysia, the Pelangi Beach Resort recreates the casual simplicity of a Malaysian village.

Scattered among the groves of palm trees, the spacious kampong houses are raised on stilts and feature intricately carved screens and sloping scalloped wooden roofs. The batik printed bed covers and finely detailed wooden headboards continue the traditional theme. Spacious balconies overlook flamboyant tropical gardens and the sparkling waters of the bay.

The elegant Spice Market restaurant is cooly furnished with dark wood and protective shutters and serves delicious Malaysian and international food. The resident band provide a sophisticated ambience. Nyom Thai serves authentic Thai cuisine in an exotic environment. Themed evenings offer traditional Malaysian folk dancing, singing and local food. Guests need not leave the pool to enjoy a light meal or favourite cocktail at the Horizon Pool Bar. The Cenang Beach Bar on the shores and the Music Box disco offer late night entertainment.

Guests can choose from a wealth of watersports including catamaran sailing, waterskiing and jet skiing or perhaps snorkelling around one of the nearby islands. Jungle treks can also be arranged, and for those who prefer to remain close to the comforts of the resort, the Health Club with sauna and massage services provide an indulgent alternative.

Weddings ceremonies can be arranged in the marina club lounge or garden overlooking the beach.

US$130–157 (350)

US$174–440 (29)

from US$14

from US$13

Honeymoon specials
Fruit basket and sparkling wine on arrival. Guaranteed king-size bed and room upgrade subject to availability.

Local attractions
Boat excursions, jungle trekking, trips to beach of black sand, Lake of Pregnant Maiden, crocodile farm.

Leisure activities
Watersports including windsurfing, waterskiing, sailing. Two open-air pools, tennis, squash, mini adventure golf, health club with gym, steam room and suana are available at the resort. Jeep and bicycle hire. Go-kart racing. Sunset cruise.

Penang Mutiara

1 Jalan Teluk Bahang
11050 Penang
Malaysia

✈ Bayan Lepas 20km

tel +604 885 2828
fax +604 885 2829

pmr@po.jaring.my

Open all year

Member of:
The Leading Hotels of the World

Penang Mutiara is located on the prime beachfront of Teluk Behang, or 'glowing bay'. A landscaped driveway leads gradually up to the granite rendered 'porte cochere'. Here, royal blue flooring introduces the pearl-white resort perfectly, with the emerald green gardens, turquoise sea and blue sky beyond.

The hotel is a fine example of contemporary Malaysian elegance. Spacious guestrooms, each with a balcony overlooking the sea, are furnished in pastel shades with rattan furniture and a combination of carpet and parquet flooring. Warm wooden shutters and exotic fabrics lend an air of timelessness and tropical romance while the bathrooms are of a sumptuous marble with extra-deep baths.

Gracious living is the key to the cuisine as well. Delicate Cantonese, Italian and Japanese recipes

are served in a number of intimate and individual restaurants. Or a starlit dinner may be had in one of the several open-air gazebos.

For centuries, travellers and traders were drawn to these sun-drenched shores. Their influence can still be seen in the island's rich cultural heritage, in the architecture, savoured in the intoxicating aromas spilling from the markets, tasted in the spicy flavours of the magnificent food and experienced in the warm welcome extended to guests at the Penang Mutiara.

 US$150–220 (406)
 US$320–2,400 (32)
 from US$15
 US$10

Honeymoon specials
Fruit, flowers, bed decorated with petals, bottle of wine and room upgrade subject to availability. This is based on a stay of 5 nights or longer.

Leisure facilities
Pools, tennis and squash courts, volleyball, golf, disco, watersports, beauty salon.

Local attractions
Visits to butterfly farm, botanical garden, Penang Hill Railway, Kek Lok Si Temple, Fort Cornwallis, Snake Temple, international sports arena. Many traditional cultural and religious festivals throughout the year.

Mines Beach Resort & Spa

43300 Seri Kembangan
Selangor Darul Ehsan
Kuala Lumpur
Malaysia

Kuala Lumpur 20km

tel +60 3 943 6688
fax +60 3 943 5555
MBR@signature.com.my

Open all year

Tour operators/booking:
UK: Prima Sales Office

A twenty minute ride from Malaysia's capital, Kuala Lumpur, brings guests to the beautiful Mines Beach Resort and Spa. Fringed with swaying palm trees, flowers and verdant greenery, it lies behind a large shimmering lake with an inviting sand-bedded swimming lagoon of blue waters.

Effortlessly decorated in natural, soothing tones, the Asian architecture of rich wooden beams and carved panels make use of Malaysian motifs, enchanting artifacts and patterned oriental fabrics. The bedrooms are spacious and breezy. Most have balconies boasting spectacular views of the beach and lake.

Sumptuous Cantonese cuisine, Dim Sum, a tantalising mixture of the best of East and West and a variety of local dishes are available at the resort. In Kuala Lumpur any number of Malay, Chinese and Indian treats await the traveller's tastebuds.

Nearby are stimuli for the other senses including a theme park, a bowling alley, an impressive shopping centre with a canal running through its heart. The main attraction is of course, Kuala Lumpur itself.

Traditional Chinese, Malaysian and Hindu ceremonies can be arranged with appropriate costumes and music in a variety of romantic spots including the garden terrace overlooking the lagoon. A sunset cruise with serenading musicians makes for a truly memorable wedding party.

RM300–465 (174)*
RM680–1,450 (6)*
RM55–80
RM28–35

Honeymoon specials
Special floral arrangement. Room upgrade subject to availability. 10% discount for cocktails on the sunset cruise around the lake.

*Prices subject to 10% service charge & 5% government tax.

Sightseeing and leisure
Theme park includes animal kingdom, Unity Bridge, Snow Town and Fun Pub. Trips to historical town of Melaka, Hindu temple, Chinatown, old railway station and other cultural sights. Golf and swimming. Spa with facial treatments, manicure, pedicure, foot reflexology and massage. Hair stylist by arrangement.

Thailand

flying time
To: Bangkok
London: 14 hrs
LA: 19 hrs via Seoul
NY: 22–23 hrs

climate/when to go
The most comfortable
months are Oct–Feb.
A particular attraction
is the festival of
Loy Krathong, usually
held in Nov, when
thousands of little
candle-lit boats are
floated on the
country's waterways.

currency
The Baht. US dollars
are widely accepted.

language
Thai. English is also
quite widely spoken.

getting around
There is an extensive
and efficient rail system,
hire cars are cheap and
readily available.
Bangkok is best
negotiated from the
numerous boats and
ferries that ply their
trade on the canals or
in a *tuk–tuk*, a three-
wheeled motor scooter.

Conical hats in paddy fields, flocks of bicycles in city streets, grilled shrimp on sugar cane, incense wafting from flamboyant temples...

Formerly known as Siam, and still referred to proudly by Thais as Muagn Thai or Land of the Free, Thailand is a small, friendly kingdom where 20th-century modernity exists alongside a unique 700-year-old-culture. For visitors, Thailand has much to offer. Take some time to sample the exotic pleasures of Bangkok, the Venice of the East, on a cruise through its countless waterways passing glorious illuminated temples and the world famous floating market on the way. Go beyond the cities where there are some enthralling natural environments: dense bamboo forests, fields of delicate orchids, waterfalls and velvet green mangroves as well as areas of sumptious cultivated land — coconut and rubber plantations and acres of rice fields. Finally, move to the coast and discover glorious beaches, Thailand style, watched over by 40ft high Buddha statues. Whatever the location, the spiritual calm of Buddhism — over half the male population has passed through monkhood — enthuses all aspects of Thai life.

Dusit Laguna

390 Srisoontorn Rd
Cherngtalay District
Amphur
Thalang, Phuket 83110
Thailand

 Phuket 22km

tel +66 76 324 320
fax +66 76 324 174

dlp@dusit.com

Open all year

Member of:
Leading Hotels of the World

White silvery sands. Beautiful lagoons. The salty tang of sea breezes. Abundant coconut groves. Shimmering, emerald Andaman waters. In the distance a solitary boat sways gently to the rhythm of the waves. Overhead a clear sky of unbelievable blue stretching away to infinity is lit by the everlasting tropical sun. All this and more is to be found at the Dusit Laguna on the exotic island paradise of Phuket.

A classic simplicity and elegance are the hallmarks of the resort's rooms and suites. A king-size bed is crowned with a white, damask canopy. Golden brown interiors are suffused with discreet occasional lamps while outside sunlit balconies overlook magnificently landscaped gardens.

Exquisite regional and international cuisine can be enjoyed at the hotel's six restaurants. Immaculately prepared Thai dishes, freshly barbecued seafood, cool refreshing drinks and delicious snacks are all available, accompanied by Thai musicians and the famous Phuket sunset.

The wedding package including a Thai Buddhist ceremony, three Buddhist monks, photographer, room upgrade, flowers and garlands, champagne breakfast and a candlelit Thai dinner, costs from US$2,600.

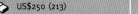

US$250 (213)
US$400 (13)
US$25–50
US$14

Honeymoon specials
Honeymooners are guaranteed a king-size bed, complimentary fruit and flowers, a honeymoon cake and a bottle of wine upon arrival. A splendid Thai wedding ceremony is available (see above).

Sightseeing and leisure
Jungle treks on elephants, Jeep safaris, canoe trips to nearby islands and visits to Wat Chalong, Phuket's largest temple. Mountain biking, sailing, scuba diving, windsurfing, fishing, canoeing, swimming, beach volleyball, tennis, table tennis and golf nearby. Beauty salon and massage by appointment.

flying time
To: Ho Chi Minh City
London: 13 hrs
LA: 18–19 hrs
NY: 20 hrs

climate/when to go
Warm and pleasant for
most of the year. The
week–long New Year fes-
tival of Tet (Jan–Feb) is a
particular attraction.

currency
The Dong. The US dollar
is the currency of choice.

language
Kinh, a combination of
Chinese, Mon–Khmer and
Tai. Chinese, English and
French are also spoken.

getting around
Internal flights, buses
and trains. The best way
to see the cities is on a
bicycle or moped.

health
The problem is not so
much the potential for
disease as the lack of
adequate medical care.

Vietnam

Vietnam is an intriguing destination. A thin strip of land along the South China Sea, it packs in ancient architecture and surrealistic volcanic bays, markets brimming with electronic gadgetary and lacquerware, brightly clad traditional dancers, quiet beaches, and paddy fields that seem not to have altered for centuries.

The Vietnamese themselves are charming, and it is locals you are most likely to meet. The cities attract business visitors, but the country is relatively untouched by tourism. A number of hotels offer top-rate service, many of them romantically restored reminders of the French colonial past. Nightlife is centered mainly in bars, in Ho Chi Minh City (Saigon) and Hanoi.

Vietnamese cooking once boasted the most subtle flavours in Indo-Chinese culinary tradition, and the delicate soups and spicy fish dishes that are beginning to reappear on restaurant menus show why. Whether you are eating in a chic hotel, or the brightly lit buzz of a small family restaurant, you will get value for your money.

Cross-country journeys can be arduous but rewards are ample. The Central Highlands rank with the most beautiful countryside in Asia; the banks of the Mekong Delta are dotted with attrac-

tive villages, each with a busy market, and the Delta Islands offer unspoiled beaches and coral diving. In the cooler upland climes of Dalat you can escape tropical stickiness. In the north, through rice paddies still ploughed using water buffalo, you come to Halong Bay, a curious world of karst rocks and volcanic grottoes.

Ho Chi Minh City (Saigon) has become a booming metropolis, but the northern capital Hanoi still has more bicycles than cars, and its Old Quarter is an alluring jumble of crumbling colonial buildings, narrow streets and pavement markets. ●

Ana Mandara

Beachside Tran Phu Blvd.
Nha Trang
Vietnam

✈ Nha Trang 1km

tel +84 58 829 829
fax +84 58 829 629

soneva-pavilion.com

Contact:
Soneva Pavilion Hotels & Resorts UK
tel +44 181 743 0208

Open all year

In Vietnamese, the name Ana Mandara means 'beautiful home for the guests', and this establishment certainly lives up to its name. Proudly located on the brink of the ocean, surrounded by gleaming yellow sands, Ana Mandara is as close to the gentle waters of the south China sea as it is possible to be. The resort itself reflects the image and feel of a bygone Vietnamese village, with its graceful architecture, atmosphere of serenity, and simple, native wooden furnishings.

The rooms are clean and spacious with Vietnamese-style decoration. All have garden or sea views and private covered terraces, some with direct access to the beach.

Guests can enjoy the natural pleasures of the soft beach outside, join in one of the many beach games hosted by the hotel, or simply browse through the large selection of books in the library. A massage in one of the specially built pavilions is an ideal way to relax and unwind.

For dining, there is the lobby Veranda Bar with neighbouring bamboo garden, or the cool, relaxed atmosphere of the open-air restaurant.

The beautiful stone church in the centre of the city is an ideal location for a wedding, and receptions for up to 130 can be held afterwards at the hotel.

 US$137–179 (64)
 US$263 (4)
US$16–22
US$10

Honeymoon specials
Three nights in a deluxe villa including breakfast. Fruit, champagne, island trips including lunch at a Vietnamese bamboo village on Tre Island. Candlelit dinner in the bamboo garden. City tour by Cyclo, Ana Mandara souvenir. Complimentary massage and air transfers. The package costs US$795 per couple.

Sightseeing and leisure
Visits to major tourist attractions including Cham Po Nagar Temples, Hon Chong Promontory and Ba Ho Falls. Excursions to neighbouring islands. Organised city tours and guided countryside treks. Motorbikes and bicycle rental. Health club with fitness room and massage pavilions. Swimming, tennis, volleyball and badminton, and all watersports.

South Pacific

PAPUA NEW GUINEA

NORTHERN
TERRITORY

Cairns

QUEENSLAND

WESTERN AUSTRALIA

SOUTH
AUSTRALIA

Brisbane

NEW
SOUTH
WALES

Perth

Sydney

AUSTRALIAN
CAPITAL TERRITORY

Adelaide

VICTORIA

Melbourne

TASMANIA

Hobart

'Sheer beauty so pure it is difficult to breathe...' Rupert Brooke

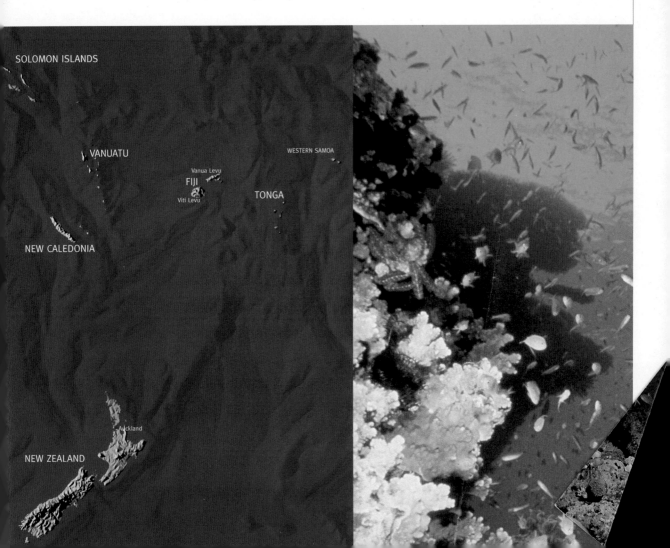

SOLOMON ISLANDS

VANUATU

WESTERN SAMOA

Vanua Levu

FIJI

Viti Levu

TONGA

NEW CALEDONIA

Auckland

NEW ZEALAND

Australia

Australia, the world's largest island, provides most of the ingredients for a romantic holiday. The country which boasts single cattle stations which are as large as the average British county also contains more than its fair share of hideaway resorts.

Those on the Great Barrier Reef, delicately coloured coral islands running for more than 1,200 miles off the Queensland coast, are Utopian. On islands such as Hayman and the smaller, more intimate Orpheus, north of Townsville, you can languish in a degree of luxury found in few other places. Back on shore, you can happily while away days, if not weeks, in places like Port Douglas and the Daintree National Park.

Touchdown for most travellers to Australia, though, is still Sydney, which is very much in the first division of the world's great cities and

Snorkelling amongst the shimmering corals and fish of the Great Barrier Reef, sipping sundowners on the shores of the Pacific, sybaritic cities, vast untamed wildernesses and intense steamy jungle...

flying tim,
To: Cairns,Sydney, Perth.
London: 19–20 hrs
LA: 14 hrs
NY: 22 hrs

climate/when to go
Oct–Mar, when the weather is hot and sunny on the mainland. Tasmanian weather is less reliable, fresher with more chance of rain. 40% of Australia is in the tropics so temperatures are more manageable May–Sept.

currency
The Australian Dollar.

language
English.

getting around
Distances are vast, but Australia has a well developed network of internal air services. For those with time on their side, there are good trans-continental train services: it takes about 65 hours to travel from the East coast to the West.

a major plaground in the South Pacific. No city, apart from Venice, is so dominated by water, the shoreline bending its way around bays and creeks for a total of 150 miles. Sydneysiders as well as visitors take to the water — hopping on the ferry to Manly or going on a harbour cruise under the coat-hanger Harbour Bridge and past the Opera House.

Outside the city, less than an hour and a half's drive away, there are guest houses offering escapism and romance in the Blue Mountains, which really are blue, the colour provided by the hazy, eucalyptus-laden air. Alternatively, heading south through the Southern Highlands brings you to Bowral and the quaintly named Tilba Tilba, a picturesque little place where a group of settler homes have been converted into galleries aand antique shops.

Just as romantic is the Victorian town of Metung, situated at the point where Gippsland Lakes, Australia's largest inland waterway, meets the Tasman Sea on the beautiful Wilderness Coast. Further on, the Wilson's Promontory National Park, which has miles of walking tracks and beaches, as well as wildlife, dips a testing toe into the Bass Strait.

Across the Bass Strait, about one fifth of Tasmania has national park status. The island has magnificent coastal scenery and although the climate here is not as reliable as elsewhere in Australia, the food is. The whiff of salt and fish greets you when you arrive in Hobart, the island's understated capital — the fish comes from Mures, a harbourside restaurant which serves *sushi*, along with the best John Dorey and chips you are ever likely to taste.

The Observatory Hotel

Sydney
Australia

 Kingsford-Smith Airport 15km

Contact:

89–113 Kent Street
Sydney
NSW 2000

tel +61 2 9256 2222
fax +61 2 9256 2233

Open all year

This deluxe 5-star hotel is located in the charming Rocks district of Sydney. The 100 spacious and comfortable rooms and suites have been designed with the utmost attention to detail. Luxury marble bathrooms feature oversized baths, heated towel racks and large vanities. Colonial-style sash windows and period balconies admit gentle breezes and afford charming views of Observatory Hill and historic Walsh Bay. The hotel boasts a magnificent drawing room, which provides a tranquil environment for reading, having afternoon tea or simply relaxing. Equally comfortable is the Globe Bar, its club-like atmosphere enhanced by a library of leatherbound books, deep lounge chairs and antiques. Galileo Restaurant offers modern Australian cuisine with a rustic Italian influence.

The Day Spa, Health and Leisure Club includes a 20-metre pool, mirrored by a ceiling of fibre optic lights, designed to recreate the constellations of the Southern Hemisphere. Guests can work out in the gym and enjoy the sauna, steam room, float and facilities. A day spa offers a wide range of face, body spa, massage and therapy treatments.

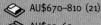 AU$465–540 (79)
AU$670–810 (21)
AU$55–65
AU$18–25

Honeymoon specials
Champagne, breakfast, canapés and bath oil.
The package cost from AU$1,605 per couple.

Leisure facilities
Day Spa, Health and Leisure Club including massage, facials, pedicure, body wraps, etc., by appointment. Gym, float tank and swimming pool.

Local attractions
The Opera House, Harbour Bridge and Darling Harbour are all within a 10 minute walk. Visits to the bustling markets in the Rocks district and botanical gardens and Observatory Hill. Sea plane to Berowra Waters. Twilight Cruise on the Harbour.

Fiji

Fiji and Western Somoa, Vanuatu and Tongo... Magical names and magical places to visit, too. It is harder to find anywhere more remote than these lonely outposts in the South Pacific, but what they lack in ease of access they more than make up for in the sheer beauty of their setting.

Of the islands, Fiji is probably the most staunchly pro-British — a surprise since it is not much more than a hundred years since the islanders greeted visitors not with today's friendly smiles but with cannibal

Swinging palms and rainbow-hued reefs, waterfalls tumbling into remote lakes, beautiful, delicate birds that flutter and chatter in the lush green canopy...

forks. Portraits of the Queen hang in shops and government offices, and scones and trifles are available in tea shops. The first European sighting was by the Dutchman Abel Tasman in 1643, followed by Captain Cook in 1774 and Captain Bligh, who sailed through the group in 1779 after the mutiny on the Bounty.

Today, on Viti Levu, the main island, there are modern hotels, marvellous beaches, coral reefs and rose-tinted sunsets — a sophisticated tropical idyll.

For the more authentic Fiji try the Yasawa islands, first sighted by Captain Bligh on his epic journey and also the setting for the film 'Blue Lagoon'. Just a scenic 30-minute flight by light aircraft from Nadi international airport, the Yasawas present turquoise-fringed reefs, thatched villages, rainforests and razor-like peaks, and more of the most perfect soft sandy beaches.

If Fiji is the most British Pacific island, lovely Western Samoa is the most Polynesian. The best known Briton associated with Western Samoa is Robert Louis Stevenson, who spent his last years here and is buried outside the capital, Apia.

There are two main islands in Western Samoa: Savai'i and Upolu — Savai'i being the legendary Hawaiki, the place from where the original Polynesians set out to conquer the Pacific. Today the island's exports are rugby players and tourism, attracting people from all over the world to admire the things the great romantic Brooke admired a century ago: the beautiful beaches, the high waterfalls and inland lakes, the lush, green countryside and, not least, the Samoans themselves. There can be few such kind, welcoming warm-hearted people on the planet.

flying time
To: Fiji/Western Samoa
London: 22–25 hrs
LA: 12 hrs
NY: 18 hrs

climate/when to go
Tropical, pleasant all the .
May–Nov are is the coolest
and driest period. In the
wetter months rainfall is
usually restricted to short,
sharp downpours.

currency
The Fijian dollar and
Western Samoan tala.
Foreign currency and traveller's cheques are accepted
at main hotels. US dollars
are welcomed almost everywhere.

language
English is generally spoken
along with the indigenous
South Pacific languages.

getting around
Freqeunt inter-island air services. Often islands can be
reached by ship or launch.
On the ground, taxis are
available in main centres,
bus services are often hap-
hazard.

NaiTasi Island Resort

PO Box 10044
Nadi Airport
Fiji

Nadi Int. 21km

tel +679 669 999
fax +679 669 197

rayjo@compuserve.com

Open all year

Tour operators:
UK:Visit Australia
US:South Seas Adventures

Situated on the Fijian island of Malolo in the South Seas renowned for its white sandy beaches, colourful native villages and spectacular views is the beautiful island resort of NaiTasi .

Island-style bures and spacious villas are set amidst gardens of tropical plants and palms, very close to the beach. All are comfortable and decorated according to local custom.

Two restaurants and bars provide international cuisine, as well as regional favourites including sweet potatoes and rice. Being on the coast, fresh seafood is always on the menu.

The resort offers a number of wedding packages. Couples can be married in a variety of romantic locations including on the beach at sunset or on a sand bar at low tide. All the trimmings are arranged upon request from hiring traditional Fijian wedding dress for the bride and groom to wedding serenades.

Many activities are available including sunset cruises, night fishing trips, snorkelling on the Barrier Reef and visits to local villages. Walking is a favourite pastime and there are many fascinating trails weaving in and around the island and varying in length and difficulty. Guests even have the opportunity to try their hand at weaving, beachcombing and classic Fijian cookery.

 US$177 (28)
 US$237 (10)
 US$10–30
 US$8–20

Honeymoon specials
For US$860 a complete wedding package is available with licence, minister, costume, flowers, island serenaders, cake and champagne. Wedding dinners can be arranged at US$45–60 per person.

Sightseeing and leisure
Coral reefs, village trips, island hopping, cruises, bushwalks, deserted islands, Shell Village, Musket Cove and Plantation. Watersports, diving, horseriding, and even cookery.

Tokoriki Island Resort

PO Box 10547
Nadi Airport
Fiji

✈ Nadi Int. 29km

tel +679 661 999
fax +679 665 295
tokoriki@is.com.fj

Open all year

Tour operators:
UK: Anderson's Pacific Way

This romantic, exotic hideaway resort nestles in the Mamanuca island chain, 29km from Nadi and surrounded by crystal-clear waters, pristine coral reef and white sandy beaches.

Accommodation is in traditional Fijian huts or bures, with floor-to-ceiling wooden louvres, high ceilings and thatched roofs. Cool tiled floors, elegant cane furniture and spacious west-facing patios create a relaxing tropical atmosphere.

Guests are invited to a traditional Fijian feast with entertainment, and to explore the surrounding islands by boat or helicopter. There are many watersports on offer, including game fishing and even shark feeding.

Couples may plan a romantic getaway to a deserted island, with a champagne picnic, and return to dinner under the stars at one the resort's fine restaurants.

Staff are able to arrange weddings against a glorious backdrop of a Fijian sunset, provided guests stay four consecutive nights.

 FJ$380 (23)
 FJ$55*
 Included

Honeymoon specials
Shell lei greeting on arrival, welcome fruit punch, happicoats, fruit plate and coconuts in room on arrival, full board, a day on honeymoon island with picnic, a private candlelit dinner at the honeymoon lookout. The package costs from FJ$1,800 and is based on a stay of 5 nights in the beachfront bure.
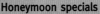
*This price includes breakfast, lunch and dinner

Sightseeing and leisure
Floodlit all-weather tennis court, croquet, indoor games, paddle boats, windsurfing, sailing lessons, handline fishing, coral viewing, fish feeding, snorkelling, bush and mountain walking, volleyball are all included. Waterskiing, banana boat rides, scuba diving, game fishing, helicopter trips and visits to local village are all available for a fee.

Index to Hotels and Resorts, Cruise Lines and Safaris

a guide to the index: `XX` is the reference code for brochure ordering (see p3 or card insert).

OOO is the page number.

Travel Agents and Tour Operators
United Kingdom & Ireland

Abercrombie & Kent
Tel +44 171 730 9600
Fax +44 171 730 9376

Africa Archipelago
Tel +44 181 780 9482
Fax +44 181 780 5838
worldarc@compuserve.com
www.tanzania-web.com/worldarc

The African Connection
Tel +44 1244 329 556
Fax +44 1244 310 255
andrewmitcltd.demon.co.uk

Anderson's Pacific Way
Tel +44 1932 222 079
Fax +44 1932 246 140

Argo Holidays
Tel +44 171 331 7070
Fax +44 171 331 7065
holidays@argotvl.co.uk
www.argotvl.co.uk/argo

Beachcomber
Tel +44 1483 533 008
Fax +44 1483 533 532
ob@bctuk.demon.co.uk

British Airways Holidays
Tel +44 1293 723 161
Fax +44 1293 722 624

BVI Club
Tel +44 1932 220 477
Fax +44 1932 229 346
bvic@vch.co.uk
www.vch.co.uk/villas/

Cadogan Holidays Ltd
Tel +44 1703 237 77 21
Fax +44 1703 636 569

Caribbean Connection
Tel +44 1244 341 131
Fax +44 1244 310 255
Brochure Line +44 1244 329 556

Caribtours
Tel +44 171 581 3517
Fax +44 171 225 2491

Carrier Travel
Tel +44 1625 582 006
Fax +44 1625 586 818
africa@carrier.co.uk

Cazenove & Lloyds Safaris
Tel +44 181 875 9666
Fax +44 181 875 9444
cnl@cazlloyds.demon.co.uk

Celebrity Cruises Ltd
Tel +44 500 332 232
Fax +44 171 412 0908
Brochure Line 0990 902 901

Concorde Hotels
Tel +44 171 630 1704
Fax +44 171 630 0391
www.concordehotels.com

Connect AB Ltd
Tel +44 1753 684 810
Fax +44 1753 681 871

Elegant Resorts
Tel +44 1244 897 011
Fax +44 1244 897 760

First Choice Holidays
Tel +44 161 745 7000
Fax +44 161 588 680

Group Promotions Ltd
Tel +44 181 900 1913
Fax +44 181 795 1728
sales@group-promotions.co.uk

Harlequin Worldwide Travel
Tel +44 1708 852 780
Fax +44 1708 854 952
harlequin@harlequin-holidays.co.uk
www.harlequin-holidays

Insignia Resorts
Tel +44 181 490 5791
Fax +44 181 994 6475

Kuoni Travel
Tel +44 1306 740 500
Fax +44 1306 744 222
Brochure Line 07000 458 664

Lynn Girling Associates
Tel/Fax +44 181 994 9160

The Moorings
Tel +44 1227 776 677
Fax +44 1227 776 670
email themoorings@moorings.co.uk
www.moorings.co.uk

On Safari
Tel +44 171 823 5900
Fax +44 171 259 9949

Passenger Shipping Association
Tel +44 171 436 2449
Fax +44 171 636 9206

Prestige
Tel +44 1425 480 400
Fax +44 1425 471 140

Prima Sales Office
Tel +44 171 936 2332
Fax +44 171 353 1904

Principal Promotions
Tel +44 171 485 5500
Fax +44 171 485 6600
principal@ppuk.demon.co.uk

Roxton Bailey Robinson
Tel +44 1488 683 222
Fax +44 1488 682 977
rbuk@aol.com
www.roxtons.com

Royal Caribbean International
Tel +44 1932 820 210
Fax +44 1932 820 286
Brochure Line 1932 820 210

Seafarer Cruising & Sailing
Tel +44 171 234 0500
Fax +44 171 234 0700
holidays@seafarer.itsnet.co.uk

Superclubs
Tel +44 1749 677 200
Fax +44 1749 677 577

Southern African Travel
Tel +44 171 630 9900
Fax +44 171 630 0100

Thomas Cook Holidays
Tel +44 1733 332 255
Fax +44 1733 505 784

Thompson Holidays
Tel +44 990 502 399
Fax +44 990 502 399
Brochure Line 01509 238 238

TTI Ltd
Tel +44 1367 253 810
Fax +44 1367 253 812
ttisafari@btinternet.com

Unique Vacations Ltd
Tel +44 171 581 9895
Fax +44 171 823 8758

Visit Australia
Tel +44 1424 722 152
Fax +44 1424 722 304

Hotel Groups

USA & rest of the world

Abercrombie & Kent
Tel +1 630 954 2944
Fax +1 630 954 3324

Africa Travel Inc.
Tel +1 818 5077 893
Fax +1 504 596 4407
Brochure Line +1 800 421 8907

Central Reservations Office
Tel +1 402 333 1500
Fax +1 402 334 7812

(RSA) Classic Safari Camps of Africa
Tel +27 11 465 6427
Fax +27 11 465 9309

Couples Resort
Tel +1 305 668 0008
Fax +1 305 668 0111
couplesresorts@worldnet.att.net

Frontiers International
Tel +1 412 935 1577
Fax +1 412 935 5388

Gogo Worldwide Vacations
Tel +1 201 934 3500
Fax +1 201 934 3888
Brochure Line +1 1800 526 0405

International Communications Consultants
Tel +1 203 431 0150
Fax +1 203 431 6125

International Lifestyles
Tel +1 954 925 0925
Fax +1 954 925 0334

(Egypt) International Spa & Fitness Association
Tel +20 703 838 2930
Fax +20 703 838 2936

The Meridian Group
Tel +1 757 340 7425
Fax +1 757 340 8379

The Moorings
Tel +1 800 437 7880
Fax +1 813 530 9747
yacht@moorings.com
www.moorings.com

Premier World Marketing
Tel +1 305 856 5405
Fax +1 305 858 4677

(Kenya) Richard Bonham Safaris
Tel +254 2 882 521
Fax +254 2 882 728
bonham.lukeett.gn.apc.org

Silkcut Travel
Tel +1 1730 230 200
Fax +1 1453 835 525

South Sea Adventures
Tel +1 303 440 8675
Fax +1 303 417 0557
Brochure Line +1 800 576 7327

(US) Spa Finders
Tel +1 212 924 6800
Fax +1 212 924 7240

Sue's Safaris
Tel +1 800 541 2011
Fax +1 310 544 1502
Email suesaf@earthlist.net

(US)Superclubs
Tel +1 954 925 0925
Fax +1 954 925 0334
Brochure line 1-800-GO-SUPER
www.superclubs.com

(UK) Best Loved Hotels
Tel +44 1454 414 786
Fax +44 1454 414 796

(It) Charming Hotels
Tel +39 8711 940
Fax +39 8711 955

(Ger) European Castle Hotels & Restaurants
Tel +49 6326 70000
Fax +49 6326 700022
email: zzz.europeancastlehotels.com
www.european/castle.de

(UK) Grand Heritage Hotels
Tel +44 171 244 6699
Fax +44 171 244 7799
email: sophiat@netcomuk.co.uk
grandheritage.com

(Fr) International Hotel Association
Tel +33 1 4489 9400
Fax +33 1 4036 7330

(It) ILA
Tel +39 8711 940
Fax +39 8711 955

(UK) Johansens
Tel +44 171 490 3090
Fax +44 171 490 2538

(UK) The Leading Hotels of the World
Tel +44 800 181 123
Fax +44 171 353 1907
hrihotel@idt.net
www.ihw.com

(US) The Leading Hotels of the World
Tel +1 800 223 6800
Fax +1 212 758 7367
hrihotelhaven.ios.com

(Cyprus) Muskita Hotels
Tel +357 5 310 222
Fax +357 5 310 887
4seasonsdeal.cylink.com.cy
www.smarttraveller.net/hotels/4slicy/

(UK) Orient Express Hotels
Tel +44 171 620 0003
Fax +44 171 620 1210

(US) Orient Express Hotels
Tel +1 516 746 8049
Fax +1 516 746 8056

(UK) Pangkor Laut Resort
Tel +44 1628 771 171
Fax +44 1628 783 379

(UK) Preferred Hotels & Resorts
Tel +44 181 348 0199
Fax +44 181 347 8998

(UK) Relais & Chateaux
Tel +44 171 287 0987
Fax +44 171 437 0241
relaislondon@easynet.co.uk
www.relaischateaux.

(US) Relais & Chateaux
Tel +1 212 856 0115
Fax +1 212 856 0193
nyrelais@aol.com

(UK) Small Luxury Hotels of the World
Tel +44 1372 361 873
Fax +44 1372 361 874
www.slh.com/foh/

(UK) Soneva Pavilion Hotels & Resorts UK
Tel +44 181 743 0208
Fax +44 181 743 6788
100673.2725@compuserve.com

(UK) Utell International
Tel +44 181 661 2263
Fax +44 181 661 1234

(US) Utell International
Tel +1 402 398 3200
Fax +1 402 398 5484
Brochure Line Freephone 180044 Utell

(UK) Unique Hotels
Tel +44 1453 835 801
Fax +44 1453 835 525

Elegant Resorts

Your honeymoon should be a once in a lifetime experience which is why we, at Elegant Resorts, go to the ends of the earth to create blissful individually tailor-made honeymoons to the most exotic destinations and in the most luxurious hotels around the world. Our philosopy is to provide the finest quality holidays backed by a personal service that is second to none.

We pride ourselves on offering a unique collection of some of the most splendid destinations — some wild, some remote and simple, others sophisticated and opulent and with every conceivable amenity.

Whether you dream of a yacht in the Caribbean, a romantic tour of Tuscany, a sleek city break or an exotic adventure in South East Asia, we will take care of every detail, leaving you free to concentrate on each other.

Our team of experts, with their highly creative approach, extensive knowledge of world-wide venues and unrivalled attention to detail, can provide a programme tailor-made to meet all objectives.

All our brochures reflect the exclusivity of our holidays and each one is full of imaginative ideas for discerning travellers.

Call us now on +44 1244 350 408 for a copy of our brochure and let Elegant Resorts make your dream come true!

Contact:

Elegant Resorts Ltd
The Old Palace
Chester CH1 1RB

Tel: +44 1244 350 408
Fax: +44 1244 897 750

TRAVEL

T·E·L·E·V·I·S·I·O·N

When it comes to discovering holiday venues, even in the most remote corners of the world, Travel Television has done its homework — many times over!

In fact, during the past 15 years, in search of the perfect holiday, we have discovered the most romantic hideaways, the most exciting destinations and had the most chilling and thrilling adventures! Whatever your taste, budget or preference, Travel Television has been there, done that and even got the T-shirt! Now it's your turn!
In this book you will find some of the most incredible honeymoon venues, and superb resorts and hotels imaginable.
But how can you make absolutely sure of choosing the right one for your romantic holiday of a lifetime?

Simply, check out our internet site, www.HolidayNet.com. and find added information for your chosen destination, like climate, excursions, even local tit-bits, where to shop and eat out. You may even see a preview on video of your hotel, resort or destination. All hotels in this book are listed on HolidayNet, some even have their own web-sites, so you can plan your very special trip.

Dial up www.HolidayNet.com and start your own discoveries...

Holiday Destinations Live!